TOYS
OF THE
SIXTIES

A
PICTORIAL
PRICE GUIDE
BY
BILL BRUEGMAN

EDITED BY
JOANNE M. BRUEGMAN

CAP'N PENNY PRODUCTIONS, INC.
AKRON, OHIO

Second (Revised) Printing
Copyright 1991, 1992 by Bill Bruegman
All Rights Reserved
Published in Akron, Ohio by Cap'n Penny Productions

Photography by Bill Bruegman
Front cover photography by Tom Bosshard of Pro Color, Akron, Ohio.
Layout by Christine Giustino of X-Graphics, Akron, Ohio.

Library of Congress Catalog Card Number 91-76882
Bruegman, William R. III
    Toys of the Sixties, A Pictorial Price Guide/by Bill Bruegman
ISBN 0-9632637-2-2

Manufactured in the United States of America

ACKNOWLEDGEMENTS

The following people proved invaluable to me in this endeavor by providing me with guidance and advice based on their various skills and their friendship: Tom Bosshard of Pro Color, Lisa Adair and Jerry Weaver of Sharon Printing, Mark Wallace, Fred Toerge, Carl Toerge, Bob Lev, Ken Sharp, Lisa Meilander, Caryl Krusinski, Ryan Brown, Jim Madden, Gordy Dutt, and Keif Fromm. I also wish to thank Christine Giustino for long hours of laying out, and tearing up, and laying out again, the pages of this book. I especially give my appreciation to Paul Matheis for contributing his writing skills to compose the introduction and the article "The Toy Industry".

Finally, I lovingly acknowledge my wife Joanne, without whose support and long hours of typesetting, proofreading, and editing this book would not have been possible.

DEDICATION

This book is dedicated to my Mom and Dad, Fran and the late Bill Bruegman, Jr., with thanks for providing me with a secure and wonderful childhood that enables me to remember fondly the era in which I grew up.

TABLE OF CONTENTS

INTRODUCTION

The years from 1960-69 were a dizzying kaleidoscope of change. It was a decade in which post-World War II America was rocked by upheavals in the arts, politics, economics, human rights, mores and morality. These changes hit home for middle America in everyday life, from fashion and popular music to social rituals such as dating, courtship and marriage.

Post-war prosperity brought a huge increase in the number of children born. In hindsight, sociologists and trend-spotters tagged this swelling birthrate as the "baby boom."

For the youth of that era, the Sixties was a wonderland of sights, sounds and colors-- primarily due to the overwhelming impact of television. Baby boomers became so numerous that they were actually a prime target for advertisers. TV sponsors would go to any length to reach this huge audience of young consumers. Logically, what product would children have wanted most? Toys, of course.

Commercials for a new generation of toys glutted the airwaves after school, on Saturday mornings and in seemingly round-the-clock barrages before Christmas. Manufacturers knew where their bread was buttered. In no time, toy packaging carried the banner "As Seen on TV," which almost guaranteed record sales.

Adults soon discovered that kids didn't just want the products advertised; they also wanted to be part of the shows they watched, whether it was Gomer Pyle, Lost in Space, or The Flintstones. Kids would be ecstatic to get something--a lunchbox, board game or replica prop--to feel closer to their electronic heroes' world. The result was that millions of kids pleaded, pestered and pressured their parents into buying them whatever flashed before their impressionable eyes on the TV screen.

Over 20 years later, those baby boomers have grown up. However, the playthings of childhood continue to hold a fascination for them. Obviously, there are associations between favorite toys and memories of a simpler, happier time, place or event. Just having an item again, or acquiring one that was unattainable when originally issued, can bring a great sense of pleasure and fulfillment. There is a kind of magic that springs from those Sixties toys. They may have been mass-produced out of cardboard and plastic, but there was a great deal of pride, craftsmanship, and--rarest of all--imagination that makes them unforgettable.

Television has grown up, too. From a novelty item, it has become, in many cases, the dominant design element in home decors. The voracious appetite of the medium has kept many of the Sixties' programs and characters alive for three decades. At first, syndication brought old TV favorites back to life on local stations, generally small UHF channels. With the video revolution of the 1980's, many cable systems (such as USA, Nickelodeon, and The Family Channel) use some of these shows as staples of their programming schedules.

The "second looks" are not just fun for the sake of seeing old shows again. They also allow a glimpse back at life during the late Fifties and Sixties. Our own homes may not have been as ideal as those of the Stone family on <u>The Donna Reed Show</u> or the Cleavers of <u>Leave It To Beaver</u>, but for many of us these were our perceptions of how life should have been.

Today, all the artifacts are there--the cars, the clothes, the customs--acting as signposts to a place that grows more distant in memory each day.

Further, many series episodes actually show the great toy trends of that era. Beaver Cleaver reflected the early Sixties monster craze when he and his buddies bought sweatshirts depicting a horrible creature. Agent Illya Kuryakin was attacked on the stairs of U.N.C.L.E. HQ by Ideal's Robot Commando, modified to fire lethal rockets! A dazed Herman Munster once mistook Marx' battery-operated Frankenstein for his new son. Remember the <u>My Three Sons</u> episode where Chip Douglas found a lost dog and was rewarded with what seemed like every toy in the 1963 Mattel catalog? Chip's generous haul was first seen inside a well-stocked toy store, then gloriously piled up in the Douglas back yard.

The kids who grew up laughing at the castaways on <u>Gilligan's Island</u> or thrilling to the Caped Crusaders' exploits on <u>Batman</u> now have children of their own. Again, because of the home video explosion, many vintage TV shows are enjoyed by a second (or in some cases, third) generation. Therefore, many age groups are attracted to Sixties collectibles. In the collectors' market, overwhelming demand has outpaced the relatively limited supply of goods, causing fierce competition and soaring prices.

Because the value of some Sixties items has increased as much as 500% in less than ten years, a third group is also snapping them up: Investors.

Toys and collectibles have weathered two recessions in the past decade and come through them wildly profitable. That kind of track record is very attractive to investors in today's unstable economy. Besides, toys are so much more fun than stocks or bonds, or even traditional antiques such as coins, furniture or Depression glass.

For whatever reason, the hottest items in the collecting field today are those legendary toys of the Sixties.

ITEMS NOT COVERED IN THIS BOOK

Items logged in <u>Toys of the Sixties</u> are divided into twelve general topics. Naturally, it is impossible to include every toy produced between 1960-69. To make <u>Toys of the Sixties</u> concise and more valuable as a resource, some forms of collectibles are not covered.

The rule for exclusion is simple: You won't find it here if there is already a definitive, specialized source. The obvious example is comic books; many fine reference books and price guides already exist on the subject.

Collectibles <u>not</u> included in <u>Toys of the Sixties</u> are:

* Comic Books
* Big Little Books, Little Golden Books, Whitmans, and other small children's books
* Movie and TV stills
* Posters
* <u>TV Guides</u>
* Non-character-related vehicles such as trains, commercial trucks and farm machinery
* Baby dolls, fashion dolls and other dolls intended primarily for girls

REGARDING PRICES IN THIS BOOK

The prices in <u>Toys of the Sixties</u> have been compiled from a combination of factors, including the author's experience, sale prices of specific items from the Toy Scouts, Inc. Mail Order Catalog, typical prices at collectible shows, dealer price lists, ads appearing in collectibles periodicals, auction results, and extensive correspondence with collectors involved in trading, buying, and selling.

The prices quoted in this book are for Near Mint or Mint items, still in their original packaging, if any, and are collector, or retail, prices.

There will generally be a high and low range for the prices quoted in this book. This reflects geographical price variations of the marketplace. The approximate value of a toy not in its original packaging, but still in very clean and near mint condition would be one half the value of the lowest end of the price range. Ever-increasing demand for scarcer items or a newly discovered warehouse find of items previously difficult to obtain may have an upward or downward effect on prices, therefore it is imperative to keep in mind that this book serves as a guide in an appraisal and does not set the market value. Collectibles, like the stock market, work on the premise that the item is only worth what someone is willing to pay for it. The broader your clientele, the better chance you have for receiving a higher price.

GRADING TOYS

Collecting toys requires a particular state of mind. It's a curious brew of nostalgia, aesthetics and investment strategy. Because there are so many diverse motives for collecting, one or more of the triad mind-set can dominate. Some collectors want an item because they had one like it as a kid. Others may stumble across a piece and think it looks "cool" or visually pleasing. Still others purchase collectibles because they're sure the items will appreciate quickly.

No matter what an individual's reason is for collecting, everyone agrees that the most desirable pieces are those in near-perfect, or "mint", condition.

Unfortunately, items turn up more frequently in less-than-mint condition than they do in factory-fresh shape. Some of the paint may have worn off, a decal may have been scraped away, or the nose on a character's face might have been broken. Moving parts may no longer move. Detachable accessories could be missing. In other words, at the opposite end of the scale are the real beaters.

Between the pristine mint examples of an item and those that are pretty well trashed are literally thousands of possibilities. Beyond the two extremes, it is rare that two collectors completely agree on the state of an item. A flaw that may seem insignificant to one person may make it totally unacceptable to another. Because of the wide-spread difference of opinion on condition, there has never been--and more than likely will never be--a universal standard of grading accepted by all buyers and sellers. However, general terms have been coined and adopted throughout the market to help evaluate items for the pruposes of trade, resale or appraisal. Many of these terms are commonly used in other types of collecting (i.e. cards, comics, and posters.)

The following scale is used to describe merchandise for sale in the mail order catalog of Toy Scouts (available for $3.00 from Toy Scouts, Inc., 137 Casterton Ave., Akron, OH 44303)

MINT: Flawless; like new and, in most cases, unused.

NEAR MINT (NM): Only slight detectable wear, usually very minor. Overall appearance is like new in every way.

FINE (FN): There are no major defects or damage, but some overall, general wear is apparent. It has not been abused and displays well. An item in Fine condition usually has a good resale value, and is generally for collectors who want a well-preserved item at an affordable price.

VERY GOOD (VG): Shows use but no serious damage. However, there may be evidence of fading, worn paint or heavy creases. Although the item is still displayable, the majority of collectors will retain a VG item until they can later upgrade it.

GOOD (G): Obviously worn, with some minor damage in the form of stains, faded colors, chips in paint, missing piece(s), minor dent(s), tear(s), etc. Good items are displayable, but their collectible value is limited.

THE TOY BUSINESS

Creating, manufacturing and marketing toys is far from a laugh-a-minute fling. It's a risky game played for <u>very</u> high stakes. The business is seasonal by nature, critically dependent on Christmas for the lion's share of its sales. Kids--the primary consumers--are a fickle, constantly changing audience. What's in now can be old hat next week. Most toys have a shelf life of just one year because kids always look forward to getting a new, different toy each Christmas. A toy company might have a runaway hit one year and a disastrous flop the next. Enough of this flip-flopping of financial fortunes could ruin a business in no time.

In the Sixties, toy manufacturers were armed witha a new weapon with which to wage war in the marketplace: Television.

As the decade opened, the toy industry underwent a transition, complete with growing pains. The main cause of this turbulence was advertising toys on Television. TV advertising revolutionized traditional merchandising methods. It opened the door for manufacturers to walk right into the homes of children across the country and make them aware of toys they might otherwise never have known existed. Millions of dollars were poured into producing elaborate commercials to sell toys.

The landmark product that demonstrated how powerful selling via TV could be was the introduction of the **Barbie Doll** in 1959. **Mattel's** massive campaign proved wildly effective not only in terms of sales figures, but also by breaking price barriers. They were able, sucessfully, to sell a toy at higher price levels than were ever before attempted.

Barbie also set the pace for other big-plastic/high-priced toys, such as **Mr. Machine, King Zor** and **Robot Commando.** All three were designed by **Marvin Glass** for **Ideal** between 1961-63, and proved to be powerhouse sellers. Mr. Machine alone was reported to have earned $12 million for Ideal. This phenomenal achievement was simply due to a winning ad campaign.

Despite a mild recession in 1960-61, toy manufacturers generally prospered, thanks in large part to Television. Unfortunately, some companies who used TV as an advertising tool did so irresponsibly by greatly exaggerating the qualities and capabilities of their products. Chief offenders included ads by **Ideal** (for its **Robot Commando, Jet Fighter** and **Steve Canyon Flight Helmet**) and **Remco** (with its battery-operated warships and submarines.) Toy missiles looked like they could soar high into the sky and hit targets with amazing accuracy--sometimes in mid-air! Gun and cannon barrels apparently smoked after firing. Products appeared in diorama settings that were grandiose beyond any kid's wildest imagination.

A typical "mom-and-pop" store of the Sixties.

These unrestrained flights of commercial fancy looked great, but were deceptive and deplorably unrealistic. Parents and retailers were outraged. A midwestern department store executive asserted that "a toy should be presented as a toy, not as the eighth wonder of the world." **The National Association of Broadcasters** agreed. In June, 1961, the NAB proclaimed that often there was "little resemblance between the commercial and the end product," and set mandates that toys be depicted honestly.

Naturally, commercials remained an integral part of overall advertising campaigns. In 1965 alone, the NAB cleared 215 different toy commercials to run on networks and local stations.

For some companies, just strategically choosing their commercial spots wasn't enough. Beginning in 1959 and continuing through the early Sixties, Mattel sponsored an entire 30-minute weekly kids' show. Over the years, this featured Harvey made-for-theater cartoons and TV originals with Beany and Cecil. Taking Mattel's lead, Ideal pacted with animation giant **Hanna-Barbera** to create a custom-made show solely as a vehicle for their products. The groundbreaking program was called **"The Magilla Gorilla Show,"** debuting in January, 1964. At the time, Ideal vice-president **Abe Kent** said: "We're giving the trade wider opportunities for year-round sales and building the foundation for customer acceptance for all our toys and games--even the non-TV items." Ideal President **Lionel Weintraub** added, "We feel that this unprecedented support will be of considerable benefit, not only to ourselves, but to the entire toy industry as well."

PLUG THAT TOY

(Above) **Structo** *metal trucks were plugged by* **Joey Bishop** *on his late night talk show in the Fall of 1969. Structo, with years of declining sales, aimed its sales campaign at an all adult audience, based on market research that revealed over 2/3 of all buying decisions of such metal trucks were made by grown-ups.*

(Upper left) TV stars of popular kids shows also promoted merchandise based on their shows. **David McCallum** *of* **The Man From U.N.C.L.E.** *addresses fans at an* **Ideal** *toy promotion at* **Topps** *stores in New York in 1965.*

(Left) **Captain Kangaroo,** *a long-time favorite of children, endorsed many toys over the years for his show sponsors, and with great success.* **Play-Doh** *sold particularly well on his show in the early '60's.*

Ideal advertised Magilla's television strangth to promote confidence and even stronger selling power within the industry.

"Magilla Gorilla" was an immediate ratings hit. In New York City, it was the highest-rated kids' show on the air. Ideal's success with "Magilla" led to the follow-up **"Peter Potamus Show"**, which premiered in September of "64. **Milton Bradley** sponsored the popular **"Shenanigans"** show with host **Stubby Kay**. These shows paved the way for later merchandise-based shows such as **"He-Man"** and **"The Transformers"** in the 1980's.

Not only did the way toys were advertised change, but also the traditional means of distribution was altered. In the Fifties, over 90% of all toys produced went from the manufacturer to the whoesalers to the retailers. Starting in 1959, discount stores began popping up. Discounters bought directly from the manufacturer in huge quantities, especially TV-advertised toys. Since discount stores bought in such volume, they could buy items for much less than wholesalers would pay. In turn, they could sell merchandise for less than could wholesalers.

Big chain stores and department stores were also buying directly from manufacturers in quantity and at cut rates. Some manufacturers, such as **Marx**, would customize their "hot" items for a volume retailer such as **Sears**--with a package deal agreement that forced Sears to take their slow-moving items, as well.

In fact, Louis Marx's company was so powerful that he wouldn't even sell to most wholesalers unless they bought in massive quantities, with a no-return policy. The quantities were far greater than they could ever hope to sell.

The bottom line was that wholesalers found themselves in a real bind. Manufacturers only wanted to move the most product they could in order to turn a profit, even if that meant selling to discounters and by-passing wholesalers. This meant wholesalers had less of the year's hot items and more slow movers to try to sell to retailers. Some wholesalers took a page from Louis Marx's book and tried to offer package deals to their retail customers. No one wanted to be stuck with old or sluggish merchandise, which cost a great deal to warehouse and had to be disposed of at a loss.

Like guppies being eaten by sharks, the small, independent "mom and pop" stores were vanishing. Their limited buying power forced them to continue dealing with wholesalers. As a result, they had to pay more for merchandise and pass the higher cost along to their customers. For example, a discount store might price a toy at half of what its "mom and pop" competition across the street could afford to do--and the discounter could still make a profit. Some small independents actually bought merchandise for their own stores right off the shelves of a discount store for less than they could get it from their wholesaler!

Further complicating the dilemma for "mom and pop" was the advent of shopping malls in the mid-60's. These sparkling, new suburban developments kept consumers away from downtown, inner-city areas where most independents were located. Smaller stores survived for a while by selling staple

HI! I'M MAGIC MARXIE...

—and I don't mean to brag, but I'm going to be the most popular little character in America this fall. As the TV spokesman for Marx Toys, I'm going to sing my way into more homes, make friends with more kids and sell more toys than anyone in the history of the toy business!

Louis Marx' close relationship with large department and chain stores allowed him to spend almost nothing on advertising within the industry itself. This ad ran for years in the back of trade publications of the '60's and essentially 'says it all.'

items which were not subject to seasonal whims. These products included train sets, race sets, wheel goods (such as bikes, wagons and peddle cars), chemistry sets and sporting goods. In 1963, there were 4,278 toy and hobby stores in this country. Of those, 75% were independently owned. Ten years later, only 10% of those remaining in business were independent. Today, they are all but extinct. This trend continued as even today large toy companies and toy chains are being bought out by mammoth conglomerates. Today, worried members of the industry wryly muse that at future toy fairs there will be one buyer (**Toys-R-Us**) and one seller (**Hasbro**).

1964-66 proved to be watermark years for the industry as a whole. The nation's economy was strong. Unemployment was at its lowest in eight years. The future for toy consumption looked promising, as parents were still producing baby-boomers at the rate of 4 million each year. During this time, TV character licensing boomed. Manufacturers began creating better quality, more colorful and visually-exciting packaging for their products. Freelance toy designer **Stan Weston** came up with a cultural breakthrough in 1964. Prior to that time, boys were never allowed to play with dolls. However, Weston came up with a military doll--more than just a toy soldier--that sold six million units its first year out. The product? **Hasbro**'s original version of **GI Joe**. Weston nearly duplicated his own success two years later with Ideal's **Captain Action**.

From the pinnacle of the "go-go" years, the last third of the decade turned dark and disappointing. Political turmoil, student unrest, urban rioting and protests against the Vietnam War plummeted the country into a state of anxiety. Reflecting the downswing in the national mood, the decade's earlier vibrant creations and designs with flair gave way to stagnancy. There were no fresh, exciting concepts to cause trends or sensations. Rising labor costs forced many firms to stop manufacturing here and and find cheap labor forces overseas. Printing and paper costs also rose sharply, creating the need for inexpensive, less-attractive packaging.

As plastic became universally accepted for producing toys, companies that still made metal toys also found themselves hurting. Plastic was far less expensive to use, and companies such as **Structo**, which specialized in metal cars and trucks, couldn't compete and folded.

Fortunately, the earlier years of the Sixties left a rich legacy that continues to be cherished by those who grew up then and by anyone who appreciates the dynamic style of the era.

Stan Weston, inventor of the GI Joe and Captain Action dolls was also the licensor for the Man From U.N.C.L.E. and Marvel Super-Heroes as well as consultant to leading toy companies in the Sixties.

SIXTIES STORE DISPLAYS were creative works of art and marketing ingenuity, the likes of which have not since been duplicated.

SURVIVORS OF THE SIXTIES

Many toys have come and gone in the last three decades. Despite this whirl wind of change, a stalwart few have weathered the storm to remain as staples in America's tumultuous toy industry today.

ETCH A SKETCH (Ohio Art, 1960) Prior to the Etch A Sketch, Ohio Art was known as the world's largest manufacturer of metal and tin toys. In 1959, the company purchased "L'Ecran Magique" from French toy designer Arthur Grandjean at the Nuremberg Toy Fair. The re-christened toy has since sold more than 50 million pieces, and boasts over 10,000 members in the Etch A Sketch Club.

FRISBEE Originally named "Pluto Platter" in 1957, the Frisbee received its present name in 1958. "Frisbie! was the cry college kids in the East used to signal the flight of their empty pie tins from the Frisbie Pie Company. By 1970, these Frisbees that Ed Headrick originally designed were so popular among college students that flying disc courses were being offered at universities. Even the US Navy investigated the use of Frisbee-like discs molded into flares to be launched from planes...a $400,000 study! With 100 million discs produced, and twelve books and seven periodicals published on the subject, the Frisbee has been a Wham-O success story.

GI JOE (Hasbro 1964) "Our decision to market this item was a move based on guts alone," recalled Stephen Hassenfeld of Hassenfeld Brothers (Hasbro) on the introduction of GI Joe to the toy market in 1964. After a year of preparation, Hasbro showed promotional models of the doll and its packaging to select buyers in early 1964. The response, at best, was lukewarm: the idea was a precedent, and there was nothing to compare it to. "Boys won't play with dolls," was the general reaction. The power of TV and Hasbro's clever advertising, however, convinced boys all across the country when commercials started airing in July. Advertised as a soldier and not a doll, commercials were laced with plenty of actual World War II film footage, and scenes showing GI Joe were on a sandtable battleground diorama to create realism. GI Joe proved not only to be a runaway hit, selling over six million dolls its first year, but also won the New York International Film and TV Festival's "Best TV Commercial of 1964" award.

SILLY PUTTY (1950)   Discovered by accident while working on a chemical plastic for the government, Silly Putty became an instant success and has continued to delight children through generations.   At a world toy exhibit in Russia in the early 60's, it was the single most fascinating item for the Russians, both young and old.

BARREL OF MONKEYS GAME (Lakeside 1965) This simple game of skill involved hanging a barrel-full of little, plastic monkeys hand-over-tail to form a chain. It was first introduced in 1965 with surprisingly good response and has become a perennial best seller in the toy industry.

COLORFORMS In 1951, Harry Kislevity, an art student, created a new toy which children could use to make a collage by adhering plastic pieces to a laminated surface.   Colorforms were originally marketed in the 1950's with licensed characters including Barbie, Sesame Street favorites, and Mickey Mouse. They also began advertising at that time and are the longest running TV-advertised toy brand in history. Presently, the original Colorforms set is being distributed through the Museum of Modern Art.

PLAY DOH (1956)   The idea for a modeling compound for children became a new product called "Play Doh" in 1956.   Manufactured by Rainbow Crafts, Inc. of Cincinnati, the company had sold 100 million cans by 1964.   This famous children's modeling material has grown in popularity throughout the world and is today being produced in London, Paris, and Milan.

BARBIE (Mattel 1959) Ruth Handler, who, with her husband Elliot, founded the Mattel toy company, is the woman we have to thank for that ultimate favorite of little girls, the Barbie Doll. Barbie was the first toy to be mass-marketed via television, and commanded never-before-imagined heights in pricing with its help. An instant success, Barbie launched Mattel from a small conventional toy company to a big league player. Throughout the Sixties, myriads of Barbie accessories and doll variations were produced. Today, Barbie is a billion-dollar industry and makes up 75% of all M a t t e l ' s   b u s i n e s s .

SEE 'N SAY (Mattel 1966) An extension of the concept of the pull-string talking puppets, See 'N say is a pre-school level toy that "teaches by talking". Children can listen to exciting sounds such as airplanes, fire engines, and trains. Original See 'N Says include "The Bee Says...","The Farmer Says...",and "The Clock Says...". Just rotate the pointer to a picture and pull the Chatty Ring to hear the sounds.

LEGO BUILDING BLOCKS (1962) Introduced from Europe, it was an immediate sell-out in ten U.S. test cities and became the third fastest selling toy in 1963. Although the architectural concept of Legos has changed from buildings to mostly space ships and other moving machines, Lego remains a popular and strong seller in the toy industry.

HOT WHEELS (Mattel 1968) Sixteen different cars were originally introduced, all with mag wheels, red stripe racing slicks, customized engines, torsion-bar suspension and moving parts. Also, four plastic action sets were introduced: two race sets, a stunt set with a loop-the-loop track, and a speed track set.

MATTEL: SURVIVOR OF THE SIXTIES

The following is from and interview with toy designer Fred Toerge, who worked for Mattel from 1964-67 and was instrumental in designing the Switch 'N Go Race Set line, Agent Zero-M Secret Agent Line, and many other favorite toys of the day. Fred left Mattel in 1967 to become Vice President of Raymond Lowery, Inc., and used his industrial design talents to help create the interior of Skylab.

I guess my first question to you is, how about giving me a quick history of the Mattel Toy Company that you know, and tell me what brought you to work for them?

I went to work for **Mattel** at the end of the year in 1964. I went there because a friend of mine named **Fred Adickes** had gone there the year before. At that time Mattel was really a new company as far as leading technology in the toy industry. That was because of a guy named **Jack Ryan**. He was a Yale graduate and was a very brilliant electronic engineer working in the defense industry--I think he worked for Sperry Missile. By chance Jack had gone to a trade show and met an inventor who had invented a voice mechanism for a doll which enabled a doll to talk randomly by pulling a cord. Jack was clear enough to see that this was a whole new form of toy, so he tied up with the inventor and decided he'd sell this idea to a toy company. His thought was to find a toy company that wasn't yet fully entrenched, one that was on the growth curve and that was willing to take chances. So, he looked around and Mattel, at that time, had just gotten out of the garage operation--it was something like 13 million a year. The company was founded by the **Handlers, Elliot and Ruth,** a mom-and-pop operation, and they were really doing a bunch of junk like everybody else...conventional toys. Jack contracted with them, as they could see the appeal of something like this. Jack was smart enough that he said, "I'll tell you what, let us sell this, I'll set up an R & D operation, and you pay me 2% on all the toys that we develop." They went for it. When I went to Mattel, Jack had been there probably around three and a half years. The company was just around 100 million then, a year. And really Mattel was, under Ryan, the first company to take advantage of modern technology and even try to upgrade toys. If you look at toys of that time, they're all traditional, inanimate objects. Mattel came out with all sorts of unique technology-based toys. As a matter of fact, we had a whole staff...there was a fellow who did nothing but acoustic research, there was one who did nothing but electronic research, we had one that was involved in chemistry. These are very, very, far-out people who weren't really interested in these toys at all. They were just looking for the gimmicks to take advantage of, natural phenomena and such, and then we would develop toys around them. Thinking back, when I was there we did the **James Bond** stuff, which was the first transforming toy. We took normal objects like cameras and fountain pens and such, and they'd all turn into lethal weapons. This went on, and then ten years later the Japanese were doing the **Transformers**.

*I'm looking in the 1966 Mattel toy catalog and I see that on the **Zero-M** you have, actually three pages of items. I notice in looking at them that on the **Agent Zero-M Snubnose with Shoulder Holster** there are bullets. It says there are "Shootin' Shells"--now I guess you didn't have the kind of constraints that toy makers came upon later. You were allowed to put things like that and not have parents worrying about kids shooting their eyes out.*

We didn't have the proliferation of lawyers you have now. All those toys would be bases for a crippling loss. Take that **Sonic Blaster** there. Something like that, if a kid took and sold that to another kid, that would be the end of it. But at that time we had a friendly nation. We didn't have all these problems. We were doing welding machines, vacuum form machines, where you have the intensity of power shock where any kid could conceivably lose an eye. Today, you can't do this.

Now, what was the idea behind the Switch 'N Go? Was that just a take off on road racing sets at the time or was it more the idea of free form driving the cars? What was it?

At that time road racing was a big thing. And road racing, as you know, had become so static and actually the cars went so fast that it was difficult for little kids to keep them on the track. The interest span of the kid...I think you yourself can remember having trouble on those road racing sets. It was just too much for a kid. So we were trying to get something that would be much slower and have more play value where you could change the layout, a flexible layout. And it was just interesting itself. You could switch it with air pressure and the car had the built in second gear. But there's a good example. We worked on that for maybe a year. Every time we'd show it to Ryan the impression was, "Real cute and it has a lot of play value, but it needs a schtick. What is the finale? It's gotta have a finale or you just can't play it." He thought that way. If he looked at the Switch 'N Go, we had this situation where you would chase the car and if you caught up to it...

You'd hit its bumper and flip it over.

Right.

How about the Chatty Kathy? Again, that was the idea of having something that could talk using a small record. I noticed in looking through this catalog the pull string dolls. Were they a success for the company?

Absolutely. All those **See 'N Say** toys came from that same basic package.

What toys were being developed when you were there that they thought were going to be big break throughs which ended up being a big bust?

Switch 'N Go.

Why do you think that happened?

Well, I think it's all a product of the time. If you look at the time, you're looking at the Sixties now. Up to that point, up to the late Fifties, children played with toys up through their twelfth year. In the 60's, television was really becoming predominant and we got all these musical fads, the **Beatles** and such, and kids were being redirected from child play to adult play. When Switch 'N Go came out...I don't really think you could interest a kid in a toy like that much past the age of nine. So our market really shrunk demographically.

*So TV really had a lot to do with...making or breaking toys. I know that with the Switch 'N Go they tried the Lost in Space model and they also had a **Batman** from the TV show. Neither of those were really able to help in any way. I could imagine they probably cost a lot just to get the merchandising rights.*

Well, that whole Batman thing was a fiasco. Batman, the show, really didn't generate the kind of following they thought it was going to.

How about the Vroom engines? What was the idea behind that?

It was the same idea as making a bicycle look and sound like a motorcycle. Once again, kids past the age of nine had no interest in things such as this. So once again it was a dead market.

Did Mattel tend to try to epitomize the California feel of the times? The surf and so on?

No. The big market was the East Coast at the time. Demographics. More people lived in the East than did in the West.

*Is that why Mattel didn't go with traditional? Like at the time you were doing this **Marx Company** was still putting out playsets and using traditional army men and stuff like...*

Well, no. If you look at Marx, Marx was working on schlocky merchandise at a very low profit margin. And Ryan's stuff, the apparent value...if you have something that intrinsically has some built in features you can charge more money for it. We broke a lot of barriers. At that time you couldn't sell a doll for over ten dollars. A doll over ten dollars was unthinkable. Well, we sold **The Walking Doll** for sixteen dollars simply because it had features that the other dolls didn't have. The thing that makes you wonder, though, is I remember that doll, as I say cost sixteen dollars, so that meant it would have to be built for two dollars. Probably $1.90 hard cost. And the box that the doll was merchandised in, in order to make it impressive and in order to make it believable with full photography, the box cost $2.25. So the box cost more than the doll.

*Now the **Hot Wheels** that came in the late 60's...*

That was a fluke. When I started there, they were making 100 million a year, and a year and a half later, they're doing 140 million a year. They're a very, very, successful company. And in those days, the trend was, "How do we buy up other companies and diversify them?" So Mattel went into a situation where they were buying up dissimilar companies. They bought a music company, one that made musical instruments. They bought several companies. One of them was a plastic laminating firm in New Jersey that made plastic lunchboxes. Cheap little schlocky deals. And Elliot came around and said, "What are we going to do? We've got to increase the use of these plastic cases." So we started thinking of all the things we could do with these plastic cases. And one of the thoughts was that, at that time, **Matchbox** was the only company that made these little miniature solid die-cast cars. So we thought maybe we could do a series of carrying cases that open into garages and play parks and all that would carry these cars and sell them through Matchbox. And as a result we got a bunch of these cars that were lying around and we started thinking, what could we do that would make the cars better? And at that time, they didn't roll at all. So

So somebody came up with the idea of how could we make this a low friction bearing where the thing would really go? That's where Hot Wheels came about. Strictly accidental.

And it was a really profitable accident.

You bet it was!

What brought about the development of the Thingmaker and I want to know, was that a failure for the company?

No. That went pretty well. The thing was, the company was being so successful in other areas. And look at it today, it's a one product company. They do a billion dollars a year and three quarters of it's **Barbie**

Why are they a one product company now?

Because of Barbie's success. When you get to be that big, you start having all sorts of marketing survey and everything. When you're small and scrambling, you try anything. When you get big and successful you say, "Let's concentrate on our high volume, high profit items." All the innovation we were going through when I was there...as a matter of fact a couple years later, Jack Ryan left, and it all died. There was no need for it. The marketing and distribution was so great at the time that they could sell anything. Just so happened that the Barbie dolls and the See 'N Say and all the traditional lines would carry the company. There was no reason to innovate anymore. In the last ten years they haven't done a darn thing that's new.

What brought up the plastic goop for the Thingmakers? Was that just a fluke again?

That was that same guy I was talking about. That chemist. I can't remember the details, but we were looking for something you could mold and something that wasn't toxic. There were problems with that Thingmaker because it picked up a lot of bacteria after you used it awhile, and built up all sorts of poisonous, not poisonous, but unhealthy situations. If it had stayed in the market for a long time, I think they would have had a lot of suits.

That's funny because I remember from the ones I bought they would get kind of a gross film on them after awhile. I guess all the heat regenerating, and little bits of plastic. Do you think that those days are gone forever? I mean, toy companies aren't going to have that kind of money....

It's not the money. We're living in a litigious society. You can't do anything, anything at all ...I mean to do...that catalog you're looking at now, to have product liability on that would have been more than the net worth of the company. Just couldn't do it. When I was a kid we used to buy lead soldier sets where you actually melted lead over the stove and poured lead soldiers. You couldn't do that today.

Your time at Mattel was pretty fulfilling for you as an artist, wasn't it?

Oh, I enjoyed it. It was the only company I ever worked for.

It's a very creative place.

Yeah, well, that was the whole idea. Ryan's idea of staffing the place, he had a psychological test for everybody to get in, and the hooks in the test were to identify people who were aggressive, belligerent, and who didn't work well with others, because he thought the only way you could really have creativity is to have people fighting each other. We had an awful lot of fist fights, a lot of action going on.

Really? There were a lot of disagreements going on?

Oh, yeah!

Did Mattel pay close attention to its competition and sometimes borrow ideas from other companies and twist them around a little bit?

Everbody does that.

Because I noticed with plastic figures a lot of companies use the same molds...they tweak them a little bit this way or that way.

Marx was notorious for that. Marx was the biggest knock-off artist in the business.

Did you ever have any run-ins? Did you guys ever have any law suits with Marx Company?

No. There was no reason to. By the time you get to court, it's already four years later and the toys are already past age. That's why the knock-off artists survive, because there's no reason to take them to court.

The Zero-M line did fairly well, didn't it?

Yeah. A lot of the stuff was hit or miss, like their spring-loaded bicycle. I thought that was going to be a big one, but it was just toooo dangerous. I was always kind of working on the outside of the limit. Stuff I was working on wouldn't have come to fruition.

Did TV have a big bearing on Mattel? Did they see it as a medium to sell their toys?

Absolutely. I think they were the first to realize that.

I recall as a child that their commercials were always a lot more interesting than other toy companies. They had a lot more to them. It was almost like a live action thing with toys.

They had a very good marketing department. What they did set the tone for the rest of the industry. They were spending more on TV advertising than the rest of the industry combined when I was there. Look what's happened since. (END)

ASSORTED GOLD NUGGETS

This chapter contains toys which are not related to any television or licensed characters. All the characters in this chapter were created by the toy companies themselves. As the power of television grew, the toy industry experienced a staggering wave of licensed character toys, making toy production an expensive and risky venture. Companies had to guess at which shows they thought would be hits if they were going to secure licensing rights early enough to manufacture the product in time for the show's running. Some companies went back to designing their own toys again just to stay in the game. Within this first chapter are both super-hit toys which made toy history and changed the industry, as well as toys that, despite big budgets and large promotions, flopped. One can see the change in trends and technology over the decade when reading this chapter, and no, it's not your imagination, the early part of the Sixties definitely had more exciting and imaginative toys to offer. Licensed television characters began changing the industry by 1965. It was easier for companies to re-make a gun and change the packaging featuring a TV character than to design a new toy.

MIS-2

MIS-2. BATTLE OF THE BLUE & GRAY PLAYSET (Marx 1960-65) One of the most popular of all of the Marx playsets is the Civil War "Blue & Gray" set. Issued in a variety of sizes and box designs, it always contains dozens of Confederate and Union soldiers molded in blue and gray plastic, shell firing cannons, wagons, caissons, horses, figures of Grant, Lee, Davis and Lincoln and battlefield accessories. Some sets contain colonial tin litho mansions, plastic bombed out mansions, ambulance wagons, record, miniature metal pistol, bridge and a unique figure of a soldier flying from his shot horse which is falling head first to the ground. Sets with any of the above added features are more desirable to collectors. Most boxes are approximately 28x14x4" deep. Our photo shows set number #4658. **$500-1000**

MIS-1

MIS-3

MIS-1. "AWK-AWK" KENNER'S GOONEY BIRD DOLL (Kenner 1964) When Kenner created it's mascot gooney bird in 1964, it appeared on all the Kenner commercials and even wound up in the form of a 12" bendable vinyl figure. Cleverly packaged in a TV shaped box with its head and feet sticking out, it sold well the first six months then steadily declined and was discontinued by late 1965. **$50-75**

MIS-3. CHANGEABLE CHARLIE (Halsam 1950s-60s) A popular toy for over a decade, Changeable Charlie consists of 13 wood blocks with all four sides of each block painted in a different facial feature of a different character. Blocks can be rearranged into several different characters. Box is 6x7x2" deep. **$10-15**

MIS-4

MIS-6

MIS-4. CLANCY THE GREAT CHIMPANZEE (Ideal 1963)
Large plastic 27" battery-operated monkey features a hidden
switch in his palm which, when pressed, would allow him to
move forward on his roller skates as he nods his head from
side to side while producing monkey noises. Clancy also
features a removable trick hat which can be placed upright
in his hand to catch tossed coins. When he catches a coin,
he skates forward. Ideal's battery-operated Clancy was the
company's pride and joy of 1963. Hoping to follow the same
successful sales of former battery-operated powerhouses
like Mr. Machine (1960), Robot Commando (1961) and King
Zor (1962). Unfortunately, the cute money didn't have the
ruggedness of earlier creations and sales were dismal at
best. It was removed from production in 1964. Box is
29x10x10". Coins included. **$100-200**

MIS-6. CRIME BUSTER ACTION POLICE GUN (Topper
1965) During the early to mid-Sixties, Topper was the
dominant force in creative new action guns. The 26" long
Crime Buster gun was like most topper guns in that it had
multiple working features such as clip-fed machine gun
bullets, Roit-Spray attachment that shot four bullets at once,
working Smoke Grenade launcher and Signal Missile, tracer
barrel that sparks and a built-in siren. Gun also includes
CrimeBuster Cartridge Belt and Police Badge. Box is 28x15"
$75-125

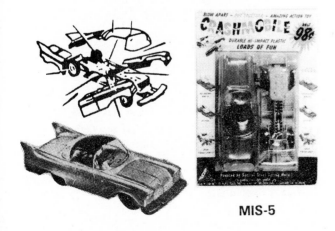

MIS-5

MIS-7

MIS-5. CRASHMOBILE (Tri-Play 1961)
Plastic 7" spring-powered car crashes apart upon impact
and can be reassembled. A variety of Crashmobiles were
made including a "Weird-oh" safari jeep and an Aston-Martin
"007" spy car. Comes on 8x11" display card. **$25-50**

MIS-7. CRUSADER 101 MOTORIZED CAR (Deluxe
Reading 1964) Large 30" long battery-operated, remote-
control red plastic convertible car with chrome trim and
black and white interior. There is a detailed 8" figure which
sits behind the wheel of the car. The car is controlled by a
remote control box and can move forward or reverse at
variable speeds. Wheels can be turned manually to allow car
to drive in a circle. The trunk of the car opens and contains
a workable jack and spare tire. Box is 11x30x5" deep.
$175-225

MIS-8

MIS-8. DANDY THE LION (Irwin 1963) Plastic 25" battery powered mechanical lion obeys commands to stalk forward or backward, rear up on its hind legs and growl- all by the touch from a "magic" training whip. Created by legendary toy designer Marvin Glass, who also designed Mr. Machine, Robot Commando and Rock'em-Sock'em Robots. Box is 26x20x27". **$200-300**

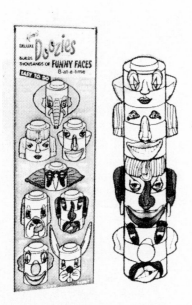

MIS-9

MIS-9. DOOZIES (Kenner 1961)
Doozies consist of circular styrofoam stacking sections and vacuform facial pieces. Facial pieces are applied to each section and stacked upon each other like a totem pole. In the late Fifties and early Sixties, totem poles were an object of fascination for children and toy manufactuers alike, appearing as cereal premiums, model kits and plastic statues. Kenner capitalized on this interest with Doozies. Doozies come in a variety of ways. Our photo shows the "Animal and People" Deluxe Doozie set. **$20-35**

MIS-10

MIS-10. EASY-BAKE OVEN (Kenner 1964)
One of the all time best selling non-doll toys for young girls was Kenner's Easy-Bake Oven. An instant sell-out when first introduced in the winter of 1964, Kenner tripled production to one million units in 1965! A continually good seller, the Easy-Bake Oven continued production into the early Seventies. The 16x18" plastic oven's most unique feature is that it bakes with just two ordinary light bulbs. There is no oven door, the pans slide through a cooling chamber and out a slot. Set includes three baking pans, plastic kitchen utensils and packaged baking mixes. Box is 22x17x8". **$35-50**

MIS-11

MIS-11. ETCH-A-SKETCH MAGIC SCREEN (Ohio Art 1960) One of the surviving toys of the Sixties that is still in mass production today due mainly to its appeal to kids and adults alike. Art exhibits, tournaments and an Official Fan Club with over 10,000 members are proof of this toy's popularity. It's hard to believe that Ohio art, then the world's largest toy manufactuer of metal toys, passed on producing the Etch-A-Sketch when it was first offered them by French toy designer Arthur Grandjean in 1959. Since its premiere in 1960, Etch-A-Sketch has sold more than 50 million units world wide. The Etch-A-Sketch features a plastic 8x10" cased screen with two control knobs, one which makes a straight horizontal line, the other a stright vertical line. When both knobs are turned at the same time, a curved line is achieved. Drawing can be erased by turning the screen upside down and shaking it. The first issue box came in a rectangular window display box. A year later, the design of the box was changed slightly, featuring beveled sides. our

MIS-14

MIS-12

MIS-14. FLYING FOX- JET PROP AIRLINER (Remco 1959-60) Large 20" long plastic airliner with four motorized jet prop engines, each individually controlled by the cockpit control panel to which the plane is attached. Other features include blinking landing lights, landing gear and high pitched jet whine. Plane can also tilt to simulate diving, banking and climbing. Wingspan is 19". Box is 20x21x12" deep. **$200-300**

MIS-12. FIREBIRD-99 SPORTS CAR DASHBOARD (Remco 1960) Dashboard toys became very popular in the early Sixties, and the Remco Firebird 99 was the most successful seller. Battery-powered, the 99 features working windshield wipers, real electric horn, blinking turn signals, a speedometer that accelerates and decelerates, a glove box that opens and adjustable rear view mirror. Made in bright yellow and red plastic-- the two colors that toy companies universally regarded as key colors in making and selling a toy. Box is 9x11x8" deep. **$20-30**

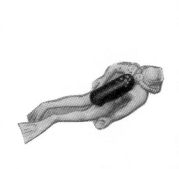

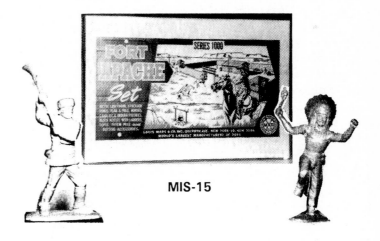

MIS-15

MIS-13

MIS-13. THE FLIPPY FROGMAN (Inco 1964) 5" black plastic frogman dives and surfaces by way of baking soda tablets which are included. Diving frogmen and submarines operated by baking soda were first introduced by Kelloggs' as cereal give-aways in the Fifties. The television series Sea Hunt renewed interest in frogmen and baking soda-powered sea-diving toys. Figure comes on 5x10" display card. **$15**

MIS-15. FORT APACHE PLAYSET (Marx 1950-70s) The longest continued production run of any of the several hundreds of playsets manufactured by Louis Marx, "the king of playsets". This set remained in a constant state of change in an effort to keep the set new and appealing to kids. The fort dwellers range from small 54mm frontiersmen to large 60mm 7th Cavalry troops. All sets include plenty of Indians, of course. Special Sears exclusive sets could contain as many as 300 pieces while others remain relatively simple at 100 pieces. Our photo example shows set #3680. **$100-400**

MIS-16

MIS-16. FREEZE QUEEN DAIRY STAND ICE CREAM
MACHINE (Kenner 1966) Kenner's enormous success with the Easy-Bake Oven created a wave of food-making toys, many of which Kenner itself introduced to an infatuated market. The Freeze Queen featured a new principle of using no batteries or electrical plug-in cords, but simply a canister which could be pre-frozen in any refrigerater freezer. Packaged mixes are poured into canister and mixing handle is pumped a few times to make actual ice cream in about ten minutes. Set includes 10x12' plastic Dairy Stand machine, mixer, cone dispenser, 24 cones, milk shake glass, mixing bowl, two canisters and eight mixing packets. Box is 16x14x8" deep. **$35-50**

MIS-17. "FRISBEE" FLYING DISC (Wham-0 1960s)
Wham-o revolutionized the toy world and created a cult following of fans that is still present today with its invention of the Frisbee. Created in 1957 and originally called the "Pluto Platter", it was an instant success and had the same sudden impact and craze phenomena as did the hula-hoop (which Wham-o made in 1958). Original first issue Frisbees were simple in design and molded in red plastic. Marketed as a flying saucer. Frisbee's from the Sixties had the names of the nine planets around it's outer rim, a raised center simulating a domed cockpit and came on a 9x12" display card. **$35-45**

MIS-18

MIS-18. FROSTY SNO-CONE MACHINE (Hasbro 1963-
70s) Tall 16" white plastic snow man-shaped ice shaving machine with manual turning crank in back. Comes with flavored syrup packets, paper cups, candy toppings and shovel-shaped spoon. Box is 11x17x6" deep. **$20-25**

MIS-19

MIS-19. FUZZY WUZZY SOAP (Aerosol Corp. 1966)
The soap that grows fuzzy hair also has a free toy inside its center. The Aerosol Company promoted the fact that the more a child would wash his hands, the quicker he/she could find his free toy. The toys are the same as those found in gum ball machines of the Sixties, including Rat Fink figures. Fuzzy Wuzzy soap comes in the shape of a Bear, Cat and Monkey and packaged in a 2x4" window display box designed like a circus cage. **$10-15**

MIS-20

MIS-20. GAYLORD THE WALKING BLOODHOUD (Ideal
1963) Gaylord was part of Ideal's battery-operated animal series that also included Clancy the Great, Smarty Bird and Odd Ogg. All four of these highly promising 1963 releases were overshadowed by the enormous success of a game they almost didn't produce at all- Mouse Trap! Gaylord's main feature is that he will walk forward when his leash is pulled upward and is even designed to walk up shallow steps. There is a small magnet in his mouth which allows him to "pick up" his bone. Box is 12x30x12" and is designed like a doghouse complete with a cut-out side panel for door. **$125-175**

MIS-21

MIS-21. GETAWAY CHASE GAME (AMF 1968)
Race set designed in the "Roaring Twenties" fashion with two old time sedans in hot pursuit. Also included is a cardboard stand-up city. Object is for the police car to catch up with the gangster car. Box is 24x20". **$35-50**

GIRDER & PANEL BUILDING SET (Kenner 1960s)
Originating in the late Fifties, Kenner's building sets increased in popularity every year to a point at which, during the early Sixties, there were over 50 variations of these sets. Our photos feature examples from the three most popular series.

MIS-22

MIS-22. GIRDER & PANEL SET BOX SET $35-60, CANISTER $25-50

MIS-23

MIS-23. GIRDER & PANEL AND BRIDGE & TURNPIKE BOX SET $75-100, CANISTER $45-75

MIS-24

MIS-24. SKY RAIL: FUTURISTIC CITY GIRDER & PANEL BOX SET $100-150, CANISTER $65-185

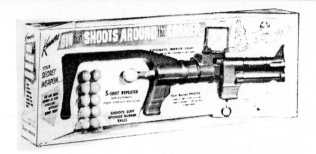

AIM and SHOOT
without being seen
SHOOT AT RIGHT ANGLE IN EITHER
DIRECTION...STRAIGHT AHEAD...
OR AT ANY ANGLE IN BETWEEN

MIS-25

MIS-25. THE GUN THAT SHOOTS AROUND CORNERS
(Kenner 1964) 24" plastic air gun with pivoting mid-section which allows the user to actually shoot around corners. Original issue gun came in solid colors. In 1965, the gun was produced in camouflage and a deluxe set was issued featuring six different projectiles (bazooka shell, bola shell, etc.) plus a pistol that could shoot around corners. Boxes are 32x9x4". **$50-75**
DELUXE "COMBAT OUFIT" SET w/pistol $75-125

HAMILTON INVADERS (Remco 1964)
This science-fiction playset was well conceived and should have been a good seller for years. The two main sets featured giant 10" mutant insects with pull-string action which allowed them to scurry across the floor while producing a hideous squeal. Also included were Blue Defender soldiers and a futuristic missile-firing tank or helicopter. What Remco didn't take into account when it designed the Horrible Hamilton insects was that mothers were absolutely appalled at the mere sight of them! They were, in fact, too horrible even to consider purchasing. Accessory sets were made containing the tank or helicopter with Blue Defender soldiers and were also packaged in colorful window display boxes with the pieces arranged in an action diorama. A child's helmet and pistol were made, each packaged separately. Sales for Hamilton Invaders remained dismal and by 1965, Remco discontinued the line all together.

Hamilton's Science Fiction Invaders Battle Mighty Earth Defenders!

12" Torpedo Tank shoots 2 torpedos 20 ft.!

MIS-26

MIS-26. HAMILTON INVADERS PLAYSET (with 10" green bug or orange spider) $150-200

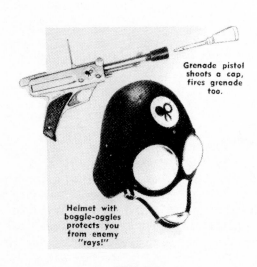

Grenade pistol shoots a cap, fires grenade too.

Helmet with boggle-oggles protects you from enemy "rays!"

MIS-27

MIS-27. HAMILTON INVADERS ACCESSORY SETS (vehicles and soldiers) $50-75
MIS-28. HAMILTON INVADER "BLUE DEFENDERS" ACCESSORY SET (soldiers only) $50-75
MIS-29. HAMILTON INVADERS HELMET $25-40
MIS-30. HAMILTONS INVADERS GRENADE PISTOL $35-50

MIS-31

MIS-31. JOHNNY WEST DOLL (Marx 1964)
When GI Joe became the hottest selling boys' toy of that year, several other toy companies jumped on the bandwagon and began producing their own lines of action dolls. Marx introduced Johnny West the Cowboy, its first western doll, which was to develop into a series of over a dozen more called "Best of the West" and remained in production throughout the Seventies. Molded in solid light brown plastic with flesh color head and hands, the Johnny West doll stood 11" tall and came with 20 pieces of equipment. Box is 7x12". **$35**

MIS-32

MIS-32. JIMMY JET (Deluxe Reading 1960)
Large, 24x22x14" plastic jet cockpit features a moving flight simulator screen which allowed the "pilot" the feeling of actually flying. A silhouette of the plane appears on the screen which is controlled by the steering column. Dial and levers also could be turned and pulled for added realism. Available only through select grocery stores, Jimmy Jet was still extremely popular and a good seller at $12.88! **$200-**

MIS-34

MIS-34. KING ZOR DINOSAUR (Ideal 1962)

Ideal was the leader in innovative battery-operated big plastic toys in the early Sixties with solid gold hits like Mr. Machine (1960) and Robot Commando (1961). King Zor was the follow up to this succession of hits and was the most mechanically advanced up to that time. Standing 16" tall and 30" long, this green plastic reptile features a hidden cannon on its back that shoots plastic balls as it moves forward. When the dinosaur bumps into something, it will stop, change direction and continue in a forward motion. The tail is actually a target with a circular tip which, when hit by a dart from the provided dart gun, causes the dinosaur to roar and shoot cannon balls in retaliation. Box is 17x32x12"deep. **$500-600**

MIS-33

MIS-33. JUNGLE HUNT FOR BIG GAME HUNTERS GAME (Hubley 1963)

Large 25x22x8" tall plastic jungle diorama features a 4" safari hunter and five wild animals. Battery-powered, the hunter can actually aim and shoot at the animals, and if the shot is a bulls' eye, the animal falls over. The hunter is able to turn by way of a remote control pistol grip at the front of the diorama. The animals can move about and are protected at times by trees and brush cover. The object is to bag all five animals before timer goes off. Hubley, better known for its metal cars and gun sets in the Forties and Fifties, tried to diversify their product line in the early Sixties and hired legendary toy designer Marvin Glass to create a series of large plastic diorama games based on coin-operated arcade games found in amusement parks (they also produced Golferino). Over-priced at $15, however, (that was a lot of money for a toy in 1963!), sales were, at best, bleak, and the series was quickly cancelled. Hubley was purchased two years later by the Gabriel Toy company. Box is 25x24x9". **$100-150**

MIS-35

MIS-35. MAGIC ROCKS (1960)

Offered almost exclusively as a mail order toy advertised in comic books, Magic Rocks sold astoundingly well throughout the Sixties. Magic Rocks consist of a colorful bag of small pebbles, magic solution and planting tweezers. Rocks are placed in a jar, covered with the solution, and grow into colorful undersea rock-type formations. Box is 5x7". **$20-25**

MIS-36

MIS-36. MATEY BUBBLE BATH (Pruitt Corp. 1960)

What made this particular bubble bath unique in its day was that it came with a free toy. From plastic soldiers to small pirate ships, Matey offered a wide variety of inexpensive plastic toys and remained a leading seller of bubble bath until Colgate/Palmolive introduced its overwhelmingly successful "Soaky" figural bubble bath containers in 1963 (**note:** see "Soakies" in this chapter). Our photo shows Matey box with free eye glasses/false nose disguise. **$25-50**

MIS-37

MIS-37. MATTY MATTEL TALKING DOLL (Mattel 1960)

Matty was Mattel's official mascot in the late Fifties through the early Sixties. Matty was among the very first pull-string talking dolls when it was designed by Mattel in late 1959. Standing 15" tall, the doll was stuffed, and its hard vinyl head wore the Mattel Crown. Doll is programmed with 11 different phrases such as "You can tell it's Mattel, it's swell." Window display box is 8x16x5" deep. **$75-100**

MOTORIFIC CAR AND TORTURE TRACK SET (Ideal 1964)

When the Motorific car was first introduced in 1964, it was promoted as a car that would drive indoors or outdoors and no racing track was offered with it at all. Twelve different car body styles were sold individually in a 6x9" window display box, each with a motor and chassis. The cars ran on two AA cell batteries which powered the motor, turning the back wheels. The front wheels could be positioned to turn right or left. In 1965, Ideal introduced the "Torture Track", a plastic one lane highway filled with obstacles such as hills, curves, collapsable brick walls, ramps and unfinished bridges. These obstructions were designated "tests" which the motorific car

was to pass through successfully. Five different sets of varying sizes were produced, each containing a Motorific car. The results were staggering, with sales nearly tripling the first year alone. Several more sets followed, as did car body styles, accessory sets, semi-trucks and more, and all remained in production through the late Sixties. In an age when racing track sets were the standard electric slot cars with a figure-8 track, the Motorific Torture Track broke new ground. Our photo example shows the deluxe-size Torture Track made in 1965.

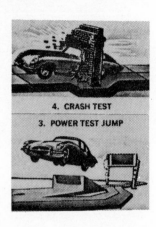

MIS-38

MIS-38. MOTORIFIC GIANT DETROIT TORTURE TRACK
(1965 deluxe set) $50-100

MOTORIFIC CAR: $20-35

MIS-41

MIS-41. ODD OGG (Ideal 1963)
Odd Ogg was a half-turtle, half-frog plastic 14" mechanical creation of toy designer Marvin Glass. Odd Ogg is something of a game as well as a toy, the object of which is to successfully roll balls at him, hitting a center control ball beneath his mouth which will cause the toy to make a low croaking sound and move forward. If balls miss the center bar, Odd Ogg opens his mouth and makes a loud "raspberries" sound and moves several feet backwards. Five plastic balls are included. Box is 15x8x8" deep. **$100-150**

MIS-39. MODEL MOTORING RACE SET (Aurora 1960)
The H/O slot car and race track craze Aurora started in the Sixties is a phenomenon all it's own. Aurora could not produce enough race sets to meet demand and consistantly sold out year after year with sales averaging about $20 million a year. Aurora made it's race sets right up until it's demise in 1975. Tyco since has bought the rights to use the Aurora logo on their race car sets. Aurora made numerous sets in those 15 years. The price value we give is for an average size race set made between 1960-69. **$100-200**

MIS-42

MIS-40

MIS-40. MR. MACHINE (Ideal 1960)
Mr. Machine was the first of a string of hits for Ideal Toy Company and free-lance designer Marvin Glass. Mr. Machine was created by Glass after an argument with one of his ex-wives, who told him that their marriage failed because he was nothing more than a working machine. Taking this insult for inspiration, Glass went to his studio in the wee-hours of the morning and drew mock-up designs of what was to become his semi-autobiographical robot, Mr. Machine. It was to become the biggest selling mechanical toy up to that time. Mr. Machine stands 16" tall and is powered by a spring motor wound up by a large key on his back. He walks, swings arms, rings a bell and sounds an alarm. The outer covering of the robot is made from clear plastic, allowing complete visibility to the inner working gears and springs. The robot could also be disassembled and reassembled. Box is 14x17x14". **$200-300**
(**Note:** Mr. Machine was re-issued in 1977 but does not disassemble and will be dated "1977".)

MIS-42. ROCK 'EM-SOCK 'EM ROBOTS (Marx 1961)
Created by free-lance toy designing legend Marvin Glass, the Marx Company had an instant hit on their hands and the robots remained in production for five years, were re-issued in the Seventies, and have been re-issued today (sporting different heads). A 12x12" yellow plastic boxing ring contains the two 10" tall red and blue robots. There are two control grips on opposite sides of the ring to control a robot to move forward, backwards, sidways and each arm can throw a punch. When a robot is hit squarely with an upper-cut to the jaw, its head will spring up producing a whining sound indicating a knock out. Box is 22x14x13". **$100-125**

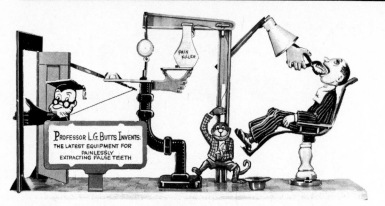

MIS-43

MIS-43. RUBE GOLDBERG ANIMATED HOBBY KITS

(Multiple 1964) Rube Goldberg's cartoon strip character Professor L.G. Butts and his crazy inventions were brought to life in the form of four intricate and fully working plastic assembly kits. Multiple produced these kits based on the huge success Ideal was having with their "crazy invention" games such as Mouse Trap and Crazy Clock. Ironically, Marvin Glass, the toy designer who created those games for Ideal, got his inspiration from Rube Goldberg! Each kit comes in a 5x12" box. Kits produced include: **Painless False Teeth Extractor, Automatic Baby Feeder, Signal for Shipwrecked Sailors, Back Scrubber & Hat Remover. EACH: $25-35**

MIS-45

MIS-45. SILLY PUTTY (Binney-Smith 1950-present)

Silly Putty, like the Etch-A-Sketch and Frisbee, are super-star success stories that remain as popular today as they did when they first hit the store shelves. Dating back to 1950, Silly Putty was a consistently strong seller through the Sixties. So much so, in fact, that other toy companies, such as Colorforms, began imitating it and manufactured their own brand of putty. Silly Putty's most unique feature is that it can lift a print from paper and transfer that print onto another paper. Silly Putty's trademark is that it always comes in an egg-shaped plastic container on a 4x7" card. **1st ISSUE (1950) $35-50, 1960s ISSUE: $15-20**

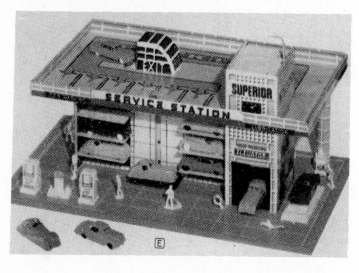

MIS-44

MIS-44. SUPERIOR SERVICE STATION PLAYSET

(Superior 1960) The popularity of gas station playsets goes back to the mid-Fifties and almost every boy growing up either had one or knew a friend who did. Most sets were made of colorful tin litho and would range from one story to three stories high. All came with plastic cars and figures of gas pump jockeys and mechanics. More imaginative sets had elevator lifts taking cars to upper decks. Our photo shows the "Superior Service Station", set #866. Box is 24x18x4" deep. **$50-100**

MIS-46

MIS-46. SILLY SAND (Funtastic 1966)

8x14" colorful box contains three bags of colored sand which, when added to water and funneled into the provided plastic squeeze bottle, make colorful globs of wet sand. Kids loved it- moms hated it. It was wet, messy and left stains everywhere. Although the set also included a styrofoam base from which to work, children seemed to want to expand their creative horizons to larger locations inside their homes, leaving a disaster area in their wake. Some wise mothers had the perception to see what could be in store and passed on buying the set altogether. As a result, Silly Sand's sales suffered, despite large television commercial campaigns, and was out of production by late 1967. **$25**

MIS-47

MIS-47. SLINKY (James Industries 1950-present)
The Slinky, like many of the successful toys that have lasted through the years, is quite simple in concept and design and yet seems to capture the imagination of children year after year. Created in the Fifties, Slinky remained popular throughout the Sixties. Variations have been made on the Slinky through out the years, including an animal series which consisted of a plastic front and back of and animal with a slinky body. There are several stories as to the origin of the Slinky and we may never really know which is the correct one. At the peak of Slinky's success, its creator disappeared never to be heard from again. Early issued Slinkies come in a 3x3x2.5" deep box. **$10-15**

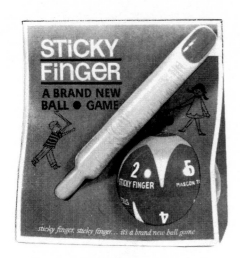

MIS-48

MIS-48. STICKY FINGERS (Mascon 1965) Sticky Finger
was a new concept in toy ball games. It consisted of an oversized 16" plastic index finger with a suction cup at the tip and trigger at the bottom. The Sticky Finger Ball is caught by the suction cup of the finger and the trigger is pressed to release and throw the ball. Two sets were available, one feature one Sticky Finger club and the larger set featuring two fingers. Both came on 14x18" display card. This was Mascon's (who normally made toy phones and banks) only big hit toy, and four years later, they folded.

MIS-49

MIS-49. SPIROGRAPH (Kenner 1968)
The concept behind Spirograph, making pattern line designs, wasn't new, but Kenner refined the idea and packaged it in such a way that it became the best selling toy in America and England in 1968. It also won Britain's "Educational Toy of the Year" Award, the 1968 "Artistc Oscar" in Paris, France, and was awarded the "Design Idea of the Month" by Design News in the United States. Spirograph consists of two large transparent plastic rings, 18 small transparent plastic wheels, and two transparent racks, all of which had tiny gear-like teeth on the outside rim. Each wheel has holes in which a color pen is to be placed. Wheels are placed against the rings, interlocking the teeth, and the wheel is turned by the pen to create an almost endless variety of line patterns. Box 9x13". **$15-20**

MIS-50

MIS-50. STRANGE CHANGE MACHINE "LOST WORLD"
(Mattel 1967) Mattel introduced a new and advanced concept to its line of Thingmaker sets in 1967 with the Strange Change Machine. Instead of pouring a liquid plastic goop into a mold to make a figure, the Strange Change Machine features a plastic square chip that, when placed in the machine, will transform into a creature of a prehistoric nature. The figures can be crushed and re-used again and again. Each set contains the Strange Change Machine, vacu-form plastic terrain and 16 plastic chips. box is 15x7x10" deep. **$50-100**

MIS-53

MIS-51

MIS-51. SUPER CITY GIANT BUILDING SET (Ideal 1967)
Ideal tried to capitalize on the success of their Motorific cars
by offering a city which was in scale to the cars. The set
was much like a Kenner Girder and Panel set and had the
added features of figures and a working fountain.
Unfortunately, the building sets which were so popular in
the early Sixties were now boring to young boys in the late
Sixties, who found more excitement in action dolls, battery-
operated wonders and TV character-related guns and toys.
The times were changing, due primarily to the impact of
television--nearly every family owned a TV set by the mid-
Sixties. The Super City remained in production less than
one year. Box is 24x20". **$50-75**

MIS-53. SUPER-STUFF (Wham-0 1966)
The Wham-O Company was known for inventing unusual
playthings, but Super-Stuff is by far its most off-the-wall
creation of the Sixties. Super-Stuff was a pink powder which
comes bagged and in a cottage-cheese style plastic
container. When water is added to the powder, it becomes
a half-pound pink blob that can stretch, bounce, blow
bubbles, and a variety of other things. Non-toxic with a
minty aroma, Super-Stuff could be chilled in a refrigerator
between uses to maintain its form and freshness. Comes in
poly bag with 5x6" header card. **$25-50**

MIS-54

MIS-52

MIS-52. STUKA DIVE BOMBER EGINE-POWERED PLANE
(Cox 1962) 18" long lightweight plastic airplane powered by
small .049 Thimble-Drmoe engine. Meticulously detailed with
reaer cockpit guns which swivel and a bomb that can be
dropped in flight. Comes in 25x20" window display box.
$50-100

MIS-54. SUPERBALL (Wham-0 1965)
Bouncing rubber balls made an incredible come-back in
1965 when Wham-O introduced its tiny black ball of zectron
with 50,000 pounds of compressed energy. Superball had
the ability to bounce as high as 100 feet into the air. Millions
were sold in the first six months alone. Imitations began
springing up everywhere, and by 1966, the market was
saturated with zectron bouncing balls of every conceivable
size and color. The original Superball was 2" in diameter and
came in a a polybag with colorful 5x5" header card. **$15-
25**

THINGMAKER SETS (Mattel 1964-68)

Mattel advanced its line of plastic vacuform machines in 1964 and introduced the Creepy Crawler Thingmaker set. This set consisted of a small electrical oven, metal molds of insects and bottles of a liquid plastic called "goop". The goop was poured into the molds and baked in the oven for about four minutes. The result was a real plastic rendition of an insect which could then be painted and have plastic wings added to it. It was an enormous success. In a year when most of the toy industry's attention was on the Beatles, a new concept in casting sets emerged to be one of the best selling toys of 1964. Only Hasbro with its newly introduced GI Joe doll, was ahead of Creepy Crawlers in sales that year. Other sets were quickly produced and remained strong sellers into the late Sixties. Sets also include cooling tray, prying tool, handle, plastic knife and instruction booklet. Boxes are approximately 15x13x4" deep.

MIS-55

MIS-55. CREEPY CRAWLERS (insects) $35-50

MIS-56

MIS-56. GIANT CREEPY CRAWLER SET #2 (giant insects) $35-50

MIS-57

MIS-57. CREEPLE PEOPLE (troll-like creatures) $50-65

MIS-58

MIS-58. FRIGHT FACTORY (monster items) $50-75

MIS-59

MIS-59. FIGHTING MEN (soldiers) $50-100
MIS-60. MINI-DRAGONS (dragons) $40-65
MIS-61. PICADOOS (matrix dot patterns) $25-35

MIS-62

MIS-62. FUN FLOWERS (assorted flowers) $25-40
MIS-63. ZOOFIE GOOFIES (goofy animals) $75-100
MIS-64. JILLIONS OF JEWELS (jewelry) $35-50
MIS-65. EEKS! (goofy monsters) $50-100
MIS-66. EVERY-THINGMAKER (20 selected molds from six sets) $100-150

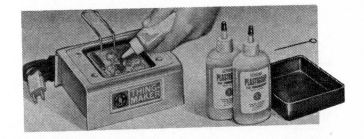

THINGMAKER TV ACCESSORY KITS (1966-67)

Mattel also made special molds which come on a 9x12" display card and contain one mold, one bottle of goop, and bottles of paint or pins and ring material.

MIS-67

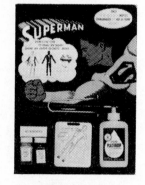

MIS-68

MIS-67. TARZAN (figure mold) **$40-50**
MIS-68. SUPERMAN (figure mold) **$50-75**

MIS-69. BATMAN (bat mold) **$50-75**
MIS-70 GREEN HORNET (hornet insect mold) **$75-125**

MIS-72

MIS-72. UNDERTAKER DRAGSTER MODEL KIT (Aurora 1964) As dragsters replaced hot rods to become the most popular race car of the Sixties, most model kit companies produced hundreds of variations. Our photo shows a classic dragster designed by Carl Casper. The Undertaker dragster was the NHRA national champion and when the model kit was produced in 1964, and remained undefeated in competition from coast to coast. Made in 1/25 scale molded in white and chrome plastic with black display base and a vampire and grim reaper figures. Box is 7x13". **$50-100**

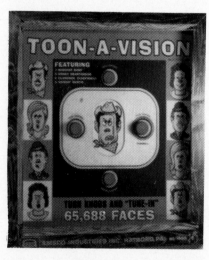

MIS-71

MIS-71. TOON-A-VISION (Amsco 1961)
Toon-A-Vision dates back to the Fifties, but actually sold better during the Sixties partially due to the company's diversifying its line to include licensed cartoon characters. Toon-A-Vision has four facial control knobs (face, eyes, nose and mouth), each with about 50 different styles. By turning one or more knobs, a total of 65,688 different faces can be created! A child would grow bored with the toy long before he could master all the possibilities the Toon-A-Vision offered. Our photo shows an early, original, non-character Toon-A-Vision from 1961 which is contained within a 14x14" cardboard frame. **$20-30**

MIS-73

MIS-73. V-RROOM! REAL MOTOR ROAR ENGINE (Mattel 1964) At about the same time as banana seats and high-rise "suicide" handlebars became the latest bicycle fashion, having a plastic rendition of a motorcycle engine that made real engine sounds also became stylish. One of the most popular models was Mattel's "V-rroom" engine. Battery-powered, the engine is mounted between the tank and frame of a bike, and a wired ignition unit is mounted to the handlebars. The engine is started by turning the key which can be revved up or left to "idle" just like a real engine. Box is 10x13". **$25-40**

CARTOONS

CAR-3

In 1959, Bill Hanna and Joseph Barbera introduced the world to a new wave of cartoon characters and met with overwhelming success. The Flintstones, Huckleberry Hound, Yogi Bear and Quick Draw McGraw all became household names overnight-- partially due to the enormous merchandising campaign that accompanied the project. Thousands of items were produced, from curtains to record players, and millions of units were sold. It was a new age for both television animation and toy manufacturers. In 1961, Popeye was dusted off, Dick Tracy and Beanie & Cecil were quickly re-vamped from comic strips into cartoons, and all were merchandised. In 1962, more new cartoon characters followed, including Walter Lantz's Space Mouse. Over 200 new cartoon characters were introduced between 1963-1965 alone, all complete with a line of merchandise. Television cartoons and the toy industry have never been the same since.

CAR-3. ASTRO BOY RECORD ALBUM (Golden 1964) Soundtrack and stories. **$25-35**

CAR-4

CAR-4. BEANY & CECIL "JUMPING DJ" GAME (Mattel 1962) 9x12" box contains vinyl figure of DJ which, when pressed down, pops up unexpectedly to decide players moves. **$40-60**

CAR-1

CAR-1. ARCHIES GAME (Whitman 1969) 12x14" box. **$20-25**

CAR-2. ARCHIE'S JALOPY MODEL KIT (Aurora 1968) 7x5" box contains all-plastic assembly kit of jalopy plus figures of Archie and Veronica. **$50-100**

CAR-5

CAR-5. BEANY & CECIL BATH MIT (Roclar 1962) 8x4" window display box contains green terrycloth childs mit in the likeness of Cecil. Also included is an assortment of small cakes of soap in the shape of Beany and Cecil. **$75-100**

CAR-6

CAR-6. BEANIE & CECIL TARGET BALL SET (1962) 14x14" colorful tin litho tray with three wood sides. There are several circular indentations into which balls fall to score points. Set comes with five colored wood balls in 15x15x3" box. **$50-75**

CAR-7

CAR-7. BEANIE & CECIL 3-D MOSAICS (1961) 8x4" box contains three bags colored crushed stone, a 5x7" pre-numbered sketch of Cecil and plastic frame. **$50-60**

CAR-8

CAR-8. BEETLE BAILEY BENDABLE FIGURE (Toy House 1963) 2.5" bendable rubber figure of Beetle comes on 6x4" display card with working compass. **$20-25**

CAR-9

CAR-9. BEETLE BAILEY "FOLD-A-WAY" CAMP SWAMPY PLAYSET (MPC 1964) 12x20x3" deep box folds open into an army camp grounds and comes with cardboard barracks, gate with Camp Swampy overhang, plastic soldiers, jeeps, trucks, exploding bridge and five 3" detailed character figures of Beetle, Sarge, Killer, Zero and General Halftrack. **$150-200**

CAR-10

CAR-10. BEETLE BAILEY "ZERO" HAND PUPPET (Gund 1960) 11" soft vinyl head/cloth body puppet of Beetle's friend Zero. Comes in 8x5x4" window display box. **$40-50**

CAR-11

CAR-11. BOZO THE CLOWN CIRCUS GAME (Transogram 1960) 8x16" box. **$25**

CAR-12

CAR-12. BOZO THE CLOWN "KID KLEANER" BUBBLE BATH (Riley 1960) 8x6" illustrated box contains powder bubble bath. **$40-50**

CAR-13. BOZO CARTOON KIT (Colorforms 1960) 10x12" box contains stick-on character figures and background board. **$35-45**

CAR-14

CAR-14. BULLWINKLE CARTOON KIT (Colorforms 1962) 8x12" box contains thin vinyl plastic character pieces that stick to illustrated background board. **$75-125**

CAR-15

CAR-15. BULLWINKLE AND ROCKY COLORING BOX (Whitman 1960) 8x12" box contains 256 coloring book pages and crayons. **$25-40**

CAR-16

CAR-16. BULLWINKLE HIDE 'N' SEEK GAME (Milton Bradley 1961) 10x19" box contains two illustrated panel playing boards and 48 playing discs. Object is to find the 16 discs with characters. **$50-75**

CAR-17

CAR-17. BULLWINKLE SPELLING AND COUNTING BOARD (Laramie 1969) 9x16" display card holds red plastic plate device with movable letters and numbers to spell and count. **$10-15**

NOTE: Also see "ROCKY & HIS FRIENDS" in this chapter.

CAR-18

CAR-18. CASPER THE GHOST LUNCHBOX (King Seeley Thermos 1966) Blue vinyl box with orange steel thermos. **$250-300**

CAR-19

CAR-19. CASPER THE TALKING GHOST DOLL (Mattel 1961) 15" stuffed doll with hard plastic face has pull-string in back of neck which allows doll to produce a variety of phrases. Doll comes in large 8x16x6" purple box designed like a haunted house with front and side windows. **$125-175**

CAR-20

CAR-20. CASPER TV PROMOTIONAL STORE DISPLAY (Harvey 1960) Large 35x26" heavy die-cut cardboard stand-up store display features Casper flying over Baby Huey, Little Audrey, Buzzy the Crow and Herman & Katnip. **$200**

CAR-21

CAR-21. CHIPMUNKS "SOAKY" BUBBLE BATH CONTAINERS (Colgate/Polmalive 1963) 11" plastic figural containers with hard plastic detachable heads. **Alvin, Theodore and Simon. EACH $20-25**

CAR-22

CAR-22. DENNIS THE MENACE CARTOON KIT (Colorforms 1960) 12x14" large deluxe-size edition set of thin vinyl plastic character pieces that affix to illustrated backgroud board. **$30-40**

CAR-23

CAR-23. DEPUTY DAWG "ACTION PUSH-OUT" FIGURES (Lays Potato Chips) Colorful 8x10" cardboard sheets contain punch-out stand-up figures of Deputy Dawg and friends plus action dioramas of henhouse, creek mud, jail house, etc., and a variety of games and puzzles. Ten different sheets were made, one available in every snack-size six pack of Lays potato chips. **EACH $10-15**

CAR-24. DEPUTY DAWG MAGIC DRAWING SLATE (Lowe 1962) 8x11" cardboard with vinyl drawing sheet. **$20**

CAR-25

CAR-25. DEPUTY DAWG PENCIL BOX (Hasbro 1961) 4x8x1" red cardboard box with snap open lid and pull-out drawer. Illustrated colored paper decal of characters on top lid. **$25-35**

CAR-26

CAR-26. DEPUTY DAWG VIEWMASTER REEL (Sawyer 1962) 5x5" illustrated envelope contains three film reels and 16-page booklet. **$20-30**

CAR-27

CAR-27. DICK TRACY JUNIOR DETECTIVE KIT (Golden Funtime 1962) 14x8" punch-out book of guns, badges, wrist-radios, etc. **$25-30**

CAR-28. DICK TRACY MASTER DETECTIVE GAME (Selchow & Righter 1961) 10x20" box contains four cardboard stand-up characters from the Dick Tracy cartoon, one villain plus 28 playing tiles of stolen loot. Object is to capture villain before he flees country and regain as many stolen loot tiles as possible. **$45-75**

CAR-29

CAR-29. DICK TRACY OIL PAINTING SET (Hasbro 1967) 26x18" box contains 22x14" pre-numbered, pre-sketched canvas, ten vials of paint and brush. **$75-125**

CAR-30. DICK TRACY PATROL SQUAD GUN SET (Mattel 1961) Set includes 28" long black/brown plastic tommy gun with side bolt action and Official Dick Tracy logo on stock, a metal .38 snub-nose pistol which shoots shells, and shoulder holster. Comes in 32x14x3" deep box. Interestingly enough, some stores in New York City and the state of Massachusetts would not carry this gun set! **$200-250**

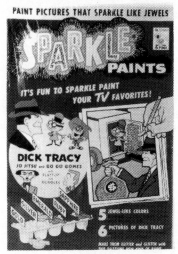

CAR-31

CAR-31. DICK TRACY SPARKLE PAINTS (Kenner 1962) 8x12" box contains six pre-numbered sketches and five vials of sparkle paint and featured characters from the Dick Tracy cartoon such as Jo Jitsu and Go Go Gomez. **$65-100**

CAR-32

CAR-32. DICK TRACY WRIST RADIOS (Remco 1961) 9x13" box contains two battery-powered plastic wrist-radios about 2x3.5x1" in size. A variety of wrist-radios were made during the Sixties, many by Remco. **$50-100**

CAR-33

CAR-35

CAR-33. DONDI POTATO RACE GAME (Hasbro 1960)
10x18" box contains playing board, pieces and spinner.
$35-50

CAR-35. FIREBALL XL-5 ACTIVITY SET (Magic Wand
1963) Set contains four 10x10" color cardboard sheets with
punch-out character figures, XL-5 spaceship, space sleds,
space monsters, etc., which can be applied to colorful
space background. Box is 10x14". $150-175

CAR-34 (1960)

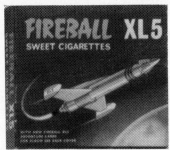

CAR-36

CAR-36. FIRBALL XL-5 CANDY CIGARETTES (1963)
(British distribution.) Sweet candy cigarettes. Box is 3x3".
$25

CAR-34 (1968)

CAR-37

CAR-34. FELIX THE CAT GAME (Milton Bradley 1960)
9x17" box. This game was re-issued in 1968 with a different
box lid design. $35-40
1968 Re-issue $20-25

CAR-37. FIREBALL XL-5 GAME (Milton Bradley 1963)
10x20" box. $45-60

CAR-38

CAR-41

CAR-38. FIREBALL XL-5 LUNCHBOX (King Seeley Thermos 1963) Comes with steel thermos which came in two different sizes. **Box $50-100, Thermos $25-35**

CAR-39

CAR-39. FIREBALL XL-5 MAGNETIC DART GAME (Magic Wand 1963) 15x18" window display box contains colorful tin litho target and four magnetic darts. **$100-150**

CAR-40

CAR-40. FIREBALL XL-5 SPACE CITY PLAYSET (MPC 1964) Large 38x17x6" deep box contains 20" long silver plastic XL-5 spaceship with detachable nose cone and slide open doors for space sleds and figures, a 36" long working launch ramp, cardboard Space City, eight character figures including two extra figures of Steve Zodiac and Venus which sit on space sleds, plus several accessories including missile and satellite launchers, astronaut figures and space cars. **$500-750**

CAR-41. FIREBALL XL-5 SPACESHIP (MPC 1964) MPC also repackaged the above playset and sold the spaceship with figures in a smaller boxed set which contained all eight character figures and two jet sleds. Box is 22x10x10". **$350**

CAR-42

CAR-42. GEORGE OF THE JUNGLE GAME (Parker Bros. 1968) 10x19" box. Object is to get George safely through the jungle and back to his hut. **$40-50**

CAR-43. GUMBY FIGURE (Lakeside 1965) 5" green bendable rubber figure comes on 6x4" display card. **$35**

CAR-44

CAR-44. GUMBY'S JEEP (Lakeside 1966) Yellow metal 8" long jeep with decals reading "Gumby's Jeep" on hood, both sides of jeep and seats. Fold-down windshield and rubber tires. Box is 10x6x6". **$50-75**

CAR-45. GUMBY & POKEY "PLAYFUL TRAILS" GAME (C0-5 Company 1968) 10x20" box contains playing board and eight miniature figures of Gumby and Pokey (Gumby wearing a cowboy hat). Object of game is for Gumby to successfully ride Pokey into his corral without being "bucked off". **$45-60**

CAR-46

CAR-46. HASHIMOTO-SAN GAME (Transogram 1963) 10x17" game. Object is to be the first player who successfully ties down Dangerous Cat. **$25-35**

CAR-47

CAR-47. HASHIMOTO-SAN PAINT BY NUMBER SET COLORING (Transogram 1964) 10x17" window display box contains six pre-numbered sketches, brush and paint palette holding eight paints. **$50-65**

CAR-48

CAR-48. HECTOR HEATHCOTE CARTOON KIT (Colorforms 1964) 8x12" box contains plastic vinyl character parts that affix to illustrated backgroud board. **$35-50**

CAR-49

CAR-49. HECTOR HEATHCOTE "THE MINUTE-AND-A-HALF MAN" GAME (Transogram 1963) Object of the game is to take Hector safely through the Revolutionary War and receive the most medals. 10x20" box contains four Hector figures, 20 battle cards, 44 medal cards, cannonade and marble. **$65-100**

CAR-50

CAR-50. HECTOR HEATHCOTE SHOW MAGIC SLATE (Lowe 1963) 8x11" cardboard slate w/plastic sheet also features Silly Sidney and Hashimoto-San. **$20-30**

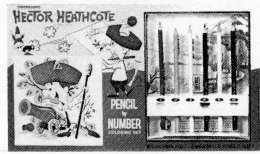

CAR-51

CAR-51. HECTOR HEATHCOTE PENCIL BY NUMBER COLORING SET (Transogram 1964) 10x17" window display box contains 12 pre-numbered sketches, six pencils and pencil sharpener. **$50-75**

CAR-52

CAR-52. HECTOR HEATHCOTE SHOW RECORD ALBUM (RCA/Camden 1964) Soundtrack and show also featuring Silly Sidney the Elephant and Hashimoto-San. **$20-25**

LINUS THE LIONHEATED

Originally a cereal box character on the box of Post's Crispy Critters, Linus grew in popularity, having his own Saturday morning cartoon show and a variety of toys produced in his honor.

CAR-53

CAR-53. LINUS THE LIONHEARTED "UPROARIOUS" GAME (Transogram 1965) 10x19" box also features other Post cereal characters like **Honey Bear, Truly the Mailman, Granny** and three others. Game includes four stand-up figures of Linus, vinyl Granny bag and playing cards. **$75**

CAR-54. LINUS THE LIONHEARTED TALKING HAND PUPPET (Mattel 1965) 12" plush puppet with hard plastic face has pull string that activates concealed voicebox, producing a variety of phrases. Window display box is 7x12x5" deep. **$40-50**

CAR-54

CAR-55

CAR-55. LINUS THE LIONHEARTED TRAY PUZZLE (Whitman 1965) 11x14" frame tray puzzle. **$12-20**

CAR-56

CAR-56. MIGHTY HERCULES GAME (Hasbro 1963) Hasbro as a rule made few board games, and those that were produced were small inelaborate games that sold for under $1.00. Hasbro spared no expense however, when it produced the Mighty Hercules game, which is equal to the quality of Transogram and Ideal deluxe-made games. Box is 10x20" and contains four cardboard stand-up figures of Hercules, ten illustrated villain cards, ten illustrated Hercules cards and playing board. Object of the game is to be the first player to avoid the clutches of Hydra and Wilamene and safely reach the top of Mount Olympus. **$100-150**

CAR-57. MIGHTY HERCULES MAGIC SLATE (Lowe 1963) 8x11". **$20-35**

CAR-58

CAR-58. MISTER MAGOO CAR (Hubley 1961) 9" long battery-operated yellow tin litho car with cloth top. Full vinyl figure of Magoo sits behind the wheel. Car moves forward with a shaky, jerking motion. Box is 10x8x5" deep. **$250-350**

CAR-59

CAR-59. MISTER MAGOO "VISITS THE ZOO" GAME (Lowe 1961) 10x20" box contains cardboard figures of Magoo and zoo animals. Object is to get Magoo safely through the zoo. **$35-50**

CAR-60

CAR-60. THE NEW ADVENTURES OF PINOCCHIO GAME (Lowe 1960) Based on the short-lived puppet animation cartoon, this unique game features remote-control magnetic movement which guides Pinocchio figure across the playing board. Object is to help Pinocchio find the Blue Fairy and turn him into a real boy while avoiding the clutches of the villainous Fox and Cat. Box is 12x15". **$50**

CAR-61

CAR-61. PEANUTS "STUFF-N-LACE" DOLLS (Standard Toykraft 1961) 14x9" window display box contains two cloth Peanuts characters, stuffing and lace. Two sets were produced, one featuring Charlie Brown and Lucy, the other featuring Linus and Snoopy. **$35-50**

CAR-62

CAR-62. PEANUTS "SNOOPY" GAME (Selchow & Righter 1960) 10x20" box contains 16 cardboard discs, each with an illustration of a different breed of dog, Snoopy disc, spinner and playing board. Object is to get each dog back to his home. **$40-50**

CAR-63

CAR-63. ROCKY & HIS FRIENDS CARTOON KIT (Colorforms 1961) 8x12" box contains plastic vinyl stick-on character parts which affix to illustrated background. (**Note:** Two diffent contents exist, although the same box lid design is used. One set depicts an outer space theme with background board showing a rocket landing on moonscape and character pieces with space gear. The other set has a landscape background board and non-space equipped character pieces.) **Space set: $100, Non-Space set: $50**

CAR-64

CAR-64. ROCKY & BULLWINKLE PRESTO "SPARKLE" PAINTING SET (Kenner 1962) Deluxe 18x12" boxed set contains six tubes of watercolors, five tubes of "jewel-like colors with glitter mixed in the paint to give the finished painting that "sparkle" look. Set also includes six pre-numbered sketches and three 8x10" comic strip panels. **$100-150**

CAR-65

CAR-65. ROCKY & HIS FRIENDS SEWING CARDS (Whitman 1961) Set includes six 6x8" color illustrated cards with small holes along the outline of the character which can be sewn along and "traced" by yarn. Seldom featured characters like **Captain Wrongway Peach Fuzz** and **Cloyd and Gidney Martians** are included. **$75-100**

CAR-66

CAR-66. ROGER RAMJET COLORING BOOK (Whitman 1966) 8x11", 120 pages. **$25-30**

CAR-67. ROGER RAMJET TRAY PUZZLE (Whitman 1965) 11x14" frame tray puzzle. **$25-30**

CAR-68

CAR-68. ROGER RAMJET FUN FIGURES (AMF 1965) Rubber Bendable figures ranging in size from 3" to 5" of Roger Ramjet, Yank & Doodle, Dan & Dee, Lance Crossfire, Lotta Love, Noodles Romanoff, Solenoid Robot and General Brassbottom. **EACH: $25-45**

CAR-69

CAR-69. SILLY SIDNEY CRAYON BY NUMBER SET (Transogram 1963) 10x17" window display box contains ten pre-numbered sketches and 24 crayons. **$35-50**

CAR-70

CAR-70. SPACE ANGEL GAME (Transogram 1965) 10x17" box. Object is to deliver fleet safely home. **$30-60**

CAR-71

CAR-73. SUPERCAR GAME (Milton Bradley 1962) 9x17" box contains ten cards, spinner, playing pieces and board. Object is to be the first player to get to the most disaster areas. **$25-40**

CAR-72

CAR-72. SUPERCAR BATTERY OPERATED CAR (Remco 1962) Supercar was the first of British creator Gerry Anderson's puppet animation adventures to be seen by American audiences. Kids fell in love with the entire concept and merchandising soon followed. (A year later Anderson would release Fireball XL-5). By far the most elaborate toy made from the show was Remco's rendition of the car. Battery-powered, this 11" orange plastic car was programmed by small directional discs which, depending on the disc used, would drive forward in a figure 8 pattern, loop-to-loop pattern and so on. Four discs were included with the car, each containing two directional programs. There is a full plastic figure of Mike Mercury behind the wheel. The box itself is hollow on the bottom and the car sits on top of the box, protected by a clear plastic dome-like cover. Box measures 10x12x6" deep. **$200-300**

CAR-73

CAR-73.   STINGRAY   FRICTION-POWERED   SHIP
(Lakeside 1966) 12" blue, black, and yellow futuristic looking
submarine is friction-powered and features a bobbing
peiscope when in motion. Rear exhaust is a translucent red
plastic. **$350-500**

CAR-74

CAR-74.   SUPERCAR ROAD RACE GAME (Standard
Toykraft 1962) 12x15x2" deep window display box contains
plastic intricate maze with small tin litho character pieces
which are moved about with a magnet stick. Do not be
alarmed if you find the tin litho pieces to be Bullwinkle and
his gang instead of Supercar character pieces. There was
a production error at the Standard Toykraft factory which
resulted in almost 30% of these sets containing incorrect
pieces! This has little to no effect on the value of this game.
$50-100

CAR-75

**CAR-75. THE ZANY ZOO ADVENTURES OF TENNESSEE
TUXEDO GAME** (Transogram 1963) 10x20" box contains
four stand-up figures each of Tennessee, Chumly and the
Professor, five cards, 31 animal tiles, spinner and board.
Object is to capture mice and zoo animals. **$150-200**

CAR-76

CAR-76. TENNESSEE TUXEDO MAGIC SLATE (Saalfield
1963) 8x11" cardboard back with plastic draw sheet.   **$40**

CAR-77

CAR-77.   TENNESSEE TUXEDO SCHOOL BAG (Ardee
1969) 12x10" plastic vinyl briefcase-style school bag with
5x7" color illustration on front of bag. **$75-100**

CAR-78

CAR-78.   TERRYTOON'S "HIDE N' SEEK" GAME
(Transogram 1960) 9x17" box features several Terrytoon
characters   including **Tom Terrific, Dinky Duck, Heckle &
Jeckle** and more. Comes with die-cut cardboard character
heads, spinner and board. **$35-65**

CAR-79

CAR-79. TWINKLES "HIS TRIP TO THE STAR FACTORY" GAME (Milton Bradley 1961) Twinkles the flying elephant was one of the very first cereal box characters to have his own cartoon show and merchandising line. He set the pace for other cereal companies to create their own unique mascot characters on countless brands of cereal. The Twinkles game was the first commercial item produced on Twinkles and sold moderately well. The object of the game was to be the first player to collect the most stars before Twinkles arrives at the star factory. Game includes five cardboard die-cut character head playing pieces, magic stars, board and dice. **$75-125**

CAR-80

CAR-80. TWINKLES & FRIENDS-KING LEONARDO & HIS SHORT SUBJECTS WASTE PAPER BASKET (1960) Colorful tin litho childs waste can stands 12" high and features Twinkles and his friends on one side including two other General Mills cereal mascots (The Trix Rabbit and the Frosty-0 Bear). The other side features King Leonardo and six of his subjects. King Leonardo is holding a General Mills banner. **$100-150**

CAR-81

CAR-81. UNDERDOG GAME (Milton Bradley 1964) 10x19" box. Object is to be the first player to save Polly Purebread. **$20-30**

CAR-82

CAR-82. UNDERDOG TRAY PUZZLE (Whitman 1965) 11x14" frame tray puzzle features Underdog saving Sweet Polly Purebread from the clutches of the evil Simon Bar Sinister. **$12-20**

CAR-83. WIZARD OF OZ GAME (Lowell 1962) Object of the game of course is to follow the yellow brick road to see the Wizard. Box is 12x15". **$35-50**

HANNA-BARBERA

HB-6

HANNA-BARBERA BOARD GAMES
We've compiled below the 25 most important Hanna-Barbera board games made during the Sixties.

HB-1.   ATOM ANT "SAVES THE DAY" GAME (Transogram 1966) 10x17" box. **$75-100**

HB-2.   BAMM-BAMM "COLOR ME HAPPY" GAME (Transogram 1963) 10x17" box. **$35-60**

HB-3.   DICK DASTARDLY & MUTTLY GAME (Milton Bradley 1969) 9x16" box. **$25-40**

HB-6. FLINTSTONE'S HOPPY THE HOPPAROO GAME (Transogram 1965) 10x20" box. **$50-75**

HB-7

HB-7.   HUCKLEBERRY HOUND'S "BUMPS" GAME (Transogram 1961) 10x17" box. **$35-45**

HB-8.   HUCKLEBERRY HOUND "WESTERN" GAME (Milton Bradley 1960) 9x16" box. **$35-50**

HB-4

HB-4. DINO THE DINOSAUR GAME (Transogram 1961) 10x17" box. **$35-50**

HB-9

HB-9. JETSONS "FUN PAD" GAME (Milton Bradley 1963) 12x12" box. **$50-85**

HB-10.   JETSONS "ROSIE THE ROBOT" GAME (Transogram 1963) 10x20" box. **$100-150**

HB-5

HB-5. FLINTSTONES "STONE AGE" GAME (Transogram 1961) 10x17" box. **$20-35**

HB-10

HB-11.   JETSONS "SPACE AGE" GAME (Transogram 1962) 10x20 box. **$100-125**

HB-12

HB-12. JONNY QUEST GAME (Transogram 1964) 10x20" box. **$100-150**

HB-13. LIPPY THE LION GAME (Transogram 1962) 10x17" box, **$50-100**

HB-14. MAGILLA GORILLA GAME (Ideal 1964) 10x20" box. **$50-100**

HB-15. MUSHMOUSE & PUMPKIN PUSS GAME (Ideal 1964) 10x20" box. **$35-75**

HB-16

HB-16. PEBBLES FLINTSTONE GAME (Transogram 1962) 10x17" box. **$35-65**

HB-17

HB-17. PETER POTAMUS GAME (Ideal 1964) **10x20"** box. **$75-150**

HB-18

HB-18. QUICK DRAW McDRAW "PRIVATE EYE" GAME (Milton Bradley 1960) 10x20" box. **$25-40**

HB-19

HB-19. RICOCHET RABBIT GAME (Ideal 1965) 10x20" box. **$100-150**

HB-20. RUFF & REDDY AT THE CIRCUS GAME (Transogram 1962) 10x17" box. **$35-45**

HB-20

HB-21. SNAGGLEPUSS GAME (Transogram 1962) 10x17" box. **$35-50**

HB-22. TOP CAT GAME (Transogram 1962) 10x17" box. **$50-75**

HB-23. TOUCHE TURTLE (Ideal 1964) 10x20" box. **$100-150**

HB-24. WACKY RACES GAME (Milton Bradley 1969) 10x16" box. **$25-45**

HB-25. WALLY GATOR (Transogram 1962) 10x17" box. **$45-75**

HB-26

HB-26. YOGI BEAR "GO FLY A KITE" GAME (Transogram 1961) 10x20" box. **$25-45**

HB-27

HB-31

HB-27. **ATOM ANT HALLOWEEN COSTUME** (Ben Cooper 1965) 10x12" window display box contains one-piece fabric bodysuit and mask. **$25-50**

HB-28. **ATOM ANT PUSH UP PUPPET** (Kohner 1965) 3" plastic jointed mechanical puppet which moves when bottom underneath base is pressed. **$15-20**

HB-31. **BIRDMAN HALLOWEEN COSTUME** (Ben Cooper 1967) 10x12" window display box contains one-piece fabric bodysuit and mask. **$20-35**

HB-29

HB-32

HB-29. **BAMM-BAMM DOLL** (Ideal 1963) 16" tall vinyl plastic posable doll dressed in leopard skin suit that buttons with bone; hat and club. Comes in 14x12x5" deep window display box. Inside of box is designed like his room. This doll came in two sizes:
Large 16" Bamm-Bamm $150-200
Small 12" Tiny Bamm-Bamm $100-150

HB-32. **DUM DUM & TOUCHE TURTLE DRIVE TOY** (Marx 1965) 3" hard plastic figure of Dum Dum riding on top of Touche Turtle, who is designed more like a scooter than a turtle. Friction drive action allows toy to roll across surfaces. Box is 4x4". **$35-50**

HB-30

HB-33

HB-30. **BATHTIME BUBBLE FUN** (Milvern 1965) 4x10x2" deep window display box contains 20 packets of soap powder, each with a different illustration of Hanna-Barbera characters. **$25-50**

HB-33. **FLINTSTONES-WELCH'S STORE DISPLAY POSTER** (Welch's 1962) 18x22" color poster features all the Flintstone characters promoting Welch's Fruit Drinks. **$50**

HB-34

HB-37

**HB-34.   FLINTSTONES MECHANICAL SHOOTING
GALLERY** (Marx 1962) Colorful 14" tin litho target set with
clear plastic dome. The main target is a plastic dinosaur
head with open mouth. There is a 6" plastic pistol attached
to the front of the target set that shoots small metal pellets.
Comes in 24x8x8" box. **$200-250**

**HB-37.   HANNA-BARBERA GIVE-A-SHOW PROJECTOR
SET** (Kenner 1963) 11x18" box contains plastic battery
powered slide film projector and 16 color slide strips.
Kenner made a variety of Hanna-Barbera sets, each with a
predominate illustration of a certain character on the box lid
(Jetsons, Jonny Quest, Huck Hound, etc.). Our photo
shows the Flintstones set. **$35-50**

HB-35

HB-38

**HB-35. FLINTSTONES PRE-HISTORIC ANIMAL RUMMY
PLAYING CARDS** (Ed-U-Card 1960) 3.5x3.5" box contains
color playing cards of Flintstone characters and dinosaurs.
$10-20

HB-38. HUCKLEBERRY HOUND BUTTON (1960)
3" diameter color button with yellow background reads
"Huckleberry Hound for President". **$8-15**

HB-36

HB-39

HB-36.   FLINTSTONES TILE SQUARE PUZZLE (Roalex
1962) 3x3" black plastic frame contains 15 illustrated square
tiles and one empty tile space. Object is to rearrange tiles
to form correct illustraions of Fred, Wilma, Barney and
Betty. Comes on illustrated 5x8" card. **$25-30**

HB-39. HUCKLEBERRY HOUND TV WIGGLE BLOCKS
(Kohner 1962) 14x9" window display box contains ten small
2x2x1" plastic TV sets with flicker-flasher images of Huck
and friends in the picture screen. **$75-125**

HB-40

HB-40. HUCKLEBERRY HOUND AND QUICK DRAW WALL PLAQUES (1960) 11" figural wall hanging plaques molded in hard plastic and colorfully painted. **EACH: $10-20**

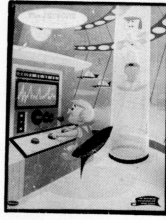

HB-44

HB-45

HB-44. JETSONS ASTRO WIND-UP HOPPER (Marx 1963) 4" tall grey tin litho figure of Astro with hard vinyl brown ears, grey plastic antenna tail and accented face highlights. When toy is wound up, body bobs up and down and legs "hop". **$300-350**

HB-45. JETSONS TRAY PUZZLE (Whitman 1963) 11x14" frame tray puzzle features George and Elroy. **$20-25**

HB-41   HB-42

HB-46

HB-41. HUCKLEBERRY HOUND STORY VIEWER AND FILM SET (Sawyer 1960) Small 2x1x1" plastic viewer and long rectangular film strip come attached on 4x8" display card. **$12-15**

HB-46. JONNY QUEST CARD GAME (Milton Bradley 1965) 6x8" box. **$35-50**

HB-42. HUCKLEBERRY HOUND & FRIENDS TV DINNER TRAY (1960) 13x18" metal serving tray with fold away legs has painted cartoon scene on top. **$35-50**

HB-43

HB-47

HB-43. JETSONS LUNCHBOX (Aladdin 1963) Blue dome top box with space graphics of Jetsons. Comes with steel thermos. **Box $400-650, Thermos $75-100**

HB-47. JONNY QUEST COLORING BOOKS (Whitman 1965) **EACH $25-30**

HB-48

HB-48. JONNY QUEST CRAYON BY NUMBER SET
(Transogram 1965) 17x10" window display box contains six pre-numbered sketches and 16 crayons. **$100-125**

HB-49

HB-49. JONNY QUEST PAINT BY NUMBER SET
(Transogram 1965) 10x17" window display box contains six pre-numbered sketches and six colored pencils. **$100-125**

HB-50

HB-50. MAGILLA GORILLA PLASTIC STICK-ONS
(Standard Toykraft 1964) Similar to a colorforms set. Thin vinyl plastic body parts of characters can be arranged on 8x8.5" illustrated board. Comes in 9x13" window display box. **$25-50**

HB-51

HB-51. MAGILLA GORILLA "TWISTABLES" (Ideal 1964) 8" posable stuffed doll with soft vinyl face. Comes in 10x5x4" deep window display box. **$35-50**

HB-52

HB-52. PEBBLES BUBBLE BATH (Roclar 1963)
4x10x2" deep box with flip-up display lid and 3-D pop-up figures of Fred and Wilma bathing Pebbles. Box contains 24 packets of powder bubble bath soap in four different colors. There are four different packet illustrations of Pebbles. **$50-75**

HB-53   HB-54

HB-53. "BABY" PEBBLES DOLL (Ideal 1962)
16" tall plastic posable doll with saran hair upswept into a ponytail and kept in place by plastic bone. Doll is dressed in two-piece outfit with leopard skin top with matching robe and blanket. Box is 9x16x5" deep. **$200-250**

HB-54. "TINY" PEBBLES DOLL (Ideal 1964)
12" vinyl plastic rendition of the 16" Pebbles doll. Comes in 12x14" window display box. The inside of box is designed like her room. **$150-200**

HB-55

HB-55. PEBBLES AND HER CRADLE (Ideal 1964)
Large 18x16x8" deep window display box contains 12" Pebbles doll and plastic rocking log cradle. **$250-325**

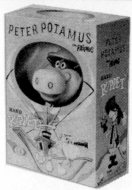

HB-56   HB-57

HB-56. PETER POTAMUS HAND PUPPET (Ideal 1964)
11" soft vinyl head/cloth body puppet comes in 10x5" window display box. **$35-45**

HB-57. PETER POTAMUS "TWISTABLES" (Ideal 1964)
8" posable stuffed doll with soft vinyl face. Comes in 10x5" window display box. **$35-50**

HB-58

HB-58. PETER POTAMUS FRAME TRAY PUZZLE (Whitman 1965) 11x14". **$10-20**

HB-59

HB-59. QUICK DRAW McDRAW MAGIC RUB-OFF PICTURES (Whitman 1960) 8x16" box contains 14 6x8" glossy cardboard slates with black/white illustrations which are colored by the included "Magic Crayons". Wipe-off tissues included so slates may be re-used. **$40-60**

HB-60

HB-60. RICOCHET RABBIT CHANGE PURSE (Estelle 1964) 3" diameter white vinyl zipper change purse with embossed color illustration of Ricochet on front. Comes on 6x4" display card. **$15-25**

HB-61

HB-61. RUFF & REDDY KARBON KOPY SET (Wonder Art 1960) 18x12" box contains tracing set which consists of several color comic strip drawings resembling comic book pages and several sheets of carbon paper. Also included is a 8x10' sheet of 16 sequence illustrations that can be cut out and placed in order to make a flip-the-page moving picture book. **$75-125**

HB-62

HB-62. RUFF & REDDY "REDDY" STUFF DOLL (Knickerbacher 1960) 15" stuff plush doll with hard plastic face. Comes with red collar with "Reddy" embossed in white letters. Illustrated 3x4" tag attached to collar features Ruff & Reddy on scooter above their name logo. **$75-100**

HB-63

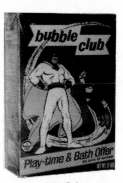

HB-64

HB-63. SPACE GHOST JIGSAW PUZZLE (Whitman 1967) 8x10" box contains 100 piece puzzle. **$20-25**

HB-64. SPACE GHOST & FRANKENSTEIN JR. BUBBLE BATH (Purex 1966) 9x6" color illustrated box features Hanna-Barbera tee-shirts and nightlights on back of box. **$50-75**

HB-65

HB-65. WACKY RACES "COMPACT PUSSYCAT" MODEL CAR KIT (MPC 1969) 9x5" box contains all-plastic assembly kit of Penelope Pitstop's "Compact Pussycat" race car. Molded in metallic purple and yellow. **$75-125**

HB-66

HB-66. YOGI BEAR MAGIC RUB-FF PICTURES (Whitman 1961) 8x16" box contains 14 glossy 6x8" cardboard slates with black/white illustrations of Hanna-Barbera characters which are colored, wiped clean and re-colored with included crayons and tissues. **$50-60**

51

GAMES

In 1963, a very significant breakthrough was made with the debut of a game which changed the way boardgames had always been played. The playing board was re-designed into a large, working plastic diorama of crazy, interacting contraptions which, through a chain reaction of events, would trap the opponents' playing piece. The game was called "Mouse Trap" and it became the best selling game of 1963 and 1964 and still remains in production today. Other game manufacturers soon followed suit, adding plastic dioramas, figures, houses, ghosts, and eyeballs into their games, abandoning the standard and more conventional playing board and creating a glut of big boxed games with plastic inventions.

GA-2

GA-2. BARBIE'S LITTLE SISTER SKIPPER GAME (Mattel 1964) Object is to be the first player whose horse wins the Best of Show Award. Box is 10x22" **$20-25**

GA-3. BARBIE "KEYS TO FAME" GAME (Mattel 1964) Object is to build careers and win Keys to Fame. Box is 8x8" **$20-25**

GA-4

GA-4. BASH GAME (Ideal 1967) Object is to strike out sections of the funny man with hammer and score points before he topples. Box is 9x10". **$15-20**

GA-1

GA-1. BARBIE QUEEN OF THE PROM GAME (Mattel 1960) Throughout the Sixties, toy companies began capitalizing on their own creations by introducing them on what would otherwise be a generic toy (wallets, tote bags, etc.) Some of the more visually appealing and elaborate examples are found in the games. The Barbie Queen of the Prom game was the first of its kind and was very successful for several years. The object was simple: be the first player elected to become queen of the prom. Activities such as shopping, parties and school clubs were featured. Box is 10x23". **$20-30**

GA-5

GA-5. BATTLESHIP GAME (Milton Bradley 1965) Object of this naval battle game is to sink the opponent's ships by firing a barrage of shots and calling the strike area. Game includes two game boxes, ten ships and several red and white firing pegs. This game was a continual good seller for Milton Bradley through out the Sixties and has recently been re-issued. Box is 10x19". **$15-20**

GA-6

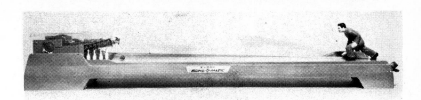

GA-9

GA-6. THE BIG SNEEZE GAME (Ideal 1968)
Object of the game is to build a house of cards before large plastic air-blowing figure "sneezes" and blows it down. Box is 10x14". **$15**

GA-9. BOWL-A-MATIC GAME (Eldon 1963)
49" long plastic bowling alley features automatic pin spotting and ball return. Bowler is operated by levers. Box is 51x10x10". **$50-100**

GA-7

GA-46

GA-7. BOOBY TRAP GAME (Parker Bros. 1965)
Object of game is to remove as many pieces from the board as possible before picking that wrong piece which willcause the spring-activated bar to snap shut. Box is 10x18" **$20**

GA-10. CAMP GRANADA GAME (Milton Bradley 1968)
Based on Allen Sherman's popular comical song. Object is to pick up and hide "icky"animals before bus breaks down. Box is 15x18". **$15-20**

GA-8

GA-8. BOP THE BEATLE GAME (Ideal 1963)
12" plastic frog trap with open mouth which snaps shut when plastic 6" beetle balls fly into mouth. Includes two plastic 20" sticks to "bop" beetles toward frog. Box is 12x15" **$35-50**

GA-11. CRAZY CLOCK GAME (Ideal 1964)
Ideal's follow-up game to Mouse Trap. Player snaps key to set off a chain reaction of crazy happenings, all aimed at making plastic sleeping man jump out of bed. **$35-55**

GA-12

GA-12. DYNAMITE SHACK GAME (Milton Bradley 1968)
Object of game is to place as many dynamite sticks into the
shack as possible before timer goes off, popping the roof off
the shack. Players wear large plastic thumbs for added
challenge. Box is 8x14". **$15**

GA-13

GA-13. ELLSWORTH ELEPHANT GAME (Selchow &
Righter 1960) Popular children's book character. Object of
the game is to be the first player to collect the most letters
and reach Ellsworth's house. Letters have questions
pertaining to good sportsmanship and good character that
must first be answered by players. Box is 10x20" **$45-50**

GA-14. FASCINATION GAME (Remco 1962)
Game includes two electronic mazes, each wired to a light
tower. The object is to be the first player to get all three of
his marbles through the maze and light the tower. Box is
10x20". **$25-35**

GA-15

GA-15. FEELEY MEELEY GAME (Milton Bradley 1967)
Find objects in box by sense of touch. Box is 12x12". **$20**

GA-16

GA-16. FISH BAIT GAME (Ideal 1965)
Ideal's third and least successful invention game from the
Mouse Trap series. Diorama game features chain reaction
of events which cause fisherman to be thrown into whale's
mouth. **$35-50**

GA-17

GA-17. FLEA CIRCUS MAGNETIC ACTION GAME (Mattel
1968) Object is to make fleas jump. Box is 15x12" **$20-30**

GA-18

GA-18. FORMULA I CAR RACE GAME (Parker Bros. 1968) Object is to be the first racer to cross the finish line. Box is 10x20" **$25-35**

GA-19

GA-19. FU MANCHU'S HIDDEN HOARD MYSTERY GAME (Ideal 1967) Object is to find the five hidden clues and be the first to locate the hidden hoard of treasure. Plastic figures included are the same Ideal used in its James Bond "Message to M" game two years earlier. Box is 15x20". **$30-40**

GA-20

GA-20. GRAB-A-LOOP GAME (Milton Bradley 1968) Grab loop from opponent's hip. This game raised a lot of eyebrows from concerned parents with teenage children.

GA-21

GA-21. GREEN GHOST GAME (Transogram 1965) Large box game contains stand-up board with diorama pieces and a large spinning ghost that screeches and points in the direction he thinks his lost son is. Box is 28x10". **$45-50**

GA-22. HANDS DOWN GAME (Ideal 1965) Object is to be last player still holding cards. Similar to the childs card game "Snap". **$15-20**

GA-23

GA-23. KA-BALA GAME (Transogram 1965) Large boxed fortune-telling game with revolving glow-in-the-dark-eye and tarot cards. Box is 24x17". **$40-50**

GA-24

GA-24. KRESKIN'S ESP GAME (Milton Bradley 1966) Test opponents ESP talents on various topics. Box is 10x19". **$15-20**

GA-25

GA-25. LIE DETECTOR GAME (Mattel 1961, 1964)
15x15" window display box contains black plastic lie detector box, peg board, suspect and arrest cards. First player to solve murder and arrest suspect wins. Repackaged in 1964 with new box design and suspect cards. **$35-40**

GA-26. LIFE, THE GAME OF (Milton Bradley 1960)
Photo of Art Linkletter on box. Box is 15x20". **$15**

GA-27

GA-27. MIND OVER MATTER GAME (Transogram 1968)
ESP game. Box is 10x20". **$15-20**

GA-28

GA-28. MISS POPULARITY GAME (Milton Bradley 1961)
Player fillsbulletin board with the most social events to win. Box is 15x20". **$30-40**

GA-29

GA-29. MOUSE TRAP GAME (Ideal 1963)
The big game of 1963 was Ideal's cleverly designed Mouse Trap, which sold millions and started the "crazy-invention" craze. Player turns crank to set off a chain reaction of events that leads to trapping a mouse. Box is 15x22. **$45**

GA-30

GA-30. MR MACHINE GAME (Ideal 1961)
A product from the overwhelmingly successful Mr Machine robot, this game features a 12" plastic figure of Mr Machine which serves as a spinner, plus four plastic playing piece figures of Mr Machine. The object is to be the first player to reach the toy factory. **$50-100**

GA-31

GA-31. MYSTERY DATE GAME (Milton Bradley 1966)
Player must be dressed for the right occasion for her mystery date. Best selling game for young girls of the Sixties. Box is 15x20". **$35-45**

GA-32

GA-32. OH NUTS! GAME (Ideal 1968)
Object is to find the hidden marbles inside walnuts. **$20**

GA-33. OPERATION (Milton Bradley 1965)
Electronic patient buzzes if mis-operated upon. Box is 10x20". This game is currently being re-issued by Milton Bradley. **$15**

GA-34

GA-34. PARK AND SHOP GAME (Milton Bradley 1960)
Object is to find a parking spot, shop the fastest and be the first back home. Box is 10x19". **$20-25**

GA-35. PLYMOUTH DRAG RACE GAME (Day 1967)
Race drivers Bobby Sox and Buddy Martin are featured. Box is 10x19". **$35-45**

GA-36. POPPIN' HOPPIES GAME (Ideal 1968)
Object is to complete figure puzzle first by catching popping little creatures of corresponding colors. Box is 18x10". **$20**

GA-37

GA-37. POP YER TOP GAME (Milton Bradley 1968)
Object is to get safely home before 5" plastic goonie bird pops top. Box is 10x16". **$20-25**

GA-38

GA-38. SANDLOT SLUGGER GAME (Milton Bradley 1968)
Mechanical 10" plastic baseball player hits ball to determine moves as in a real baseball game. Box is 10x20". **$20-25**

MIS-39

GA-39. SILLY SAFARI JUNGLE GAME (Topper 1966)
Object is to catch wild animals with crazy trap diorama. Well-detailed crazy animals included, some measuring almost 6" tall. Box is 10x22". **$50-75**

 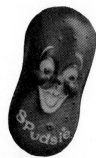

GA-40   GA-41

GA-40. SLAP TRAP GAME (Ideal 1967)
Object is to be the first player to trap a beetle. **$20-25**

GA-41. SPUDSIE THE HOT POTATO GAME (1967)
Similar to the popular Time Bomb game where players toss Spudsie back and forth and try not to be caught with him when timer goes off. **$15-20**

GA-42

GA-42. STRATEGO (Milton Bradley 1961)
A popular game for almost ten years, Statego's object was to capture enemy flag by use of wits and strategy. Box is 10x20". **$20-25**

GA-43

GA-43. TICKLE BEE (Schaper 1956-69)
Actually a product first introduced in the Fifties, Tickle Bee enjoyed renewed popularity in the Sixties, selling more than four million units in 1963 alone. The object is for Tickle Bee to pass through a maze of sharp curves and obstacles safely by way of a magnetic stick. Box is 6x12". **$15**

GA-44

GA-44. TIME BOMB GAME (Milton Bradley 1965)
5" black plastic bomb with timer. Players toss back and forth before it "explodes". Box is 8x6x6". **$30-40**

GA-45

GA-45. THE TIME MACHINE (American Toy 1961)
Each player travels through a different century with the aid of the mechanical Time Machine. Players "relive"historical events and even travel through the world of the future. Object of the game is to win the race through the centuries. Box is 22x18". **$100-125**

GA-46. TOP COP (Cadaco-Ellis 1961)
Object of the game is to be the first patrolman on his manhunt to search for clues that will capture his criminal. Box is 14x21". **$50-75**

GA-47. TRADE WINDS: THE CARIBBEAN SEA PIRATE TREASURE HUNT GAME (Parker Bros. 1959-60) **$20-25**

GA-48

GA-48. TRY-IT MAZE PUZZLE GAME (Milton Bradley 1965) Clear plastic 5x5x5" four-level maze contains a black marble. The object was to pass the marble through the maze. A popular game for kids and adults, remaining a strong seller for years. **$15**

GA-49

GA-49. TWISTER GAME (Milton Bradley 1966) Twister was the game rage of 1966, appealing to kids and sporting adults alike. Unlike all other games up to that point, Twister allowed the players to actually become physically involved in the playing of the game. The object of the game was to try to remained balanced on a 6x5" vinyl sheet with 24 colored dots. The spinner indicates on which color dot the player would place a specific hand or foot. Box is 15x14". **$20**

GA-50

GA-50. WIPE OUT! HOT WHEELS RACE GAME (Mattel 1968) Based on the popularity of Mattel's Hot Wheels metal cars, Mattel promptly produced a game featuring them. Like all racing car games, the object was to be the first to cross the finish line. Box is 12x18". **$25**

GA-51

GA-51. WOW! PILLOW FIGHT FOR GIRLS GAME (Milton Bradley 1964) Plastic beds shoot small pillows to knock over opponents' pajama team. Box is 10x20". **$20-25**

GA-52.

GA-52. YAHTZEE (Lowe 1961)
"It makes you THINK...while having FUN". Roll the dice to add up the highest score of various "poker hand" combinations. (Three of a kind, full house, etc.) A party game designed to "replace the jaded card games that now split male and female party guests into two camps", Yahtzee sold 18 million between 1960-69. Box is 10x15". **$10-15**

GA-53. ZIP CODE GAME (Lowe 1964)
20x18" box contains mail cards, dead letter mail box and four zip code racks. Players sort and discard mail cards and fill their racks with the most letters to win. Box is 12x18". **$45-65**

MILITARY

Throughout the history of toys, military-related themes have always been a popular seller. The sixties, however, saw an even greater growth in this area due to the increased interest in WWII nostalgia brought on by such television shows as COMBAT!, and the innovation and technological advances which toy companies employed to produce new toys with exciting features that captured the imagination of young boys.

AMERICAN HERITAGE GAMES (Milton Bradley 1962-65) Series of four U.S. military games that come with actual ship, airplane and soldier playing pieces. Box measures 14x20".

MIL-1

MIL-1. DOGFIGHT AIR BATTLE GAME OF WWI (1963) **$20-30**

MIL-2

MIL-2. BROADSIDES- NAVAL BATTLE GAME (1962) **$20-25**

MIL-3. BATTLE CRY- CIVIL WAR GAME (1962) **$30-40**

MIL-4

MIL-4. HIT THE BEACH- WWII GAME (1965) **$30-40**

AR/15 CLIPFIRE WEAPON SYSTEM (Ideal 1967-68) Ideal utilized the gun designs originally made for the Ma From U.N.C.L.E. television show. When the series wa cancelled, Ideal quickly repackaged them as the AR/15 se Our photo shows all three guns on store display.

MIL-5

MIL-5. AR/15 ASSAULT RIFLE SET (originally the THRUSH rifle) Large 36x14x2" windo display box contains 34" long rifle with grenade launcher grenade, bayonet, clip pouch with two magazine clips an combat badge. **$250**

MIL-6. AR/15 PISTOL SET (originally Illya gun) 18x11" window display box contains pistol, clip and combat badge. **$125-150**

MIL-7. AR/15 AUTO-PISTOL AND HOLSTER SE (originally Napoleon Solo pistol) 17x12" display card hold pistol, holster, clip and combat badge. **$125-150**

MIL-8. AR/15 STORE DISPLAY. Large 48x40" die-cut cardboard construction display with a three guns boxed and one unboxed rifle. **$750-850**

MIL-9. ATOMIC CANNON (Ideal 1959-60)

Long 42" army green plastic truck with dual front and rear cab and 17" long mobile cannon. Cabs detach to leave cannon platform ready to fire six ejecting shells. Box is 44x8x8". **$75-100**

MIL-10

MIL-10. BARRACUDA SUB (Remco 1962)

37" long light grey submarine with removable transparent top deck shows detailed interior. Sub is battery-operated and moves forward, signals red flashing light and produces a warning chime sound. Also equipped with 4 firing torpedos, 4 firing missiles, raft and 24-man crew (including 4 frogmen). Box is 41x8x8". **$175-225**

BATTLE ACTION PLAYSETS (Ideal 1964-65)

Ideal produced nine different diorama playsets with working features and called the series "Battle Action". Each set came with 3" soldiers although these were also sold separately. Some sets came in large window display boxes featuring the set, while other larger sets were produced which contained two or more sets and came in large boxes with fold-open lids. Our photo examples show both box styles.

MIL-11. FIGHTER JET STRIP.

Set contains 14" long jungle airstrip and three jet fighters, air control tower and four trees. Airstrip has triggering device in runway to launch planes. Also a lever to pre-control left or right banking of plane. **$150-200**

MIL-12. SNIPER POST.

Five-man squad in parapets that are spring-motor operated to pop up individually in sequence and open a barrage of gun fire with real sound effects. **$200-225**

MIL-13. CHECK POINT.

Set contains sentry post, truck guard and two soldiers. As truck approaches checkpoint, guard springs out of post and barricade gate raises. **$150**

MIL-14. WAR FIELD & FIGHTING MEN.

8x9" plastic battle scarred terrain base with road, bomb craters, sandbags and bunker. Six 3" figures with detachable equipment also included. Object is to overtake supply road. **$100-125**

MIL-15. TWIN HOWITZERS.

Set contains two battery-operated howitzer cannons that fire shells and produce sound, and two soldiers. Cannons set on top of large plastic hillside diorama with tunnel entrance. **$175-200**

MIL-16. MINED BRIDGE.

Set contains 14" plastic spring-operated bridge that explodes into two pieces; also includes jeep and two soldiers. **$150-175**

MIL-17. BOOBY TRAP ROAD.

Large plastic road terrain base features hidden spring activated "mine" that tosses several plastic rocks into the air when detonated. Comes with truck and two soldiers. **$200-225**

MIL-18. MACHINE GUN NEST.

Set contains 6x9" plastic bombed-out brick house with two machine guns and attached gunners. Spring-operated guns vibrate and make gun sounds. **$175-200**

MIL-19

MIL-19. ROAD BLOCK.

Set features spring-activated falling tree and machine gun nest which produces gun sounds. Also included are three soldiers and jeep. **$175-200**

MIL-20

MIL-20. BATTLEGROUND PLAYSET (Marx 1961-62)

Large 13x24x4" box contains all plastic 3" WWII soldiers, jeeps, trucks, cannons, tanks, helicopters, pillboxes, barbed wire fence, tents and minor accessories. **$150-250**

MIL-21

MIL-21. BATTLE WAGON (Deluxe Reading 1963)
35" long two tone grey battery powered battleship moves forward, flashes signal lights, fires missiles and torpedoes and catapults planes. Originally sold in grocery stores. Box is 35x10x9". **$175-225**

MIL-22

MIL-22. BATTLING BETSY MOTORIZED TANK KIT (ITC 1960) Ideal produced its own model kits for a short time in the early Sixties with the most ambitious being the 14" rendition of the Walker Bulldog tank called the Battling Betsy. Battery operated, it moves forward and reverses and climbs over obstacles. The turret rotates side to side and is programmed to fire every 15 seconds. **$100**

MIL-23

MIL-23. BIG CAT CANNON (Ideal 1965)
Large plastic retractable cannon cranks open to 35" and fires ejecting shells. Mounted on tank base. Box is 20x18x10". **$75**

MIL-24

MIL-24. BIG CAESAR ROMAN WAR SHIP (Remco 1962)
29" long white plastic ship with gold and blue trim is battery-operated to move forward as eight oars on each side row back and forth. Comes with 50 red plastic 2" Roman soldiers, two chariots, four catapults and cardboard castle fort. Box is 31x10x10. **$200-250**

MIL-25. BULLDOG TANK (Remco 1959-60)
Plastic 23" long battery-operated army green tank with aluminum barrel and rubber treads. Two control levers on back of tank allow it to move forward or reverse. Gun fires four shells and ejects empty casings. Detachable flag with star emblem. Box is 24x15x12" deep. **$100-125**

MIL-26

MIL-26. LIGHT BULLDOG TANK (Remco 1960)
14" replica of the larger Bulldog tank. One control lever in back moves tank forward or reverse. Manual spring-activated lever in back of tank fires shells. There is a yellow triangular **Monkey Division** decal on turret. Box is 13x6x7" **$50-65**

MIL-27.

MIL-27. CAMPAIGN! CIVIL WAR GAME (Saalfield 1961)
Object is to capture enemy capital. Flip side of playing board has several illustrated historical stories of the Civil War. **$40-50**

MIL-28   **MIL-29**

MIL-32

MIL-28. COMBAT GRENADES (Marx 1961)
8x12" display card holds five green plastic grenades with removable gold plastic pull-pins. **$20-25**

MIL-29. COMBAT HAND GRENADE (Esquire 1963)
8x8" display card holds cap-firing plastic grenade. Back of card has cut-out target of tank. **$15**

MIL-32. FIGHTING LADY BATTLESHIP (Remco 1959-60)
36" long two-tone grey plastic battery-operated ship features remote gun fire control, alarm siren, aircraft laucher, shell casting ejection, two airplanes, landing craft and crew. Box is 37x9x8". **$125-175**

MIL-30

MIL-33. FIGHTING TIGER DOLLS (Topper 1966)
Poseable 7" dolls with mechanized arm that swings upward to perform a function (throwing grenade, raising telephone, etc). Each doll comes with a helmet and weapon inside a clear plastic display tube. Eight dolls were produced: **Machine Gun Mike, Big Ears, The Rock, Bugle Ben, Sarge, Combat Kid, Pretty Boy and Tex.** **EACH $25**

MIL-30. DEFENDER DAN 50 CALIBER MACHINE GUN
(Deluxe Reading 1961) Huge 36" long plastic and metal machine gun in army green with chrome trim stands 35" high when mounted on swivel tripod. Barrel recoils when shooting belt is fed ejecting shells. Box is 40x15x12". **$200**

GI JOE DOLL (Hasbro 1964)
Plastic 12" jointed doll with cloth uniform came in 12x4x2" deep box with cap, dog tags, insignia stickers, booklet and membership papers to GI Joe fan club. Created by freelance toy designer Stan Weston and sold to Hasbro (Weston would create Captain Action two years later for Ideal), GI Joe was the hottest toy of 1964, selling over 6 million dolls the first year alone.

MIL-34

MIL-31. FAMOUS MILITARY MEDALS (West 1963)
Series of eight miniature reproduction 2x1" medals made of metal and cloth come on 6x8" display card that gives a brief history of the medal and why it's awarded. Primarily marketed in the backs of comic books as a mail order product. Medals include: **Iron Cross, Victoria Cross, Croix De Guerre (both France and Belgium), Legion of Honor, Order of the Crown, Distinguished Service Order and The Star of India. EACH $20-30**

MIL-34. GI JOE ACTION SOLDIER/ARMY. **$125-175**

MIL-35. GI JOE ACTION SAILOR/NAVY **$150-200**

MIL-36. GI JOE ACTION MARINE **$150-200**

MIL-37

MIL-37. GI JOE ACTION PILOT/USAF   **$175-225**

MIL-38

MIL-38. GI JOE GREEN BERET (1967)
10x14x3" window display box contains GI Joe in Green Beret outfit with camouflaged scarf and beret featuring Special Forces insignia sticker. Also field pack, M-16 rifle, field radio and booklet. **$750-1000**

MIL-39

MIL-39. GI JOE GREEN BERET MACHINE GUN OUTPOST SET (1967) 11x13x3" deep box contains two GI Joe in camouflaged outfits with berets, shell-firing bazooka and shells, 50-caliber machine gun and cartridge belts, field radio, sand bags, grenades, ammo box, camouflaged netting and two M-16 rifles. **$350-500**

GI JOE ACTION SOLDIERS OF THE WORLD SERIES

(1966-67) Hasbro made a series of six international WWII soldiers and packaged them individually in a small 4x12" cellophaned window display box and also in a larger 10x14" window display that contained extra weapons and equipment.

MIL-40   **MIL-41**

MIL-40. BRITISH COMMANDO.
Small box $500
Large box $750-1000

MIL-42

MIL-41. RUSSIAN INFANTRYMAN.
Small box $550-650
Large Box $850-1100

MIL-42. AUSTRALIAN JUNGLE FIGHTER.
Small box $500-600
Large box $750-100

MIL-43. GERMAN SOLDIER.
Small box $500-600
Large box $750-1000

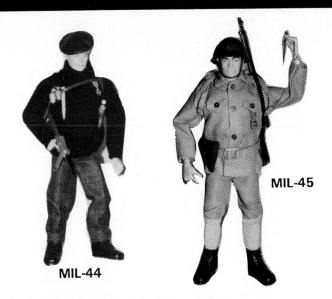

MIL-45

MIL-44

MIL-48

MIL-48. GLOBEMASTER US ARMY CARGO PLANE (Ideal 1962) Also re-packaged as **Flying Boxcar.** Plastic 22x17" grey (or army green) military cargo plane has swing-open nose with movable ramp. Cargo includes jeep, rocket launcher that fires two missiles, mobile cannon that fires six shells, truck with searchlight, truck with radar scanner and ten soldiers. Box is 24x18x10". **$75-100**

MIL-44. FRENCH RESISTANCE FIGHTER.
Small box $400-500
Large $650-850

MIL-45. JAPANESE IMPERIAL SOLDIER.
Small box $800-1000
Large box $1500-1800

MIL-46

MIL-46. GI JOE NURSE (1967)
10x14x3" cellophane window display box contained 10" jointed female nurse dressed in white Red Cross uniform with white stockings and cap and came with medical accessories including crutches, stethoscope, plasma bottle, etc. **$650-850**

MIL-49

MIL-49. GREEN BERET MODEL KIT (Aurora 1966) 13x4" box contains all plastic assembly kit of Green Beret soldier in action. **$50-75**

18" legs on swivel tripod and camouflage coloring. Rapid fire with light and realistic sound effects.

MIL-50

MIL-47

MIL-47. GI JOE DESERT PATROL JEEP (1967)
Large 28x12x10" deep box contains 25" long tan plastic jeep with 50-caliber machine gun mounted in back. Also included is a GI Joe dressed in a tan desert patrol uniform. **$500-750**

MIL-50. GUNG HO COMMANDO OUTFIT (Marx 1963)
Set includes 28" plastic replica .50 caliber machine gun with belt-fed ammo, firing sound effect and flashing gun barrel. Also plastic .45 automatic pistol with holster, knapsack, canteen, mess kit, map with case, compass, walkie-talkie and two tin dog tags. Comes in large 32x24x12" box. **$150**

MIL-51. JOHNNY EAGLE "LIEUTENANT" RIFLE (Topper 1965) Authentic styled 36" plastic and metal M-14 semi-automatic rifle shoots bullets and ejects cartridges. Rifle feeds automatically from 6-round clip. Box is 38x14x3" deep **$100-125**

MIL-52

MIL-52. JOHNNY EAGLE "LIEUTENANT" PISTOL (Topper 1965) Authentic style 10" plastic .45 pistol that shoots shells automatically from 6-round clip. Comes in 12x8" plastic display case with clear plastic lid. **$40-65**

MIL-53

MIL-53. JOHNNY EAGLE "LIEUTENANT" WALL PLAQUE (Topper 1965) Brown plastic 23x10" oval shaped gun rack with embossed scenes of WWII soldiers in battle. Box is 24x11x2" deep. **$30-45**

MIL-54. JOHNNY REB CANNON (Remco 1961) Large 29" plastic Civil War cannon comes with six cannon balls, loading ramrod, tow-rope and cloth Confederate flag. Shoots balls up to 35 feet. Box is 30x12x11". **$50-75**

MIL-55

MIL-55. JOHNNY SEVEN MICRO-HELMET PHONE SET (Topper 1965) Plastic helmet with tinted pull-down visor features built-in head phones and speaker walkie-talkie. Triangular color decal on front of helmet reads "Johnny Seven". Box is 14x10x10. **$25-50**

MIL-56

MIL-56. JOHNNY SEVEN O.M.A. GUN (Topper 1964) The biggest selling boys' toy of 1964 was Topper's Johnny Seven "One Man Army" gun, selling over 1.6 million units the first year alone. This unique gun was designed as seven guns in one (hence the name) including: Grenade Launcher, Anti-Tank Rocket Launcher, Anti-Bunker Missile Laucher, fires ten bullets as rifle on bi-pod, slide-bolt chatter action of Tommy gun, and detachable pistol that fires ejecting shells. Over three feet long and molded in green plastic with brown and black highlights. Box is 36x11x5" deep. **$200-250**

MIL-57

MIL-57. M-16 MARAUDER AUTOMATIC RIFLE (Mattel 1967) Plastic 32" long replica of the actual M-16 used in the Viet-Nam war (which Mattel also made). Rifle features side bolt action and real firing sound. Box is 33x11x5". **$40-50**

MIL-58. MIGHTY MATILDA ATOMIC AIRCRAFT CARRIER (Remco 1962) 35" long yellow and grey plastic battery-operated ship moves forward and features other actions including: working aircraft elevator lift, alarm siren, airplane catapult launcher and firing missiles. Included are 12 pursuit planes, nine bomber planes, four helicopters, tow truck and 100-man crew. Box is 38x15x16". **$200-275**

MIL-59

MIL-59. **MIGHTY MO CANNON** (Deluxe Reading 1960) 25" long green plastic cannon with aluminum barrel has remote control firing action. Box is 24x17x15". **$75-100**

MIL-62

MIL-60   MIL-61

MIL-62. **MONKEY DIVISION BAZOOKA** (Remco 1961) 39" long plastic and heavy cardboard army green bazooka with scope comes with three firing shells and cardboard pillbox target. Box is 41x12x8" deep. **$50-60**

MIL-63

MIL-60. **MONKEY DIVISION 3-IN-1 GUN SET** (Remco 1961) Looking more like a space gun than a military pistol, this plastic 10" gun has barrel extension that converts it into a tommy gun and firing grenade launcher and is battery powered for sound effects. Yellow and orange triangular decal featuring monkey in helmet with rifle on side of gun. Comes in 18x12x3" deep window display box. First of a long line of Monkey Division weapon sets by Remco. **$50-100**

MIL-61. **MONKEY DIVISION HELMET** (Remco 1961) Red and yellow plastic helmet with pull-down tinted visor, chin strap and radio antenna extending from left ear shield. Monkey decal on front of helmet. Box is 11x9x10". **$35-50**

MIL-63. **MORTAR MAN** (Payton 1962) Detailed 5" plastic green soldier figure kneeling beside working mortar. Comes in 10x8 package.

A masterpiece of military deception!

PHANTOM RAIDER™

MIL-64

MIL-64. PHANTOM RAIDER (Ideal 1963)
28" black and grey freighter can be extended into a 33" long war ship. Three hatch doors open, bringing up two missiles, two ashcan depth-charges and four torpedoes, all set for manual firing. Battery-operated to move forward. Box is 30x10x10". **$200**

MIL-65

MIL-66

MIL-65. SCREAMING MEE-MEE GUN (Remco 1965)
28" long blue plastic futuristic-looking rifle has built-in detachable pistol. Both shoot ejecting shells and 8" grenades which produce a screaming-like sound when fired. Box is 30x14x4" deep. **$75-100**
Pistol was also sold separately in 16x12x3" box. **$35-50**

MIL-66. STONY THE PARATROOPER DOLL (Marx 1964)
Stony was Marx's answer to Hasbro's GI Joe. Originally marketed as simply "Paratrooper" with unjointed legs, the Stony edition came fully poseable. Doll was 11" tall and molded in army geen uniform and came with over 20 pieces of equipment including weapons, helmet, walkie-talkie, etc. Boxes came in two sizes; 12x4x3" and a wider 12x6.5x3". **$40-75**

MIL-67

MIL-70

MIL-67. TIGER JOE TANK (Remco 1959-60) Large 23x14 green plastic battery-operated tank features forward and reverse movements and fires ejecting shells. There are two half-figures looking out of tank, one behind a .50-caliber machine gun on top of turret and the other on lower tank deck with walkie-talkie. Box is 24x14x14". **$100-150**

MIL-68. TIGER TANK (Deluxe Reading 1962-63) Large 24" long, green plastic battery-operated tank with walkie-talkie shaped remote control box. Half-figure soldier pops out of front. Box is 25x15x16". **$100-150**

MIL-70. WHIRLYBIRD HELICOPTER (Remco 1962) Battery-operated 25" long white plastic twin blade helicopter features working hoist chain. Included are plastic army truck, jeep, tank and 25 soldiers. Triangle decal on side of helicopter reads "Whirlybird". Box is 26x9x7". **$35-50**

MIL-69

MIL-71

MIL-69. TOY SOLDIERS IN A FOOT LOCKER (Lucky Products Inc. 1961-68) Somehow the ads for these soldiers always looked more promising than what was actually received! The soldiers and accessories were about 2" tall and were thin, 2-dimensional figures made of hard, brittle, olive-green plastic. The cardboard footlocker measured 6x3x2-1/2". Later, the manufacturer had to state in the ad the size and composition of the footlocker. **$20-30**

MIL-71. WORLD WAR I BATTLE SETS (Remco 1964) Remco made three different WWI playsets. Our two photo examples show the **"Doughboy"** and **"Air Aces"** sets. Each comes in a 11x20x6" window display box and contain bi-planes and soldiers. The Doughboy set also contains plastic blue tank, cannon and truck with ammo carrier. The larger deluxe set not shown features a combination of both sets in a 11x28x6" window display box.

Doughboy set $100-125
Air Aces Set $100-150
Deluxe Battle Set $150-200

MONSTERS

The source of the monster craze of the early Sixties can be traced back to the late Fifties when local television stations began replaying classic horror movies on their late night weekend formats. At that same time, a magazine called "Famous Monsters of Filmland" was published, further fueling interest in the resurrection of forgotten monsters. In 1961, the Aurora Plastics Company produced a model kit of Frankenstein which proved so successful that the company had to produce two molds and keep them running 24 hours a day to meet demand. By 1963 the monster craze was alive with merchandise ranging from T-shirts to radio speakers. Crazy "Bug-Eye" monsters were also created (see RAT FINKS & WEIRD-OHS chapter) further popularizing the fad. The monster craze lost steam in 1966 when Batman and other superheroes became the latest rage.

MON-1. BATS IN THE BELFREY GAME (Mattel 1964) Plastic 15" purple castle with orange accents designed to shoot small bats from tower. Claw-like hand scoops are used by players to catch the bats as they drop. Box is 9x16x7" deep. **$35-50**

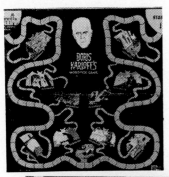

MON-2

MON-2. BORIS KARLOFF'S MONSTER GAME (Gems 1965) 10x20" box contains four die-cut stand-up figures of Karloff, 30 colorful monster tiles and playing board. **$50-75**

MON-3

MON-3. CREATURE OF THE BLACK LAGOON MODEL KIT (Aurora 1963) 13x4" box contains all-plastic 1/12 scale assembly kit molded in metallic green. **$175-250** (NOTE: This kit was re-issued in 1969 with extra glow pieces in a 12x12" square box and called " Glow in the Dark" Creature **$65-100**)

MON-4

MON-4. CREATURE OF THE BLACK LAGOON MYSTERY GAME (Hasbro 1963) 10x19" box contains four die-cut cardboard Creature figure playing pieces and playing board. Object is to get the Creature safely back to Lagoon. **$150-200**

MON-5. CREATURE OF THE BLACK LAGOON CANDY CONTAINER (Pez 1960s) 5" plastic Pez candy container with green or grey molded head of Creature. **$50-100**

MON-5

MON-6

MON-6. CREATURE OF THE BLACK LAGOON "SOAKY" BUBBLE BATH CONTAINER (Colgate/Palmolive 1963) 10" metallic green plastic figure of Creature with detachable head. **$50-75**

MON-7   **MON-9**

MON-11

MON-7. DRACULA MODEL KIT (Aurora 1962)
3x4" box contains 1/12 scale all-plastic assembly kit molded in black. **$200-250**. (**Note:** This kit was re-issued in 1969 with extra glow pieces in a 12x12" box and called "Glow in the Dark" Dracula **$50-75**

MON-8. DRACULA MYSTERY GAME (Hasbro 1963) Comes with four cardboard figure playing pieces of Dracula, spinner and board. Box is 10x19". **$75-150**

MON-9. DRACULA OIL PAINTING SET (Hasbro 1963) 14x20" box contains a 12x16" pre-numbered, pre-sketched canvas board, 14 vials of paint and brush. **$200-250**

MON-11. FRANKENSTEIN JIGSAW PUZZLE (Jaymar 1963) Scene shows Frankenstein fighting the Wolfman in a dungeon laboratory of a castle. There is a frightened couple in the background and a corpse on an examination table with a hypodermic needle stuck in its neck. Parental objection to these gruesome puzzles soon led to the discontinuation of the series. Puzzle came in two sizes:
Small 7x10" red box $50-75
Large 8x12" blue box $100-150
Frame tray puzzle $35-50

MON-10

MON-12

MON-10. FRANKENSTEIN HALLOWEEN COSTUME (Ben Cooper 1963) 10x12" box with window display lid contains one-piece synthetic body suit and mask. **$50-60**

MON-12. FRANKENSTEIN MODEL KIT (Aurora 1961)
The production of this kit marked the beginning of the Monster craze of the Sixties. An instant success, Aurora had to make a second mold and keep both running 24 hours a day to meet demand. Grey all plastic assembly kit in 1/12 scale comes in 13x4" box. **$150-225**
(**Note:** This kit was re-issued in 1969 with extra glow pieces in a 12x12" square box and called "Glow in the Dark" **Frankenstein. $75-100**

MON-13

MON-16

MON-13.   FRANKENSTEIN FLIVVER WIND-UP (1963)
Japanese-made   vinyl plastic figure in antique flivver with wind-up feature in back which causes car to move from right to left. Car measures 4-1/2x4-1/2" tall. **$200-250**

MON-16. GODZILLA GAME (Ideal 1963)
Object of the game is to kill Godzilla by hitting him in any one of his three vulnerable areas with atomic playing piece. Box is 10x20". **$100-150**

MON-14

MON-17

MON-14.   FRANKENSTEIN MYSTERY GAME (Hasbro 1963) 10x19" box contains four cardboard figure playing pieces of Frankenstein, spinner and board. Object is to get Frankenstein safely back to his castle. **$75-150**

MON-17.   GODZILLA'S GO-CART MODEL KIT (Aurora 1966) 13x7" box contains all plastic assembly kit molded in green and yellow plastic. **$1000 and up**

MON-15

MON-18

MON-18. GODZILLA MODEL KIT (Aurora 1964)
13x7" box contains all-plastic assembly kit in 1/12 scale molded in pink plastic. **$250-350**
(Note: This kit was re-issued in 1969 with extra glow pieces in a 12x12" box and called **"Glow in the Dark" Godzilla.** **$100-150**

MON-15.   FRANKENSTEIN BY NUMBER OIL PAINT SET (Hasbro 1963) 14x20" box contains 12x16 pre-sketched, pre-numbered canvas board, 14 vials of paint and brush. **$175-225**

MON-19

MON-21

MON-21. HAUNTED HOUSE GAME (Ideal 1963)
Large 19x22x8" deep box contains plastic house with cut-away view to reveal a four story, 9-room interior. Object is to find the hidden treasure while overcoming spooky encounters. **$50-100**

MON-19. GREAT GARLOO (Marx 1961-62)
Large 18" tall green plastic battery-operated monster with remote control features. Toy moves forward and backward, turns right or left, and can bend over and close his arms together which allows him actually to pick up items. Dressed in leopard trunks and chain-linked plastic green "Garloo" medallion around his neck. There are foam pads at each shoulder and on the palms of both hands. Box is 20x12x12". **$400-650**
(**Note:** Marx also made a 6" tin wind-up of this creature called **Son of Great Garloo $150-200**

MON-22

MON-22. HOOTIN' HOLLOW HAUNTED HOUSE (Marx 1963) 11x13x7" tin litho house with eight control key buttons that produce eerie sounds and actions. Spook pops up from chimney, witch opens door, screeching cat, etc. Box is 12x15x8". **$400-600**

MON-20

MON-20. GUILLOTINE MODEL KIT (Aurora 1964)
13x4" box contains all-plastic assembly kit of a working guillotine that beheads its victim. Aurora had to discontinue this kit after only eight months due to parental objection. **$350-500**

MON-23

MON-23. KING KONG GAME (Ideal 1963)
10x20" box contains cardboard figure of Kong, playing cards, spinner and board. Object is to trap Kong atop the Empire State Building. **$75-100**

MON-24

MON-27

MON-24. KING KONG MODEL KIT (Aurora 1964)
13x7" box contains all-plastic 1/12 scale assembly kit
molded in black and tan plastic. **$300-350**
(Note: This kit was re-issued in 1969 with extra glow pieces
and 12x12" box and called **"Glow in the Dark"** King Kong
$75-125)

MON-27. MONSTER PRINT PUTTY (Colorforms 1965)
6x5" display card holds plastic skull-shaped container of
print putty which, like Silly Putty, lifts prints from and
transfers them to paper. Also included is an illustrated print
book and paper. **$50-75**

MON-25

MON-28

MON-25. MONSTER OLD MAID CARD GAME (Milton
Bradley 1963) 8x6" box contains oversized photo cards of
Universal movie monsters. **$35-50**

**MON-28. MUMMY "SOAKY" BUBBLE BATH
CONTAINER** (Colgate/Palmolive 1963) 10" plastic figural
container with white body and green removable head. **$75**

MON-26

MON-29

MON-26. MONSTER LAB (Ideal 1963)
Large 28x6x6" tall battery-operated plastic laboratory
diorama with control panels at each end and a monster
inside lab. The object is to send the monster to the other
players' side of the lab. The direction of the monster is
unpredictable. As he reaches either end of the lab, his arms
shoot up, he growls and his masks pops off revealing
hideous face. Box is 30x6x6". **$75-125**

MON-29. MUMMY JIGSAW PUZZLE (Jaymar 1963)
Gruesome picture showing the Mummy carring a screaming
victim mummified from the neck down. There is an
anguished woman crying in the background and a dead
victim in the foreground with a large lizard crawling across
him. A cloaked skeleton is also in the foreground rising from
a casket. Parental objection to these gruesome puzzles
soon led to Jaymar's discontinuation of them. Puzzle came
in two sizes:
Small 7x10" box. $75-100
Large 8x12" box. $125-150

MON-30

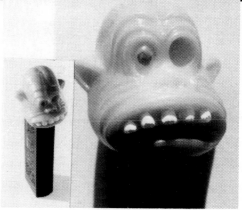

MON-33

MON-33. ONE-EYED MONSTER CANDY CONTAINER
(Pez 1960s) 5" tall plastic Pez candy container with orange molded head of a one-eyed monster. **$35-75**

MON-30. MUMMY MODEL KIT (Aurora 1963)
3x4" box contains all-plastic 1/12 scale assembly kit.
$200-250
Note: This kit was re-issued in 1969 with extra glow pieces in a 12x12" box and called **"Glow in the Dark" Mummy.**
$50-65

MON-31

MON-34

MON-31. MY NAME IS "GLOB" MODEL KIT (Lindberg 1965) Part of the Lindberg "Repulsives" model kit series, this all-assembly plastic model kit comes in 6x4" box. **$35-50**

MON-34. PHANTOM OF THE OPERA MODEL KIT (Aurora 1963) 13x4" box contains all-plastic 1/12 scale assembly kit molded in black plastic. **$200-275**
(Note: This kit was re-issued in 1969 with extra glow pieces in a 12x12" box and called **"Glow in the Dark"** Phantom of the Opera **$50-75**

MON-32

MON-35

MON-32. MYSTIC SKULL GAME (Ideal 1964)
Object of this unusual game is to put a "hex" on your opponent by sticking pins into his voodoo doll. The "Mystic Skull" dangles on the end of a limb and directs actions. Winner is the wise player who has managed to keep his doll the less filled with pin holes. Box is 12x12x5" deep. **$35-50**

MON-35. VOODOO DOLL GAME (Schaper 1967)
12x12" box contains plastic voodoo doll and large plastic base with hut with witch doctor inside. Players take turns sticking plastic pins into the voodoo doll. If the witch doctor pops out of hut, the player is eliminated. **$25-45**

MON-39

MON-37

MON-36

MON-36. WOLFMAN "SOAKY" BUBBLE BATH CONTAINER (Colgate/Palmolive 1963) 10" metallic copper-color figure with removeable hard plastic head. **$50-75**

MON-37. WOLFMAN JIGSAW PUZZLE (Jaymar 1963) Night scene shows Wolfman lurking behind a tree in a cemetary with a bloody, torn and scratched woman beneath him. Other people are fleeing the cemetary. Frankenstein and the Grim Reaper are also in the scene. Parental objection to these gruesome puzzles soon led Jaymar to discontinue this series of monster puzzles. Two sizes made:
Small box (7x10") $75-100
Large box (8x12") $125-150

MON-39. WOLFMAN MYSTERY GAME (Hasbro 1963) 10x19" box contains four cardboard playing piece figures of the Wolfman, spinner and board. Object is to bring the Wolfman safely through the moors and back home. **$150-175**

MON-40   **MON-41**

MON-38

MON-40. WOLFMAN NOTEBOOK BINDER (1963) 10x12" colorful vinyl three-ring notebook binder. Pose is taken from the Wolfman oil painting set made by Hasbro. A dracula and Frankenstein notebook binder were also made. **$25-50**

MON-41. WOLFMAN DRINKING GLASS (Anchor-Hocking 1963) 7" frosted drinking glass in shades of lavenders and light greens feature a wrap-around scene of the Wolfman lurking through the moors. **$25-30**

MON-38. WOLFMAN MODEL KIT (Aurora 1962) 13x4" box contains all-plastic 1/12 scale assembly kit. **$250-300**
(Note: This kit was re-issued in 1969 with extra glow pieces in a 12x12" box and called **"Glow in the Dark" Wolfman.**
$40-65

MUSIC, MOVIES, & PERSONALITIES

Each decade has its own distinctive style and sound, from music and movies to a host of other charismatic personalities which personify that era. The Sixties seemed to produce some of the most colorful personalities of recent times and some of the best music ever. Movies went through a cultural change, too, as the introduction of the rating system became universally used by 1969.

MUS-2

MUS-2. BEATLES "FLIP YOUR WIG" GAME (Milton Bradley 1964) Box is 20x10". **$50-100**

MUS-3

MUS-3. BEATLES MODEL KITS (Revell 1964) 6x9" box contains all plastic assembly kit of a Beatle playing an instrument and standing on a base featuring a facsimile autograph. Four kits were produced. **PAUL, RINGO: $125-175 each, GEORGE, JOHN: $175-250 each**

MUS-1

MUS-1. BEATLES DOLLS (Remco 1964)
One on the most popular selling toys made on the Beatles was the 5" figures with life-like hair. Each figure comes with an instrument with a facsimile autograph. Window display box is 4x6". **EACH: $100-125**

MUS-4

MUS-7

MUS-4. BEATLES SKATEBOARD (Surf Skater Co. 1965) 19x6" wood skateboard features photo decal of the Beatles and their logo name. Comes in illustrated 20x7" box. Two larger sizes were also available and measured up to 32" in length. **$100-125**

MUS-7. BEATLES YELLOW SUBMARINE JIGSAW PUZZLE (Jaymar 1968) 12x12" box contains 650-piece puzzle which, when assembled, makes a 19x19" picture. **$35-65**

MUS-5

MUS-5. BEATLES YELLOW SUBMARINE LUNCHBOX (King Seeley Thermos 1969) Steel box with matching steel thermos. **Box: $100-200, Thermos: $50-75**

MUS-8

MUS-8. BEN HUR PLAYSET (Marx 1960)
Hailed by playset collectors as one of the very best playsets made, the Ben Hur playset comes in two sizes: a 132-piece set including four chariots and a larger deluxe 217-piece set which includes eight chariots. Each set contains a hard plastic coliseum with pillars, two separate galleries with seats, two amphitheaters with lion cages with raising gates, a slave market, a market place, 54mm tan or cream-color Romans, gladiators, slaves and character figures of Ben Hur, Emperor and Empress. Also several accessories such as flags, pennants, wagons, lions, tigers, statues, tent, etc., were included as well as either four or eight chariots, each drawn by four horses. Box is 31x17x4". **$1000 and up.**

MUS-6

MUS-6. BEATLES YELLOW SUBMARINE MODEL KIT (MPC 1968) 6x9" box contains all-plastic assembly kit of the famous psychedelic submarine. **$150-250**

MUS-9

MUS-9. CHITTY CHITTY BANG BANG DELUXE OIL PAINTING BY NUMBERS (Hasbro 1968)
Large 26x18" window display box contains one 14x20" pre-sketched, pre-numbered canvas, eight vials of paint, brush and plastic frame. **$25-30**

MUS-10. CHITTY CHITTY BANG BANG MODEL KIT (Aurora 1968) 9x12" box contains all plastic assembly kit of the flying car in 1/25 scale and measures 12" long when assembled. **$35-50**

MUS-13

MUS-14

MUS-15.

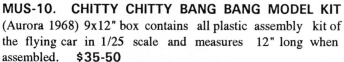

MUS-11

MUS-11. CHUBBY CHECKER LIMBO BAR (Wham-o 1962) 15x10" box contains plastic adjustable limbo bar and plastic "Fun-Pad" sheet which is placed under bar to help guide players. There is also a record included. **$50-65**

MUS-13. DOCTOR DOOLITTLE DOLL (Mattel 1967)
6" plastic vinyl posable doll with cloth suit and stuffed parrot on shoulder comes in 4x8" window display box. **$25-35**

MUS-14. DOCTOR DOOLITTLE MYSTERY CHAMBER SET (Hasbro 1967) 10x8" box contains red plastic chamber in which magic tricks (included) may be performed. **$20-25**

MUS-15. DOCTOR DOOLITTLE "PUSHMI-PULLYU" MODEL KIT (Aurora 1967) 13x4" box contains all-plastic assembly kit of the Siamese Llama. **$40-50**

MUS-12

MUS-12. CHUBBY CHECKER "TWISTER" GAME (Empire 1961) Game includes record and a Twister Belt which is tied around player and partner. Object is to be the first team to "Twist" the best. Box is 12x8". **$50-75**

MUS-16

MUS-16. THE EXCITING GAME OF THE KENNEDIES (Harrison-Winter 1962) Game deals with the Kennedy Family in the White House. Playing board is divided into sections like "Personal Image", "Social Standing", etc., and play money has picture of Joseph Kennedy. Box is 20x10". **$65**

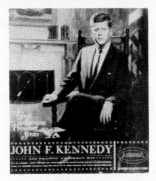

MUS-17

MUS-17. JOHN F. KENNEDY MODEL KIT (Aurora 1963) 10x11" box contains all-plastic assembly kit of the late President John F. Kennedy sitting in his rocking chair beside a fireplace. **$50-75**

MUS-18

MUS-18. MONKEES GAME (Transogram 1967) Object of the game is to be the first player to finish the Monkees Theme Song. Game includes plastic guitar, playing pieces and playing board. Box is 19x10". **$35-60**

MUS-19

MUS-19. MONKEES LUNCHBOX (King Seeley Thermos 1967) White vinyl lunchbox with matching blue steel thermos. **Box: $100-150, Thermos: $15-20**

MUS-20

MUS-20. MONKEES MONKEE-MOBILE (ASC 1967) Battery-operated 12" tin litho/metal GTO with friction drive and a switch which, when activated, plays the Monkees Theme Song. There are four plastic vinyl half-figures of the Monkees sitting in the car playing instruments. Box is 13x6x4" deep. **$350-500**

MUS-21

MUS-21. MONKEES MONKEE-MOBILE MODEL KIT (MPC 1967) 9x6" box contains all-plastic assembly kit in 1/25 scale of the Monkee-Mobile. **$35-40**

MUS-22

MUS-22. PLANET OF THE APES DOLLS (Azak 1969) ?x9" display card holds 8" posable plastic doll with cloth ?utfit. Three Apes and two Astronauts were produced. Our ?hoto shows the two astronauts Peter Burke and Alan Verdon. **EACH: $15-20**

MUS-23

MUS-23. PLANET OF THE APES GUM CARDS (Topps ?969) Set of 44 color photo cards with narrative on back. ?um Card Set: **$25-35** ?um Card Wrapper: **$10-20** ?um Card Display Box: **$50-65**

MUS-24

MUS-24. PLANET OF THE APES STATUE (1967) ?2" tall painted plaster statue of Zera. Two other Ape ?haracters were also made. **$35-45**

MUS-25

MUS-25. TWIGGY GAME (Milton Bradley 1967) "The game that makes every girl like Twiggy--the Queen of Mod". Object of the game is to score points by covering the picture of Twiggy with matching cards. Box is 20x10". **$25-35**

MUS-26

MUS-26. TWIGGY FASHION TOTE BAG (Mattel 1967) 11x14" yellow plastic vinyl carry bag with photo and designs of Twiggy on front. **$35-50**

QUISP

QUISP © JAY WARD & QUAKER OATS

PREMIUMS & CEREAL BOXES

Nothing quite started the day off right more than sitting down with your favorite breakfast cereal every morning--particularly if that cereal had a free toy inside. Nearly all the cereal premiums of the Sixties were plastic and most required assembly. From simple rings to complex shooting mechanisms, these toys, so lavishly illustrated on the front and back of cereal boxes, captured the imaginations of young children to the point where cereal was being bought for the free toy inside and not because of the brand. Mothers grew skeptical: "Are you sure you're going to eat this?" or worse: "No, I bought that for you last time and it just sat there." Like baseball trading cards, cereal toys could easily fit into a pocket and be taken to school to be swapped at recess or played with surreptitiously while less exciting subjects were being taught. Throughout the Sixties, nearly every pre-sweetened cereal offered a free toy inside its package.

PRE-1

PRE-1. CAP'N CRUNCH BANKS (Quaker 1966)
Plastic 7" color figures of **Cap'n Crunch** and **Jean Lefoot** which were available as a mail order premium. **EACH: $15-25**

PRE-2

PRE-2. CAP'N CRUNCH BUTTON (Quaker 1965)
3" diameter button with color illustration of Cap'n Crunch's head against a white background. This was part of a membership kit issued by Quaker in the mid-Sixties. **$10**

PRE-3

PRE-3. CAP'N CRUNCH HAND PUPPETS (Quaker 1964)
8" thin plastic puppet which came free inside specially marked packages of Cap'n Crunch. A series of six crew members were made: **Cap'n Crunch, Seadog, Brunhilde, Alfie, Carlyle, Dave.** Our photo shows Cap'n Crunch. **EACH: $5-10**

PRE-4

PRE-4. CAP'N CRUNCH KALEIDOSCOPE (Quaker 1964-65) Colorful 7" long cardboard kaleidoscope with illustration of all six characters (Cap'n Crunch, Seadog, Alfie, Brunhilde, Carlyle and Dave) on both sides. This was a mail order premium. **$20-35**

PRE-5

PRE-7

PRE-8

PRE-5. CAP'N CRUNCH "OATH OF ALLEGIANCE" PLAQUE (Quaker 1964) 8x10" plaque made on high-grade document paper with color illustration of Cap'n Crunch surrounded by gold leaf cluster on top and affixed seal of acceptance on bottom. The oath requires the bearer of the plaque to "be good and eat plenty of Cap'n Crunch." This is part of an early membership kit. **$10-20**

PRE-7. CAP'N CRUNCH SHIP SHAKE (Quaker 1968) Clear plastic 6" tall tumbler with red lid features color illustration of Cap'n crunch on side. This was a mail order premium. **$15**

PRE-8. CAP'N CRUNCH FIGURE RING (Quaker 1963) One of the very first premiums to be offered in Cap'n Crunch cereal was one of a series of 9 different rings, all featuring a sea-pirate related theme (Ship-in-a-Bottle Ring, 1863 Gold Coin Ring, Treasure Chest Ring, etc.). The figure ring of Cap'n Crunch is 1" tall and stands on top of ring. **$15-20**

PRE-6

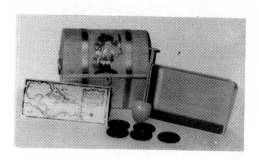

PRE-9

PRE-6. CAP'N CRUNCH SEA CYCLE (Quaker 1960s) Plastic snap-together assembly kit of working sea-cycle that is rubber-band powered and skims across water. There is also a figure of Cap'n Crunch and Seadog which sits on top and rides the cycle. Kit is 6x5" high when assembled and comes with color stick-on decals of Cap'n Crunch and Seadog. This was a mail order premium. **$25-35**

PRE-9. CAP'N CRUNCH TREASURE CHEST BANK & CEREAL BOWL SET (Quaker 1960s) 6x5x4" deep tan plastic treasure chest bank opens up to reveal a tray-like cereal bowl and shovel-shaped spoon. Also included are several plastic gold pirate coins and a paper treasure map. There is an embossed color figure of Cap'n Crunch on the top of the chest and a working lock and key holds latch closed. This was a mail order premium. **$35-50**

PRE-10

PRE-10. FIZZIES DRINK TABLETS (American Chicle Co. 1960's) Fizzies dissolved in water the same as Alka-Selzer and came in various flavors including cherry, grape and root beer. They were the rage of make-at-home drinks in the early Sixties. When first introduced, General Mills cereal offered two Fizzie tablets as a free premium in specially marked boxes of children's pre-sweetened cereals. **$50-75**

PRE-11

PRE-11. DIVING "BAKING SODA-POWERED" FROGMEN (Kelloggs 1960-61) Originally released in the late Fifties, the popular baking soda-powered frogmen soon made their way back into boxes of Raisin Bran and other Kellogg's cereals, due largely to the renewed interest in skin diving brought about by the television series "Sea Hunt". Each 3" plastic red, yellow or green frogman has a small hollow base where baking soda is stored which causes the figure to dive, then float to the surface. Three different frogmen were made, each carrying a specific piece of equipment. **EACH: $5-15**

PRE-12

PRE-12. DROOPY DOG "POPPING HEAD" FIGURE (General Mills 1960) Plastic 2" tall detailed figure of the cartoon character Droopy the Dog has a spring-loaded head which shoots several feet into the air with a press of a lever. This snap-together assembly toy came free in side General Mills cereals. **$20-25**

PRE-13

PRE-13. HANNA-BARBERA "SNAP-TOGETHER" FIGURES (Kelloggs 1960) Plastic three-piece 2" figures of **Huckleberry Hound, Yogi Bear, Boo-Boo** and **Jinx the Cat** which detached from the head and feet. These figures came free inside Corn Flakes and Sugar Frosted Flakes and there is also a figure of Tony the Tiger. **EACH: $15-25**

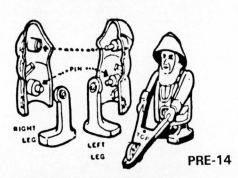

PRE-14

PRE-14. GNOMEMOBILE WALKING GNOME (Dan-Dee 1968) Plastic 1-1/2" figure with walking legs and wheelbarrow comes with a jug-shaped weight which, when tied to wheelbarrow with thread and hung over the edge of a table, will make gnome "walk". Available in Dan-Dee potato chips. **$10-12**

84

PRE-15. LINUS THE LIONHEARTED STUFFED DOLL
(Post 1965) Plush 10" doll available by mail order coupon on side panel of Crispy Critters cereal. **$20-25**

PRE-16

PRE-16. MARY POPPINS "POPPING" FIGURES (Kellogg's 1964) Two different spring-loaded plastic assembly sets were made in this series based on the popular Disney film of the same year. One set features a 1.5" figure of Mary Poppins holding umbrella which can be "popped" out of a spring-loaded chimney. The second is one of Dick Van Dyke as the chimney sweep which also pops out of a chimney. This cereal came free in boxes of Kellogg's cereals. **EACH: $20-30**

PRE-17

PRE-17. QUAKE EARTH-DIGGER CAR (Quaker 1965) Plastic 2.5" car with drill-bit front and fin in back holds a small detailed figure of Quake in his cowboy-style hat. There is a launcher that comes with the car and shoots the car forward. This premium came free in boxes of Quake. **$50-100**

PRE-18

PRE-18. QUAKE FIGURE RING (Quaker 1966) Small detailed plastic figure of Quake sits on top of plastic ring band and came free inside boxes of Quake cereal. **$50-100**

PRE-19. QUAKE MINERS HELMET (Quaker 1966) Yellow plastic miner's helmet with battery-powered light on front and embossed words "Quake" on sides. This was a mail order premium available through Quaker. **$100-150**

PRE-20. QUANGAROO FREE-WHEELER (Quaker 1964) 2" plastic snap-together figure on wheels. **$25-50**

PRE-21. QUISP CERAMIC BANK (Quaker 1960s) Colorful 6" ceramic figure of Quisp on base. **$50-100** (**Note:** Reproductions of this bank are currently being produced and are sometimes passed off as originals. The reproductions are quite good and buyers should look closely for mold flaws and edge lines.)

PRE-20

PRE-22

PRE-22. QUISP "GYRO-POWERED" FIGURE ON THREE-WHEELER (Quaker 1969) Snap-together blue plastic 2.5" long three-wheeler with detailed figure of Quisp riding. The vehicle has a white gear-edged disc and plastic pull-string which, when pulled, sends it moving in a forward direction. This premium was free inside boxes of Quisp cereal. **$50**

PRE-23. QUISP FIGURE ON UNICYCLE (Quaker 1969) Snap-together blue plastic 2.5" tall detailed figure of Quisp riding a working unicycle which is powered by a small ball under the frame. This premium came free inside boxes of Quisp cereal. **$50-75**

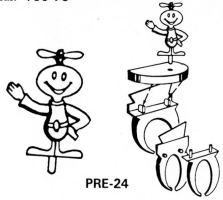

PRE-24

PRE-24. QUISP FRIENDSHIP RING (Quaker 1966) Plastic snap together ring features a 1" detailed figure of Quisp waving. **$25-50**

PRE-25

PRE-25. SO-HI "WALKING" FIGURE AND RICKSHAW
(Post 1965) Plastic 1.25" detailed figure of So-Hi (Post's mascot of Rice Krinkles cereal) pulling snap-together rickshaw. There is a small plastic box of Rice Krinkles which serves as a weight and is tied to So-Hi and dangled over the edge of a table to pull the rickshaw forward. This premium came free in boxes of Rice Krinkles. **$20-30**

PRE-26

PRE-26. TRIX RABBIT BOWL AND MUG SET (General Mills 1963) Plastic white bowl and mug with color accents. The bowl has enbossed colored pictures of the Trix rabbit in a variety of predicaments. The mug has two ear-shaped handles and a face on one side of mug. This set was a mail order premium available through Trix cereal coupons. **$25**

JUST CUT 'EM OUT   PUT 'EM IN WATER   SEE 'EM GROW TO FULL SIZE

PRE-27

PRE-27. TWINKLES SPONGE FIGURES (General Mills 1960) Set of four 5x3" thin color sponges with illustration of a character on each sponge (**Twinkles the Elephant, Fulton the Camel, Wilbur the Monkey** and **Sanford the Parrot**). The figures were to be cut out and placed in water,

which would "puff" the sponges up to make the characters three dimensional. The trademark of Twinkles cereal was the free comic book on the back of the box so very few premiums were offered inside the cereal. This premium was a mail order item available through Twinkles cereal. **$25-40**

PRE-28

PRE-28. WINNIE THE POOH SPOON HANGERS (Nabisco 1960s) Plastic 2" detailed sitting figures of **Winnie Pooh, Eeyore, Piglet, Owl, Rabbit, Kangaroo** and **Christopher Robin**. Each figure has a groove on its bottom which allows the figure to slide on, and stay affixed to, the handle of a spoon. One of each figure came free inside boxes of Wheat or Rice Honey. **EACH: $8-12**

PRE-29

PRE-29. APPLE JACKS CEREAL BOX (Kelloggs 1965) "An apple a day keeps the bullies away" was Kellogg's advertising motto for Apple Jacks when first introduced in 1965. The first issue box had a black/white comic page (which could be colored) of an Apple Jacks kid fighting bullies. **$50-75**

PRE-30

PRE-30. CAP'N CRUNCH CEREAL BOX (Quaker 1963) "Stays crunchy...even in milk" was Quaker's slogan for introducing its Cap'n Crunch cereal into the market when it first debuted in 1963. By 1965, just two years later, it was the second largest selling pre-sweetened cereal in the country. The first issue box advertised one of nine different pirate rings inside. **$75-150**

PRE-31

PRE-31. COCOA KRISPIES CEREAL BOX (Kelloggs 1964)
Hanna-Barbera's **Snagglepuss** is featured on the box as the official mascot. Back of box features cut-out Classic Antique Car trading cards. **$200-300**

PRE-32

PRE-32. CORN FLAKES CEREAL BOX (Kelloggs 1960)
Limited edition box commemorating one year birthday for Yogi Bear. There is a free Yogi Bear birthday comic book premium offered inside. **$400-500**

PRE-33

PRE-33. CRISPY CRITTERS CEREAL BOX (Post 1964)
"The one and only cereal that comes in shapes of animals". This slogan, when shown on the TV commercials, started a stampeding herd of animals across the television screen, trampling poor Linus the Lionhearted in the process. Introduced into the market in 1962, our photo shows a third year box. **$50-75**

PRE-34

PRE-34. FRUIT LOOPS CEREAL BOX (Kelloggs 1963)
"OOT-fray, OOPS lay" was the "pig latin" slogan introducing the newly conceived Fruit Loops into the market place with Toucan Sam the Mina Bird as its mascot. **$50-75**

PRE-35

PRE-35. FROSTY-0'S CEREAL BOX (General Mills 1961)
Dating back to the mid-Fifties, Frosty-0's was the equivalent of a sugar-coated Cheerio's and was very popular with children. It's mascot, the Frosty-0's Bear, first appeared around 1959. Our photo shows a 1961 box design. **$40-60**

PRE-36. LUCKY CHARMS (General Mills 1965)
"They're magically delicious" sang the impish leprechaun who, like the Trix Rabbit, could never hang on to a box of his favorite cereal. Lucky Charms hit the shelves in 1965 and although the little leprechaun has been replaced, the cereal is still around today. **$35-50**

PRE-37

PRE-37. OK's CEREAL BOX (Kelloggs 1960)
"The Best in Oats" came in the shape of little O's and K's and featured Yogi Bear on the box as the official mascot. **$200-300**

PRE-38

PRE-38. QUAKE CEREAL BOX (Quaker 1965)
Quake was introduced in 1965 along with his adversary Quisp. Quake, the earth-digging miner mascot, was created by Jay Ward of Bullwinkle cartoon fame. Quake, a corn based cereal, didn't have the taste kids wanted, and after a grand, pre-conceived, national popularity contest between Quisp and Quake cereals, in which kids were to vote for their favorite character, Quake lost. The cereal was discontinued in 1975. **$200-350**

PRE-39

PRE-39. QUISP CEREAL BOX (Quaker 1965)
Quisp debuted in 1965 and was an instant success, partially due to the witty TV commercials that flooded Saturday morning programs. The little alien mascot Quisp was designed by Bullwinkle creator Jay Ward, who was also behind those clever, animated commercials. Quisp was in production for twenty years and continues to be the most widely requested cereal of all time. Our photo shows a 1969 box which features the Quisp Gyro Unicycle premium. **$100-200**

PRE-40

PRE-40. RICE KRINKLES (Kelloggs 1960)
So-Hi, the oriental mascot for Rice Krinkles, was first introduced in 1960 and remained on cereal boxes until 1969. Our photo shows a first year box with color cut-out baseball trading cards as a premium. **$100-150**

PRE-41

PRE-41. SUGAR CRISP CEREAL BOX (Post 1960)
The Sugar Crisp Bear dates back to 1958, but he was never really perfected or fully utilized until 1965, when his features were re-vamped and he began making television commercials. Our photos show a 1960 and 1965 box.
EACH: $50-60

PRE-42

PRE-42. SUGAR SMACKS CEREAL BOX (Kelloggs 1963)
Hanna-Barbera's **Quick Draw McDraw** was the official Sugar Smacks mascot from 1963-64. Our photo shows a 1963 box. **$150-250**

RAT FINK AND WEIRD-OHS

Already a legend in the customized car show circuit, Ed Roth introduced Rat Fink in 1961 on t-shirts he airbrushed during personal appearances at these shows. Demand for this "anti-Mickey Mouse" character grew, and in late 1962, Revell approached him to produce both his customized cars and his Rat Fink character. Revell's "Rat Fink" kit was an enormous success, and plans were made for 13 more, each being available for only six months. The popularity of Rat Fink began a "crazy monster" fad in which other model kit and toy manufacturers began pumping out bug-eyed monsters on hot rods at every opportunity. The most heavily merchandised characters from these imitators were the "Weird-Ohs". The Rat Fink craze lost steam in 1964 with the "British Invasion" started by the Beatles, and by 1965 Rat Fink was all but forgotten.

RAT-2

RAT-2. RAT FINK SQUEEZE FIGURE (Macman 1964)
6" tall pink vinyl squeeze figure comes on 9x5" display card.
$75

RAT-1

RAT-1. RAT FINK HALLOWEEN COSTUME (Ben Cooper 1963) Costume consists of one piece fabric body suit with full Rat Fink illustration and logo and vacuum plastic mask. Comes in 8x12x4" deep window display box. **$150**

RAT-3

RAT-3. RAT FINK RING (Macman Ent. 1963)
Plastic 1.25" figure of Rat Fink can be detached and reattached to ring. Comes in polybag with 3x1" header card. Back of card has Official Certificate of Membership. **$10** (Note: these rings were also sold in gumball machines without packaging.) **DISPLAY BOX $100-125**

RAT-10

RAT-10. ANGEL FINK MODEL KIT (Revell 1965) $85-135

RAT-11

RAT-4

RAT-4. RAT FINK MODEL KIT (Revell 1963)
Plastic all assembly kit with photo of Ed Roth and Rat Fink on box. Box is 9x6x2" deep. This kit was fourth in a series of twelve figure kits designed by Roth for Revell and marked the beginning of the Rat Fink craze. The other eleven kits of this series are listed below in production order. **$50-75**

RAT-11. SUPER FINK (Revell 1964) **$85-135**

RAT-12. SCUZ FINK (Revell 1965) **$150-200**

RAT-13. FINK ELIMINATOR (Revell 1965) **$150-200**

RAT-14. ROBBIN' HOOD FINK (Revell 1965) **$200-300**

RAT-15. TWEEDY PIE W/BOSS FINK (Revell 1965) **$200-300**

RAT-5

RAT-5. MR. GASSER MODEL KIT (Revell 1963) **$75-100**

RAT-6. MOTHERS WORRY MODEL KIT (Revell 1963) **$40**

RAT-7. DRAGNUT MODEL KIT (Revell 1963) **$30-40**

RAT-8. BROTHER RAT FINK ON A BIKE MODEL KIT (Revell 1963) **$30-40**

RAT-16

RAT-16. MR. GASSER IN BRM MODEL RACER WITH MOTOR (Revell 1964) 9.5x6" box contains 6" plastic hot rod body, aluminum chassis, rubber tires, and 12-volt racing motor. **$75-100**

RAT-17

RAT-9

RAT-9. SURF FINK MODEL KIT (Revell 1965) **$75-125**

RAT-17. RAT FINK IN LOTUS FORD MODEL RACER WITH MOTOR (Revell 1964) 9.5x6" box contains 6" plastic hot rod body, aluminum chassis, rubber tires, and 12-volt racing motor. **$75-100**

RAT-19

RAT-22

RAT-22. DADDY THE SUBURBANITE (Hawk 1963) **$50-60**

RAT-18. ED ROTH IRON-ON T-SHIRT TRANSFERS (Insta Lettering Co., 1963) Series of 10 different 6x5" color T-shirt transfers. **EACH $10-20**

RAT-19. ED "BIG DADDY" ROTH DECALS (Insta-Lettering Co., 1963) Series of ten different characters. 4x6" decals come individually packaged on small header cards and depict various monsters on hot rods created by Ed Roth. Our photos show "Chevy-Breakfast of Champions" and "Lover Boy". **EACH $5-10**

WEIRD-OHS MODEL KITS (Hawk 1963)
Capitalizing on the success of Revell's Rat Fink, Hawk created its own crazy, bug-eyed monster kits, whose popularity inspired the marketing of games, puzzles, records and more.

RAT-23   RAT-29

RAT-20

RAT-20. FREDDY FLAME-OUT MODEL KIT (Hawk 1963) **$75-85**

RAT-23. FRANCIS THE FOUL (Hawk 1963) **$35-50**

RAT-24. DIGGER THE WAY-OUT DRAGSTER (Hawk 1963) **$75**

RAT-25. DAVY THE PSYCHO CYCLIST (Hawk 1963) **$75-85**

RAT-26. LEAKY BOAT LOUIE (Hawk 1963) **$75-85**

RAT-27. DRAG HAG (Hawk 1963) **$35-50**

RAT-28. ENDSVILLE EDDIE (Hawk 1963) **$50-75**

RAT-29. KILLER McBASH (Hawk 1963) **$100-125**

RAT-21

RAT-30

RAT-21. HUEY'S HOT ROD (Hawk 1963) **$50-60**

RAT-30. WADE A. MINUT (Hawk 1964) **$15-20**

RAT-31. SLING RAVE CURVETTE (Hawk 1964) **$15-20**

RAT-32

RAT-32. WEIRD-OH CUSTOMIZING KIT (Hawk 1964)
Three kits in one; comes in large 13x9 box and consists of
Davy, Digger and **Leaky Boat Louie** with assorted
customizing accessories such as feathers and glitter. **$150-
200**

RAT-33

RAT-33. WEIRD-OHS BOARD GAME (Ideal 1964)
Object is to cross the finish line in this frantic race of
vehicles. Box 10x20. **$50-75**

RAT-34

RAT-34. WEIRD-OHS "DIGGER" MOSAIC WALL PLAQUE
(Hawk 1963) 10x12" illustrated box contains several bags of
colored, crushed stones and illustrated hard canvas-like
board. Also made were **Davy, Freddie** and **Leaky Boat
Louie. Each $75-100**

RAT-35

RAT-36

**RAT-35. "THE SOUNDS OF THE WEIRD-OHS" RECORD
ALBUM** (Hawk 1964) Flip side features **"The Sounds of
the Silly Surfers"**, a spin-off of the original Weird-Oh series.
$30-50

RAT-36. WEIRD-OHS JIGSAW PUZZLE (Hawk, 1963)
8x6" box contains 100-piece jigsaw puzzle. Also made in
this series were: **Davy, Freddy Flame-Out, Digger,** and
Daddy. EACH $35-50

RAT-37.

RAT-37. WEIRD-OH "NUTTY MAD" FIGURES (Marx 1963-
4) Plastic 5" figures with outstanding attention to detail. Six
characters were produced: **Davy, Digger, Freddie Flame
Out, Drag Hag, Daddy** and **Endsville Eddie. EACH $20-
25** (note: figures molded in turquoise blue can be worth
$5-10 more.)

RAT-38

RAT-39

RAT-38. WEIRD-OHS HELMET (Ideal 1964)
Child's helmet made of yellow plastic with lift-up tinted sun visor and silver plastic exhaust manifolds extending from each side. Comes with sheet of Weird-Oh decals to decorate helmet. Illustrated box (not photographed) measures 10x10x9". **$50-100**

RAT-39. WEIRD-OHS GUM CARDS (Fleer 1965)
Set consists of 66 different cards, packaged in groups of five. **SET $40-50, WRAPPER $5-10, DISPLAY BOX $40-50**

RAT-40. WEIRD-OHS BASEBALL GUM CARDS (Fleer 1965) Set consists of 66 different cards, all baseball-oriented, packaged in groups of five. **SET $40-50, WRAPPER $5-10, DISPLAY BOX $40-50**

RAT-41

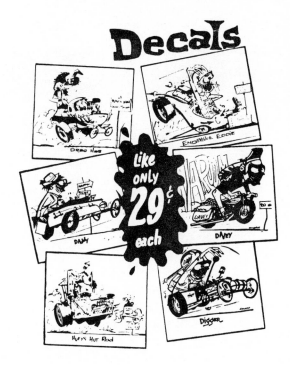

RAT-41. WEIRD-OHS DECALS (Hawk 1963)
Series of six 4x6" color decals of **Digger, Davy, Daddy, Drag Hag, Endsville Eddie** and **Huey Hut Rod.** Each comes individually wrapped in clear plastic. **EACH $8-10 DISPLAY BOX** (14X14X1") **$75-100**

RAT-42

RAT-42. WEIRD-OHS HALLOWEEN MASKS (1964)
A series of four plastic masks sold indiviually with no bodysuit or box. **Davy, Digger, Leakie Boat, Francis the Foul** were made. **EACH $15-25**

RAT-43. WEIRD-OHS VINYL CARRY CASE (Hawk 1963)
Series of four 10x7" vinyl cases with snap open lids. **Digger, Daddy, Davy** and **Endsville Eddie** were produced. **EACH $35-50**

RAT-46

RAT-46. WEIRD-OHS PAINT BY NUMBER WATER COLOR AND PENCIL BY NUMBER SET (Standard Toykraft, 1963) Large 21x12x1" deep window display box contains 12 pre-numbered pictures, eight water color paints, eight craycil pencils, water pan and pencil sharpener. **$150-200**

RAT-44   RAT-45

RAT-47

RAT-44. WEIRD-OHS PAINT BY NUMBER WATER COLOR SET (Standard Toykraft, 1963)
Large 19x9x1" window display box contains six pre-numbered pictures, eight water colors, water tray and brush. **$75-100**

RAT-45. WEIRD-OHS PENCIL BY NUMBER COLORING SET (Standard Toykraft, 1963) Large 19x9x1" deep window display box contains six pre-numbered pictures and eight craycil pencils. **$75-100**

RAT-47. WILD AND WEIRD JIGSAW PUZZLES (Jaymar 1963) A knock-off of the popular Weird-Oh characters, Jaymar produced four jigsaw puzzles, each depicting a main character. Each puzzle contained 100 pieces and came in a 8x10x2" deep box. **$35-40**

FRED FLYPOGGER MODEL KITS (Monogram 1965) At the tail end of the crazy monster craze, Monogram produced three kits designed by Stan "Mouse" Miller. Although these three kits are far superior in detail and craftsmanship to anything Hawk or Revell produced, they were introduced into the market too late. The fad for these kits had lost steam, and distribution of these kits was low. Monogram's fourth kit, "The War Mongler" was never released at all.

RAT-51

RAT-48

RAT-49

RAT-51. LINDBERG LOONYS MODEL KITS (Lindberg 1964) "The hep model in the square box" was about half the size of its competitors and came in a 7x7x1" box. Four characters were produced: **Satan's Crate, Big Wheeler, Road Hog** and **Scuttle Bucket. EACH $65-100**

RAT-52

RAT-50

RAT-48. **SPEED SHIFT** $150-200
RAT-49. **FLIP-OUT THE BEACHCOMBER** $125-150
RAT-50. **SUPER FUZZ** $175-225

RAT-52. BATFINK HALLOWEEN COSTUME (Collegeville 1965) Short-lived cartoon series but not based on Rat Fink. One piece fabric body suit and mask. Comes in 8x12 window display box. **$50-65**

601

602

603

604

605

606

RAT-53

SILLY SURFER MODEL KITS (Hawk 1964) As hot rods and surfing are closely related, Hawk produced four surfing character kits in 1964 which might sold better had they been made a year erarlier.

RAT-54

RAT-54. HOT DOGGER HANGIN' TEN (1964) 10x4" box. $40-50

RAT-55

RAT-53. FINKO'S IRON-ON TRANSFERS (Mani yacks 1964) Take-off of the popular Rat Fink characters. Each transfer came on a 8x12" T-shirt-shaped display card. Seven characters were produced. **Mr. Rat Fink, Hut Rod Harry, Side Car Charlie, Loco Lil, Johnny Jet, Dangerous Dan and Stanley Steamer. EACH $15-20**

RAT-55. HODAD MAKING THE SCENE WITH A SIX PACK (1964) 10x4" box. $40-50
RAT-56. BEACH BUNNY CATCHIN' RAYS (1964) 10x4" box $40-50
RAT-57. WOODIE ON A SAFARI (1964) 10x4" box. $65-75

NUTTY MADS (Marx 1963-64) Louis Marx saw the popularity of the Rat Fink culture grow and wasted no time creating his own line of bug-eyed monsters called "Nutty Mads". These 6" solid plastic figures were first produced in flat shades of pink and lime green. Later, brighter colors were used. There were 18 different characters made which were sold in large bins in department stores for around 15 cents each. They sold like hot cakes and soon follow-up toys were produced featuring these characters. These figures were issued in three series, with each series containing six figures. The name of each character is marked on the bottom of its base.

RAT-58. NUTTY MADS 1st Series: Roddy the Hot Rod, Manny the Reckless Mariner, Waldo the Weightlifter, Rocco the Champ, Dippy the Diver, Donald the Demon. **EACH $8-10**

RAT-59. NUTTY MADS 2nd Series: The Thinker, Lost Tee-Pee, Bull Pen, Surburban Sidney, Hogan the Cop, End Zone. **EACH $12-15**

RAT-60. NUTTY MADS Third Series: U.S. Male the Postman, Hipo-crit the Doctor, Smokey Sam the Fireman, Mudder, Gutterball Annie, Now Children the Teacher. **EACH $25-30**

RAT-61. NUTTY MAD BAGATELLE (Marx 1964) 12" tall tin litho pinball game with clear plastic casing features several characters from the first and second series of Nutty Mads. **$40**

RAT-62. NUTTY MAD MECHANICAL ARCADE TARGET GAME (Marx 1964) Colorful target set consists of 14" long tapered tin litho target with clear plastic dome cover which features several of the Nutty Mad characters. The main target is a plastic three dimensional head of Rocco with this open mouth being the central target. There is a black pistol at the front of the target that fires pellets. There are also wire supports to hold the set up. Box is 8x21x5" deep. **$75-100**

RAT-64

RAT-63.

RAT-63. MAD'S ALFRED E. NEUMAN MODEL KIT (Aurora 1965) 7x13x2 deep box contains all plastic assembly kit of Alfred with four different pairs of arms (holding nose, holding hatchet, covering ears, etc.) and a variety of signs to add color to these "idiotic customized poses". **$175-225**

RAT-64. MAD'S ALFRED E. NEUMAN BUST (Mad Magazine 1960's) White bisque china bust on base with inscription: "Mad's Alfred E. Neuman: What- Me Worry?". Mail order premium from Mad Magazine only. Two sizes were made:
SMALL BUST (3.75" tall)   **$100-150**
LARGE BUST (5.5" tall)   **$150-200**

RAT-65. MAD'S ALFRED E. NEUMAN HALLOWEEN COSTUME (Collegeville 1959-60) One piece black/red fabric body suit designed like a tuxedo with illustrated button of Neuman. Mask is very close resemblance. Comes in 8x12x3" deep window display box. **$125-175**

RAT-66

RAT-68

RAT-66. MAD STRAIGHTJACKET (Mad Magazine 1960's) Available through Mad Magazine only and made in three sizes. White canvas-like material with color illustration of Alfred E. Neuman with inscription: "What- Me Worry? I'm wearing my MADstraightjacket". Back of jacket has sewn-in false sleeves where actual sleeves can be placed creating the illusion of a real working straightjacket. There is also a red and silver metal lock that hangs in the front of jacket. **$500-750**

RAT-68. SCREWBALL- THE MAD, MAD, MAD GAME (Transogram 1961) A knock-off of the Mad Magazine format and characters, with Wally Wood- and Jack Davis-style artwork. Box is 20x10" and contains elaborate variety of playing pieces and cards. **$35-50**

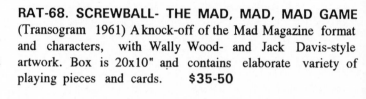

RAT-69

RAT-69. (WEIRD) CLYDE THE MUSICAL MONSTER (Merry Mfg. 1965) Packaged as "Clyde" or "Weird Clyde" in a 12x18" window display box. Clyde is a full-size plastic horn with four push-button valves and a monstrous green head with purple warts. **$75-100**

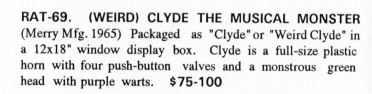

RAT-67. MAD RECORD ALBUMS (Big Top, 1960's) Several albums were made over the years, all have relatively the same collectible value.

MAD "TWISTS" ROCK 'N' ROLL	$35-50
FINK ALONG WITH MAD	$50-65
MUSICALLY MAD (RCA Records)	$50-65

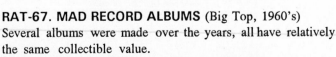

SECRET AGENTS

The spy phenomena of the Sixties began to take shape in 1962 when United Artists released its first James Bond movie, "Doctor No". Secret agents and their admirers gained a definite stronghold in 1964 when NBC aired its weekly television series "The Man from U.N.C.L.E.". By 1965, the craze hit its zenith with Thunderball (the most commercially successful Bond movie), U.N.C.L.E.'s Illya Kuryakin (a national sex symbol), over a dozen secret agent television series premiering from 1965-69, and several hit movies including "Our Man Flint" and "The Spy Who Came in From The Cold".

SPY-3

SPY-3. I-SPY CARD GAME (Ideal 1965)
10.5x6" box contains illustrated cards and pegboard. **$35-50**

SPY-4

SPY-4. I-SPY TARGET SET (Ray-Line 1965)
10x8" card contains pistol, pellets and three spy figures. **$100**

SPY-1

SPY-1. IPCRESS FILE GAME, THE (Milton Bradley 1966)
British agent Harry Palmer starring Michael Caine. This was the only U.S. item merchandised on the movie. 10x20" box. **$35-40**

SPY-2

SPY-2. I-SPY GAME (Ideal 1966)
10x20" box. **$20-35**

SPY-5

SPY-5. I-SPY GUN AND HOLSTER SET (Ray-Line 1965)
10.5x14" color photo display card contains 8" blue/black pistol that shoots small pellets (included) and black plastic shoulder holster. **$100-125**

SPY-8

SPY-8. JAMES BOND SWIMMING FINS & SNORKEL (Voit 1965) Black rubber pair of fins with embossed 007 logo on top comes in a 14x6x3" box. Snorkel features 007 logo on side and comes on a 12x5" display card. **EACH: $35-50**

SPY-6

SPY-6. JAMES BOND ACTION FIGURE DOLL (Gilbert 1964) Plastic 12" doll with spring-activated right hand that fires gun. Originally issued in black or dark blue suit with white shirt and tie. Later, in 1966-67, the Ideal Toy Company picked up manufacturing the doll (although continued as a Gilbert line) and packaged him in white T-shirt and swim trunks and added scuba mask, snorkle and fins. Box is 12x4.5x3" deep.
1st ISSUE DOLL w/SUIT $200-225
2nd ISSUE DOLL w/SWIM TRUNKS $100-125
STORE DISPLAY POSTER $50-75

SPY-9

SPY-9. JAMES BOND ROAD RACE SET (Gilbert 1965) Six large, fully-landscaped interlocking dioramas make up the race track and measure 51x34 when assembled. Enemy agent Mustang chases Aston-Martin sports car over oil slicks, washed out bridge, curves and tunnels. Box is 25x16x15". **$350-500**

SPY-7

SPY-7. JAMES BOND SHOOTING ATTACHE CASE (MPC 1965) The single most popular 007 toy made during the Sixties was the MPC's attache case. 18x12" black plastic briefcase contains shell-firing pistol with various attachments (stock, scope, silencer barrel) which convert into a sniper's rifle. A secret message decoder, code book w/booby-trap, passport, business cards and paper money are also inside briefcase. A hidden dagger slides out of the side of exterior of case and the latches which open case are booby-trapped to explode if opened incorrectly. Comes in 18x24x3" deep box. **$400-650**

SPY-10

SPY-10. JAMES BOND'S ASTON-MARTIN BATTERY-OPERATED CAR (Gilbert 1965) 12" silver metal sports car is battery-powered and features a variety of actions including working ejector seat, bullet-proof shield that raises and lowers, hidden front bumper machine guns that flash and produce sound, extending crash bumpers, revolving license plates, extending tire cutters and bump-and-go forward drive. Box is 12x5x5". **$200-300**

SPY-11

SPY-11. JAMES BOND MODEL KIT (Aurora 1966)
13x4" box contains all plastic assembly kit of Bond. **$150-200**

SPY-12. ODD JOB MODEL KIT (Aurora 1966)
13x4" box contains all plastic assembly kit. **$150-175**

SPY-12   SPY-13

SPY-13. ODD JOB ACTION FIGURE DOLL (Gilbert 1965)
12" plastic doll with spring-activated arm that throws derby. Two different box designs exist; one showing Odd Job in suit and one showing him in karate outfit. Doll also came dressed both ways. Box is 12x5x4" deep. **$200-250**

SPY-14

SPY-14. BOND VS ODD JOB FIGURE KIT (Airfix 1966)
This 1/12 scale kit features two 4" figures in hand-to-hand combat and comes in a colorful 8x4" box. **$100**

SPY-15. ASTON-MARTIN SUPER SPY CAR MODEL KIT
(Aurora 1965) This 1/25 scale kit features almost a dozen working devices including revolving license plates, ejector seat, etc. (Unlicensed model kit). **$150**

SPY-16

SPY-16. ASTON-MARTIN MODEL KIT (Airfix 1966)
This 1/24 scale kit was just as intricate as the Aurora Aston-Martin and included a weapons attache case in the trunk. **$100**

SPY-17. 007 GAME (Milton Bradley 1964)
Two versions of the box lid were originally made, one with a generic-looking James Bond, the other with a Sean Connery facsimile. Price varies little, although the Connery rendition is more desirable to collectors. **$15-25**

SPY-18

SPY-18. 007 THUNDERBALL GAME (Milton Bradley 1965)
Object of game is to find the secret area in which S.P.E.C.T.R.E is hiding the atomic bomb. Playing pieces include islands, enemy and British frogmen. **$35-45**

SPY-19

SPY-19. 007 GOLDFINGER GAME (Milton Bradley 1966)
Goldfinger and his men are trapped by James Bond and his agents, who try to capture Goldfinger. **$35-45**

SPY-20. JAMES BOND CASINO GAME (Milton Bradley 1965) 9x12x2" box contains small poker-type chips. Lid has light blue illustration sketch of Agent 007. **$35**

SPY-21. JAMES BOND CARD GAME (Milton Bradley 1965) 6x10x2" photo box lid contains red, white, and blue poker chips and deck of cards. **$30**

SPY-22. JAMES BOND "MESSAGE FOR M" GAME (Ideal 1966) Large 22x16x3" box contains four 3-dimensional diorama territories of villains (Dr. No, Goldfinger, Largo, and Rosa Klebb). There is also a mechanical box with a secret decoder and hidden SMERSH agent that pops out during course of play. There is a total of 16 miniature Bond figures in four colors each; all come with an array of weapons (cars, guns, briefcases, etc) to help subdue victims. This game was unique for its lack of a standard playing board. **$75-125**

SPY-23

SPY-23. JAMES BOND 007 SECRET SERVICE GAME (Spears 1965) 18x8" box contains 1" secret agent figures, plastic cars, playing cards and playing board. British distribution only. **$50-75**

SPY-24

SPY-25

SPY-24. JAMES BOND BEACH TOWEL (1965) Large three-color 36x20" towel with image of Sean Connery, 007 logo and facsimile signature. **$35-50**

SPY-25. JAMES BOND 007 SPY TRICKS (Gilbert 1965) 20x14" box contains ten different magic tricks, all involving cards and small plastic items such as keys, gun, etc. **$100**

SPY-26

SPY-26. JAMES BOND VAPOR PAPER & ACTION PEN (American character 1966) Color-illustrated 7x10" blister card contains vanishing paper and a versatile pen that can shoot projectiles, write secret messages, has a built-in secret whistle, and secret cap-firing booby-trap device. **$50-75**

SPY-27

SPY-27. THUNDERBALL CRAFT (Lone Star 1966) British distribution. 10x8" display box contains working 9" subcraft that dives and surfaces. **$200-300**

SPY-28

SPY-28. 007 SHOES (Hushpuppy 1965) Sean Connery-illustrated shoe box with logo. Shoes come black with logo inside. **$150-200**

SPY-29. JAMES BOND FULL-BODIED HAND PUPPET (Gilbert 1965) Vinyl 12" puppet with lower 2/3 of back body die-cut away to enable a child's hand to fit inside. Comes on 11x14 display card. **$75-125**

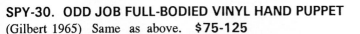

SPY-29   SPY-30

SPY-30. ODD JOB FULL-BODIED VINYL HAND PUPPET
(Gilbert 1965) Same as above. **$75-125**

SPY-31

MAN FROM UNCLE

SPY-31. NAPOLEON SOLO GUN (Ideal 1965)
The most popular of all U.N.C.L.E.toys, selling more than
four million units in its first year alone. 30x14x2" deep
window display box contains black plastic cap-firing pistol
with orange U.N.C.L.E.decal on handle. Rifle conversion
pieces include stock, scope, and silencer. Plastic triangular
badge and silver ID card also included. **$500-600**

SPY-32

SPY-32. ILLYA KURYAKIN GUN SET (Ideal 1965)
20x14x2" deep window display box contains 8" cap-firing
pistol with detachable metal clip. Also comes with triangular
U.N.C.L.E.badge, silver ID card and plastic wallet. **$250-
350**

SPY-33

SPY-33. MAN FROM U.N.C.L.E. SECRET WEAPON SET
(Ideal 1965) 23x14" window display box contains black pistol
with orange U.N.C.L.E.decal on handle, clip, black plastic
holster, silver I.D. card, badge, wallet, two demolition
grenades and grenade holster. **$250-350**

SPY-34

SPY-34. MAN FROM U.N.C.L.E. SECRET SERVICE GUN
(Ideal 1965)
12x7x2" deep window display box contains black plastic
pistol with orange U.N.C.L.E. decal on handle, plastic
holster, silver ID card and triangular badge. **$250-350**

SPY-35

SPY-35. ILLYA KURYAKIN SPECIAL (Ideal 1965)
8.5x13x2" window display box contains 3x4" cap-firing gun
disguised as a cigarette lighter. Lighter also features a radio
compartment concealed behind dummy cigarettes. **$125-
150**

SPY-36

SPY-36. STASH-AWAY GUNS (Ideal 1966)
16x20x2" deep window display box contains three plastic cap-firing guns, three holsters, two straps, triangular badge, silver ID card. **$150-200**

SPY-37. THRUSH RIFLE (Ideal 1966)
42x24x4" window display box contains 36" long plastic cap-firing silver/brown rifle featuring "ray-sight" scope which shows four targets in the sight. Targets vanish (destroyed) when trigger is pulled. Yellow THRUSH decal on rifle stock. **$500-1000**

SPY-38

SPY-38. GIRL FROM UNCLE "TRICK GADGETS" SET
(Transogram 1967) Attractive 15x22" boxed set contains several spy-type gadgets including a plastic Radio-Gun, Secret Message Comb, Whistle Code Signaler, Secret Message Writer, Decoder Guide and a Safe Book for hiding papers, and Secret Compartment Ring. **$200-300**

SPY-39

SPY-39. MAN FROM U.N.C.L.E. NAPOLEON SOLO AND ILLYA KURYAKIN DOLLS (Gilbert 1965) 12" plastic dolls with spring-loaded right arm that holds a cap-firing gun which shoots when arm is raised. Dolls also come with yellow cardboard membership card and triangular badge. Dolls sold separately. Comes in 4.5x12.5x2.5" deep photo box. **EACH $100-150**

DOLL ACCESSORY SETS
Seven different accessory sets were made by Gilbert to accompany their 12" dolls.

SPY-40   SPY-41

SPY-40. BOXED DOLL ACCESSORY SETS (Gilbert 1965)
Five different sets were made, all packaged in a 9x14x1" deep photo box. **EACH $25-45**
TARGET SET
JUMP SUIT SET
ARMAMENT SET
SCUBA SET
ARSENAL SET #1

SPY-41. CARDED DOLL ACCESSORY SETS (Gilbert 1965)
Two different weapon sets were made, both packaged on a 6x8" card. **EACH $20-30**
ARSENAL SET #2
PISTOL CONVERSION KIT

SPY-42

SPY-45

SPY-45. MAN FROM U.N.C.L.E. GAME (Ideal 1965) 20x10" box. **$25-35**

SPY-46. MAN FROM U.N.C.L.E. CARD GAME (Milton Bradley 1965) 6x10" box. **$15-20**

SPY-46

SPY-43

SPY-47. ILLYA KURYAKIN CARD GAME (Milton Bradley 1966) 6x10" box. **$15-20**

SPY-48. THRUSH RAY GUN AFFAIR GAME (Ideal 1966) 20x10.5x3" deep contains large plastic mechanical observatory with rotating ray gun, four plastic figures, four plastic diorama hideouts, four vehicles, cards, and playing board. **$75-100**

SPY-42. GIRL FROM U.N.C.L.E. DOLL (Marx 1967) 11" poseable doll comes with 30 pieces of spy equipment, disguises and clothing. Originally intended for US distribution, but when the series was cancelled, Marx shipped doll to Great Britain. Box is 12x6". **$400-500**

SPY-49. MAN FROM U.N.C.L.E. SHOOT OUT! GAME (Milton Bradley 1965)
8x15" box contains plastic marble game where the object is to be the first to spell U.N.C.L.E. **$75-100**

SPY-43. GIRL FROM U.N.C.L.E DOLL STORE DISPLAY (Marx 1967) Large 20x9x18" tall cardboard display stand features doll and all her accessories. **$750-1000**

SPY-50. MAN FROM U.N.C.L.E CREDENTIALS AND PASSPORT SET (Ideal 1965) 10x10" display card contains black plastic ID wallet with triangular badge and silver ID card, and passport with outside 2-way slide window. **$40-50**

SPY-51. MAN FROM U.N.C.L.E COLORING BOOKS (Whitman 1967) Illustrated covers. **EACH $15-25**

SPY-44

SPY-52

SPY-44. MAN FROM U.N.C.L.E. HEADQUARTERS TRANSMITTER (Cragston 1965) 8x12 box contains three-piece gold plastic transmitter, amplifier and cigarette case communicator, all with U.N.C.L.E. decals. Also included is 20 feet of transmission wire and silver ID card. **$200-250**

SPY-52. MAN FROM U.N.C.L.E. COLORING BOOKS (Watkins-Strathmore 1965) Photo covers. **EACH $25-35**

SPY-53. MAN FROM U.N.C.L.E. TRAY PUZZLES (Jaymar 1965) 11x14". **EACH $15-25**

SPY-54. MAN FROM U.N.C.L.E. JIGSAW PUZZLES (Milton Bradley 1965) 9x12". **EACH $35-50**

SPY-55. NAPOLEON SOLO MODEL FIGURE KIT (Aurora 1966) 13x4" boxed kit interlocks with Illya model (sold separately) **$150-200**

SPY-56. ILLYA KURYAKIN MODEL FIGURE KIT (Aurora 1966) 13x4" boxed kit interlocks with Solo model (sold separately) **$150-200**

SPY-57

SPY-57. MAN FROM U.N.C.L.E. CAR (AMT 1966) 9x5" box, 1/24 scale kit. **$100-125**

SPY-58. GIRL FROM U.N.C.L.E. CAR (AMT 1967) Same U.N.C.L.E car AMT produced a year earlier, the only difference is the box shows a photo of Stephanie Powers. **$100-125**

SPY-59. GIRL FROM U.N.C.L.E HALLOWEEN COSTUME (Halco 1967) Black synthetic dress, painted mask or transparent mask. **$75-125**

SPY-60

SPY-60. ILLYA KURYAKIN HALLOWEEN COSTUME (Halco 1965) Purple synthetic one-piece bodysuit and mask. Comes in 10x12" window display box. **$75-125**

SPY-61. NAPOLEON SOLO HALLOWEEN COSTUME (Halco 1965) White and black synthetic bodysuit designed like a tux, transparent mask. **$75-125**

SPY-62. MISSION IMPOSSIBLE GAME (Ideal 1968) 20x10" box. **$50-75**

SPY-63. MISSION IMPOSSIBLE VIEWMASTER REEL SET (GAF 1966) Three reels with 16-page booklet comes in photo envelope. **$15-25**

SPY-64. MISSION IMPOSSIBLE RECORD ALBUM (Dot 1966) Original soundcast recording. **$15-20**

SPY-65

SPY-65. SECRET AGENT MAN GAME (Milton Bradley 1966) 20x10" game based on the TV series starring Patrick McGoohan. **$20-30**

GENERIC TOY COMPANY SPY CHARACTERS.
During the peak spy-craze years, several toy companies took advantage of the popularity of the fad and created their own characters with extensive lines of merchandise. Listed below is a sample of toys produced.

SPY-66

SPY-66. AGENT ZERO-M CAMERA PISTOL (Mattel 1964) Looks like a camera but turns into cap-firing pistol. Comes in 8x11" open display box. **$35-50**

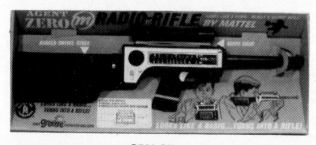

SPY-67

SPY-67. AGENT ZERO-M RADIO RIFLE (Mattel 1964) 8x5" portable radio snaps open into a cap firing 23" long rifle. Comes in 10x24x3" deep open display box. **$75-85**

SPY-68

SPY-68. AGENT ZERO-M MOVIE CAMERA MACHINE GUN (Mattel 1964) Hand-held movie camera turns into machine gun producing rapid fire sound as it snaps open. Comes in 16x12x5" deep window display box. $75-100

SPY-69

SPY-69. AGENT ZERO-M PISTOL KNIFE (Mattel 1964) Plastic 4" penknife opens up into a pistol. Comes on 8x6" display card. $35-50

SPY-70. AGENT ZERO-M INVISIBLE PEN SET (Mattel 1964) Pen writes invisibly. Comes on 6x8" display card with infared glasses with which to read message. $25-30

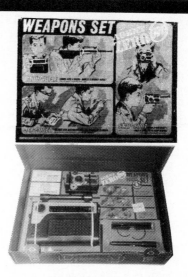

SPY-71

SPY-71. AGENT ZERO-M ATTACHE CASE (Mattel 1964) 16x12x4" deep cardboard briefcase contains Radio Rifle, Camera Pistol, Invisible Pen and Infared Glasses. There is an illustrated 12" wide paper wrapping around the briefcase describing contents. $75-100

SPY-72

SPY-72. AGENT ZERO-M NIGHT FIGHTER MACHINE GUN (Mattel 1964) 29" long black and blue camouflaged machine gun with infared scope and side bolt action comes on 30x9" display card. $65-85

SPY-73

SPY-73. AGENT ZERO-M SUPER SONIC BLASTER (Mattel 1964) 35" long bazooka-style air gun also produces a very long blasting noise when fired. Comes with three cardboard airport targets that can be toppled from a distance of 40 feet by the gun's air current. Ruled unsafe in 1965, it was quickly taken from store shelves. Comes in 12x38x5" deep display box. $150-200

SPY-74

SPY-74. AGENT ZERO-M SNUB-NOSE .38 (Mattel 1964)
Metal pistol with chrome finish and black plastic handle
comes with black plastic shoulder holster and ejecting
shells. Comes in 8x8x2" deep window display box. **$75**

SPY-75

SPY-75. AGENT ZERO-M "SPY DETECTOR" GAME
(Mattel 1964) 20x10" box contains the same detector box as
Mattel's Lie Detector game. Concept is the same and comes
with spy suspect cards, etc. The object is to arrest the spy.
$40-50

SPY-76. AGENT ZERO-M COLORING BOOK (Mattel 1964)
8x12" format. **$10-15**

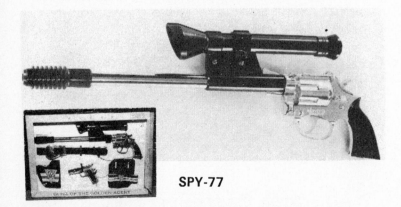

SPY-77

SPY-77. GUNS OF THE GOLDEN AGENT (Hubley 1965)
14x9" box contains .38 gold-color metal pistol with 10" barrel
with silencer and black/gold scope. Also included is a
smaller 4" gold revolver, two leather holsters with Golden
Agent logo and belt. **$65-85**

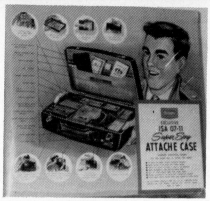

SPY-78

SPY-78. ISA-07-11 SUPER SPY ATTACHE CASE (Sears
1965) ISA stands for International Secret Agent. Colorful
14x14x5" deep box holds black plastic briefcase which
contains all surveillance devices including telescope, built-in
walkie-talkie, working camera, heligraph, decoding machine
and secret coder, plus passport aand papers. **$150**

SPY-79. ISA-07-11 ATTACHE CASE (Sears 1965)
9x14" black plastic attache case with clear plastic lid
contains luger and attachments to convert into rifle (scope,
stock, barrel extension w/clip). There are also two projectile
missiles and grenade that fire from gun. The case itself is
booby-trapped to "explode" by cap if opened incorrectly and
comes with a key to open safely. Box is 10x15". **$150-200**

SPY-80

SPY-80. ISA-07-11 SPECIAL DUTY WEAPONS SET
(Marx 1965) 12x14x3" deep box contains an M-240 Machine
Gun Pistol and attachments to convert into rifle
(scope, stock, barrel extension). Also comes with firing
grenade missile. This was a Sears exclusive and found only
in Sears department stores. **$125-150**

SPY-81

SPY-81. MIKE HAZARD DOUBLE AGENT DOLL (Marx 1965) 12" jointed doll molded in blue outfit comes with over 50 pieces of spy equipment, weapons and disguises. Some of the more interesting pieces include cloth trnch coat with secret pockets, Exploding Luggage, Stlletto Neck Tie, Comunication Receiver inside hat, Sound Gun w/Movie Camera, several facial disguises, several interchangable weapons and pistols including a bazooka laucher that actually fires and an exact replica of the famous U.N.C.L.E. gun. Box is 6x12x3" deep. **$150-250**

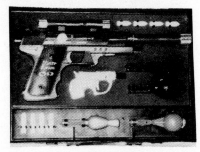

SPY-82

SPY-82. MULTI-PISTOL 09 (Topper 1965) 13x9" plastic carry case with clear plastic lid contains sharp looking blue/brown with chrome trim 8" long plastic pistol w/scope. There is a small 4" silver metal derringer that conceals inside the handle of the larger pistol and eight bullets (four long, four short) included. **$75-125**

SPY-83

SPY-83. SECRET AGENT 808 PISTOL PAK (Irwin 1966) Dummy box of cigarettes actually conceal hidden pistol which fires bullets from inside the box. Comes on 8x6" display card **$25-30**

SPY-84

SPY-84. SECRET AGENT 002 GRAB BAG AND CANDY (Best 1966) 3.5x7" illustrated bag contains three plastic toys and candy. Toys were usually animal, dinosaur, or monster figures. Display box is 8x12x5" deep.
BAG $5-10
STORE DISPLAY BOX $25-30

SPY-85

SPY-85. SECRET SAM ATTACHE CASE (Topper 1965) By far the most creative and best made spy attache case to be made during the Sixties. Heavy black 10x16" black plastic case contains 9" pistol which shoots long or short range bullets and grenade missile and comes with attachments to convert into rifle (scope, stock, barrel extension w/silencer). There is also a concealed working camera inside case which can be operated from outside the case. The case is designed so the pistol itself can be fired from within the case by a button on the outside. Color 8" wide wrapping came around case advertising all it's features. **$175-250**

SPY-86. SECRET SAM BASEBALL BAT RIFLE (Topper 1965) 29" plastic bat shoots bullets. Comes on 32x7" display card. **$50-75**

SPY-87

SPY-87. SECRET SAM EXPLODING BINOCULARS
(Topper 1965) 5x6x2" deep box contains black plastic
binoculars booby-trapped to explode in use. **$25-35**

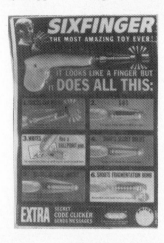

SPY-88

SPY-88. SECRET SAM "6-FINGER" GUN (Topper 1965)
6x9" display card holds plastic artificial index finger which
fires bullets. Comes with six different types of bullets,
including exploding bullets, secret message projectile bullet,
secret pen bullet that actually writes and three more. **$35**

SPY-89

SPY-90

SPY-89. SECRET SAM SHOOTING CANE (Topper 1965)
36" long plastic walking cane with gold-color plastic lion's
head handle which conceals trigger. Bullets shoot from end
of cane. Comes on 37x6" display card. **$35-50**

SPY-90. SECRET SAM SHOOTING PIPE (Topper 1965)
4.5" long brown/black plastic pipe with trigger button
concealed on smoking stem and fires when pipe in placed
in mouth and button pressed. Box is 3x5x3". **$25-25**

SPY-91. WWSA-05 GUN SET (Marx 1965)
WWSA stands for World Wide Secret Agent. 18x14x3" deep
box with pop-up display lid contains plastic black/brown
machine gun with side bolt action, .38 pistol with shoulder
holster, badge and wallet. All pieces have the WWSA-07
logo on them. **$50-100**

SPY-92

SPY-92. WWSA-05 SHORTY PISTOL (Marx 1965)
Plastic 6" pistol makes real shooting sound when fired.
Comes on 8x6" display card. **$25-30**

SPY-93. WWSA-05 SPECIAL MISSION TOMMY GUN
(Marx 1965) 18" plastic machine gun features side bolt
action and folding stock. Has WWSA logo on stock. Comes
on 11x20" display card. **$35-45**

SPY-94. WWSA-05 MINIATURE GUN SET (Marx 1965)
5x7" plastic case with clear plastic lid contains 3.5" gold
metal luger with plastic attachments to convert into rifle
(scope, stock, barrel extension and bi-pod). **$25-30**

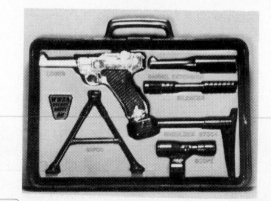

SPY-94

SPACE

The interest in the Space Race made a full orbit in the toy trade in the Sixties. The early exploits of NASA's Mercury Astronauts were widely merchandised as toys in the early part of the decade, but interest switched from space-related toys to other fads in 1964-66. Space toys began gaining momentum again in 1967 with the release of Mattel's Man is Space, Major Matt Mason, and interest peaked in 1968-70 with NASA's moon landing.

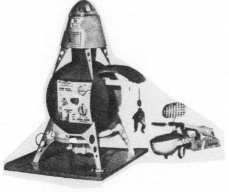

SPA-1

SPA-1. ASTRO BASE (Ideal 1960) 22" tall red and white astronaut base has working control panel that opens space lock door, extends crane and lowers astronaut into a remote control scout car. Car moves forward and turns and has two rocket missles that fire. Box is 24x12x10". **$150-200.**

SPA-2

SPA-2. ASTRONAUT SPACE HELMET (RCA-Victor 1960) White plastic helmet with pull-down tinted visor with built-in speaker phones. Helmet has silver-winged decal on front with red letters reading "Astronaut" and a blank space for name. Comes with boxed set of three 45 rpm records "Blast Off to the Moon". Comes in 14x14x12" box. **$40-65**

SPA-3

SPA-3. BIG LOO MOON ROBOT (Marx 1962)
Very tall 38" metallic green plastic robot with maroon and gold trim comes with 12 operable features including: observation see-through scanner-scope, morse code sender with chart, hidden rubber-tipped dart gun which shoots from chest, missile launcher on base of robot, secret water squirter, whistle, compass, and bell. Also has light-up eyes and swiveling head. Bends at waist and left hand shoots ping pong balls. Right hand has pinchers for picking up items, including small 5" green microphone (provided). Large crank on back which says "Big Loo Fights For You" when turned. Box has three graphic designs and measures 40x16x16". **$1000-2000**

SPA-4

SPA-4. BILLY BLAST-OFF (Eldon 1968)
4.5" tall plastic bendable figure comes equipped with battery-powered jet pack, space car, space sled, exploration tractor and lunar crawler. Box is 8x14x6". **$50-75**

SPA-5. BLAST-OFF GAME (Waddington 1969)
10x22" box contains elaborate game with plastic space capsule playing pieces, cards, and playing board that shows several planets in outer space. **$25-40**

SPA-6

SPA-6. CAPE KENNEDY PLAYSET (Remco 1966)
24x18x10" window display box contains replica launching
center with working gantry, revolving radar tower, spring-
loaded rocket, four firing missiles, loading crane, helicopter,
two trucks, and seven men. **$125-175**

SPA-7

SPA-7. CAPE CANAVERAL MISSILE CENTER PLAYSET
(Marx 1960s) Large 24x12x4" deep box contains U.S Air
Force Missile Test Center tin litho building, working missile
and rocket launches, 32 scientists and technicians and
several accessories.   There were many variations of the
Cape Canaveral playset through out the Sixties. **$100-250**

SPA-8. CONQUEST OF SPACE VIEWMASTER REEL SET
(GAF 1969) Three reel set of moon landing comes with
booklet in color photo envelope. **$15**

SPA-9

SPA-9. COUNTDOWN GAME (Lowell 1966)
10x21" box contains well-made, elaborate game with plastic
two-piece capsule playing pieces and color photo cards of
U.S. astronauts and various stages of their mission.
$30-40

SPA-10

SPA-10. GEMINI ASTRONAUT MODEL KIT (Revell 1966)
7x12" box contains all-plastic assembly kit. **$25**

SPA-11. GEMINI CAPSULE MODEL KIT (Revell 1965)
9x14" box contains all-plastic assembly kit of capsule and
two astronauts. Capsule features removable retrograde
system and detachable equipment module. Story book
included. **$50-65**

SPA-12. JANE APOLLO DOLL (Marx 1968)
8"plastic posable doll comes molded in white space uniform
with over a dozen pieces of gold plastic space accessories.
Box is 4x9". **$50-75**

SPA-13. JOHNNY APOLLO DOLL (Marx 1968)
8"plastic posable doll molded in white space uniform comes
with over a dozen pieces of gold plastic space accessories.
Also packaged by Marx as the **"U.S. Astronaut"** and sold
primarily at launch base gift shops. **$50-75**

SPA-14

SPA-14. JOHNNY APOLLO STORE DISPLAY (Marx 1968)
22x20x6" die-cut cardboard store display features doll and
all accessories. **$100-200**

SPA-15

SPA-15. MAN ON THE MOON GUM CARDS (Topps
1968-69) 99 card set first issued in 1968 as a 45 card set. In 1969, a second series set of 44 cards was released. Color photos of astronauts and moon landing with photo puzzle on back.
First Set $25
Second Set $40-60
Wrapper $10
Display box $15-25

SPA-16

MAJOR MATT MASON (Mattel 1966-69)
Mattel's "Man in Space" 6" bendable figure enjoyed enormous success for nearly five years. It also paved the way for other toy companies to switch to the production of space-related items at a time when the Viet Nam war made the previously briskly selling military toys wane in popularity. Mattel produced a long line of Matt Mason accessories, vehicles and equipment sold separately and together in deluxe sets. We list only the Matt Mason line of figures that Mattel made.

SPA-16. MAJOR MATT MASON DOLL (Mattel 1967)
10x13" display card holds Matt Mason, helmet, two-piece space sled and jet propulsion back pack. **$75-125**

SPA-17. CALISTO DOLL (Mattel 1968)
10x13" display card hold 6" bendable green alien figure and air-powered back pack with hose extender that shoots balls. **$100-150**

SPA-18. CAPTAIN LAZOR DOLL (Mattel 1968)
12" hard-plastic doll with movable arms and legs molded in metallic blue space suit with painted features. There is a pistol molded in his hand that comes with three different attachments to fit on barrel. He also comes with space helmet and space boots. Box is 14x6x4" deep. **$75-125**

SPA-19. DOUG DAVIS DOLL (Mattel 1968)
6" bendable figure in yellow space suit with helmet and Cat Trac comes on 9x12" display card. **$75-125**

SPA-20. JEFF LONG DOLL (Mattel 1968)
5" bendable negro astronaut in blue space suit with helmet and Cat Trac comes on 9x12" display card. **$175-250**

SPA-21. SGT. STORM DOLL (Mattel 1968)
6" bendable figure in red space suit with helmet and Cat Trac comes on 9x12" display card. **$75-125**

SPA-22. SCORPIO DOLL (Mattel 1968)
9" pink and purple plastic bendable alien figure with metallic eyes that light up. Comes with winged back pack powered by air pump to shoot little balls. Box is 12x4x4". **$500-750**

SPA-23

SPA-23. MARS ATTACK GUM CARDS (Topps 1962)
The most popular of all science-fiction gum cards sets. Short-lived due to parental objection to the graphic violent scenes most of the cards depicted (burning flesh, splattered brains, dying pets, etc.) Back of the card explains illustration on front. **SET (55 cards) $650-1000**
WRAPPER $250-450
DISPLAY BOX $850-1000
PROMO "ATTACK FROM MARS" DISPLAY BOX $1500 and up.

SPA-24

SPA-27

SPA-24. MARS INVADES EARTH COLOR PENCIL SET
(Crafthouse 1963) 8x12" window display box contains 12
pre-numbered sketches of Martians attacking earth and 12
color pencils. **$100-150**

SPA-27. MYSTERY SPACE SHIP (Marx 1960-61)
Heavy plastic 8" diameter spaceship actually contains a
large gyroscope operated by detachable hand crank. Once
activated, ship can roll on its edge, spin and perform
other assorted gravity tricks. Comes with a three piece
stand, 11 small 1" orange plastic astronauts and nine green
1" plastic alien figures. There is a missile launcher which
attaches to the ship and fires three missiles, plus two plastic
space cars also come with set. Box is 7x11x5" deep. **$100-
150**

SPA-25

SPA-25. MOON McDARE ASTRONAUT DOLL (Gilbert
1966) 12" plastic movable doll comes dressed in jumpsuit in
12x4" box. Six different accessory sets were made for him
and sold seperately including a space suit and a space dog.
Produced in the mid-Sixties when the Space Program had
limited appeal, the doll sold poorly and was soon
discontinued. **Doll $50-75, Accessory cards $20-35**

SPA-28

SPA-28. OPERATION X-500 PLAYSET (Deluxe Reading
1960) This set is comprised of two large space pieces. The
first piece is a 12x20x12" Base Defense System molded in
red and black plastic which features several working
missiles, radar screens and front chrome control panel with
working levers, dials and gauges. There is also an
observatory tower with armed gaurds that attach to base.
The second piece is a 16x20x12" Rocket Launcher which
fires Atlas missile with detachable head. Rocket Launcher
also features working crane and two-level control room.
There are also railroad tracks at the base of the Launcher
where train cars transport the Atlas missiles. Figures include
chimp, dog and human astronauts, crane operators,
cameramen and armed soldiers. Box is 23x16x14". **$500-
750**

SPA-26

SPA-26. MOON WALKER (Perry 1966)
Large 38" tall carboard assembly model of U.S. space
capsule that a child can stand inside, pick up sides and
walk around with. There are cut away windows and four legs
to "land" the craft when child exits. Box is 36x14x4" deep.
$35-50

SPA-29

SPA-33

SPA-33. ASTRO-NAUTILUS MAN FROM NEPTUNE (5.5" purple four-arm alien with trunk-like nose comes with trident) **$250-300**

OUTER SPACE MEN (Colorforms 1968)

Colorforms made seven different bendable alien figures, each representing a planet in our universe (Mercury excluded). Sizes ranged from 3" to 6" and came on 8x10" display card.

SPA-29. ALPHA 7 MAN FROM MARS (3" tall, comes with helmet and ray gun) **$100-125**

SPA-30. COMMANDER COMET MAN FROM VENUS (6" winged human-like alien comes with helmet and crossbow) **$150-200**

SPA-30

SPA-34

SPA-34. COLOSSUS REX MAN FROM JUPITER (6" barrel chested alien in shades of metallic greens with fin-shaped ears and spiked body joints, comes with spiked mallet) **$250-300**

SPA-31   SPA-32

SPA-35

SPA-31. ORBITRON MAN FROM URANUS (purple and red alien with exposed brains and pincher hands) **$225**

SPA-32. XODIAC MAN FROM SATURN (5" demon-like figure comes with helmet and speargun) **$200-225**

SPA-35. ELECTRON MAN FROM PLUTO (5.5" silver humanoid-looking alien comes with helmet and ray gun) **$175-200**

SPA-39

SPA-39. U.S. ASTRONAUT HALLOWEEN COSTUME (Ben Cooper 1961) 8x10" window display box contains one piece synthetic body suit with illustration of astronaut and plastic mask of man in helmet. **$20-30**

SPA-40

SPA-36

SPA-36. ROBOT COMMANDO (Ideal 1961)
Large battery operated 15" tall blue plastic robot with red dome and accents. Remote control box shaped like a microphone and features "voice activated" control and has a joystick which can be flipped to manual control. Robot moves forward and fires missiles from its head and hurls balls from its arms as eyeballs rotate in a circular motion. Box is 18x12x12" **$250-350, Store Display $500-600**

SPA-40. ZEROIDS (Ideal 1968-69)
Ideal made a series of four 6" metallic colored plastic robots powered by small "Motorific" motors which were able to move forward or backward and came with extra interchangable magnetic hands for holding, throwing and pulling. Each robot came in a 8x5x4" plastic case with clear plastic display lid which, when tilted on its side, served as a space sled the Zeroid could actually pull. These robots were immensely popular and revised variations continued up to the late Seventies. **ZERAK The Blue Destroyer, ZOBOR the Bronze Transporter, ZINTER the Silver Explorer and MIGHTY ZOGG. EACH $50-100**

SPA-37

SPA-37. SATELLITE LUNCHBOX (American Thermos 1959-62) One side of box show rocketship flying toward space station and the other side shows rocketship landing on planet. Both sides have strong shades of grey-green and blues. Steel thermos shows a variety of space ships against blue background. **Box $50-65, Thermos $25-30**

SPA-38. U.S. ASTRONAUT MODEL KIT (Aurora 1967) 13x4" box contains all plastic assembly kit of Gemini astronaut with orbit and capsule background. **$40-60**

SPA-41. ZEROID COMMANDER ACTION STATION (Ideal 1968) Large 17x14x5" box contains Mighty Zogg Zeroid plus Solar Cycle Attack Vehicle, Sensor Station with revolving space scanner and Sonic Alarm with button for coded messages. **$125-150**

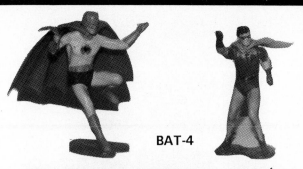

BAT-4

SUPERHEROES

Superhero related toys were almost non-existant until January of 1966 when the Batman television series first aired and instantly started a nostalgic superhero craze that lasted over two years. Over 1000 different items were produced on Batman alone. The Green Hornet was the second largest produced character, followed by Superman.

BAT-1

BAT-1. BATMAN MAGIC MAGNETIC GOTHAM CITY PLAYSET (Remco 1966) Large 36x20" box contains large table with surface illustration of two city blocks. Cardboard city includes city hall, jail, bank, nuclear plant and Batcave. Set also includes figures of Batman, Robin, Joker, Penguin, Shark and Catwoman as well as the Batmobile and Batplane, assorted police cars and vehicles. All figures are controlled by a powerful magnetic wand affixed under the table. Plot scenarios are suggested such as stopping a jail break, etc. **$600-750**

BAT-4. BATMAN PLAYSET (Ideal 1966)
Large 22x14x11" deep window display box contains 11-piece playset and includes 3" hand painted plastic figures of Batman, Robin, Superman and Wonder Woman. There are four unpainted villains (Joker, Brainiac, Key Man and Robot), a 7" long, black plastic Batmobile and Batplane (both with clear plastic windshields), and a silver plastic sonar ray disc weapon which resembles a radar dish. Pieces are arranged inside the box on a three dimensional background, creating an attractive action diorama scene. **$1000 and up.**

Note: Batman playset was also sold by Sears in 6, 11 and 23-piece sets and came in plain cardboard mailing boxes. Value of these sets would be $100, $300 and $450.

BAT-2   **BAT-3**

BAT-5

BAT-2. BATMAN POSTCARDS (Dexter 1966)
Set of eight 4x6" postcards have empty word balloons for writing message. Comes in polybag with header card. **$15**

BAT-3. BATMAN FLYING COPTER (Remco 1966)
12" plastic helicopter with 35" guide-wire control allows the user to fly copter in diving and loop patterns. Batman decals on side of copter. Box is 10x16x5" deep.
$75-100

BAT-5. BATMAN TRACE-A-GRAPH (Emenee 1966)
11x17x5" deep box contains plastic light table with Bat-decal, large envelope containing 12 illustrated sheets, tracing paper and color pencils. **$100-125**

BAT-6

BAT-6. BATMAN OIL PAINT BY NUMBER SET (Hasbro 1965) 10x15" box contains five pre-numbered sketches, ten oil paint vials and brush. **$50-60**

BAT-7

BAT-7. BATMAN COLOR PENCIL BY NUMBER SET (Hasbro 1966) 16x12" box contains eight pre-numbered sketches and twelve color pencils. **$50-75**

BAT-8

BAT-8. BATMAN "CAPTURE THE JOKER" GAME (Hasbro 1965) 15x9" box. **$35-50**

BAT-9. BATMAN GAME (Milton Bradley 1966) 10x20" box contains four cardboard Batmobile playing pieces, character cards of six villains and playing board. Object is to capture villains by operating Batmobile from Batcave. **$50-65**

BAT-10

BAT-10. BATMAN TRAY PUZZLES (Watkins Strathmore 1966) Two different 11x14" puzzles were made, **EACH $20**

BAT-11. BATMAN JIGSAW PUZZLES (Whitman 1966) 8x12" box containg 100-piece puzzle. Four different puzzles known to be made. **EACH $20-30**

BAT-12   BAT-13

BAT-12. BATMAN PUSH-UP PUPPET (Kohner 1966) 3" plastic jointed mechanical puppet which moves when bottom underneath base is pressed. **$35-50**

BAT-13. ROBIN PUSH-UP PUPPET (Kohner 1966) 3" plastic jointed mechanical puppet which moves when bottom underneath base is pressed. **$50-65**

BAT-14

BAT-14. BATMAN & ROBIN HAND PUPPETS (Ideal 1966) 12" soft vinyl head, with plastic body come in attractive 8x7x3.5" window display box. **$75-100**
Batman was also sold separately in its own box (**$35-50**) or in polybag with illustrated header card (**$25-40**)

BAT-15

BAT-15. BATMAN PUPPET THEATER STAGE SET (Ideal 1966) Marketed exclusively by Sears, this 19x11x20" cardboard theater stage set came with 12" plastic/vinyl hand puppets of Batman, Robin, and the **Joker** (only available with this set). Background of stage shows silhouetted buildings of Gotham City. **$250-300**

BAT-16

BAT-16. BATMAN TARGET GAME (Hasbro 1966) 9x12" tin litho target features the Joker as the target with

accompanying illustrations of Batman and Robin. Comes with plastic revolver that shoots three rubber-tipped darts. Window display box is 14x11x2" deep. **$60-85**

BATMAN CAPTAIN ACTION COSTUME (see CAPTAIN ACTION)

BAT-17

BAT-17. BATMAN & ROBIN SOCIETY BUTTON (World Mfg. 1966) Colorful 3.5" button reads: "Charter Member of Batman & Robin Society". Comes in polybag with illustrated 4x2" header card. **$10-15**

BAT-18

BAT-18. BATMAN SWITCH & GO PLAYSET (Mattel 1966) 14x20x4 boxed set contains 9" plastic Batmobile which is powered by pumping air into air hose track. Includes 40 feet of track hose, a bridge, cardboard figures of Batman, villains (Joker, Penguin, Riddler, Mr. Freeze), and Batcave. The Batmobile has three speeds and is designed to shoot projectiles at the targets of villains. **$400-500**

BAT-19

BAT-19. BATMAN "BATMOBILE" STORE DISPLAY SIGN
(Burry's 1969) Large 33x48" thin plastic store display sign with raised images of Batman, Robin and Batmobile. This display was to promote the Batmobile model kit made by Aurora and was offered as a premium by Burry's Cookies. **$350-400**

BAT-20

BAT-20. BATMAN BATTERY-OPERATED BATMOBILE
(ASC 1966) Japanese made 12" long tin litho blue metal car with metal/plastic figures of Batman and Robin in seats. Car moves forward with bump-and-go action while siren light on canopy flashes and rear jet exhausts blink. Box is 5x13x3" deep. **$150-200**

BAT-21

BAT-21. BATMAN FRICTION DRIVE BATMOBILE (ASC 1966) Japanese made 11" tin litho blue Batmobile is a one-seater, containing metal/plastic Batman behind wheel. Box is 14x5x4" deep. **$100-150**

BAT-22

BAT-22. BATMAN MODEL KIT (Aurora 1964) 7x13" box contains all-plastic assembly kit. **$150-200**

BAT-23

BAT-23. ROBIN MODEL KIT (Aurora 1966) 13x4" box. **$75-100**

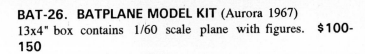
BAT-26. BATPLANE MODEL KIT (Aurora 1967)
13x4" box contains 1/60 scale plane with figures. **$100-150**

BAT-27

BAT-24

BAT-24. PENGUIN MODEL KIT (Aurora 1967)
13x4" box contains all-plastic assembly kit of Batman's arch enemy. **$250-300**

BAT-27. BATCYCLE MODEL KIT (Aurora 1968)
13x4" box contains 5" long Batcycle with figures. **$250-350**

BAT-25

BAT-28

BAT-25. BATMOBILE MODEL KIT (Aurora 1966)
13x4" box contains 1/32 scale car with figures. **$200-250**

BAT-28. BATBOAT MODEL KIT (Aurora 1968)
13x4" box contains 7" long boat with figures. **$300-350**

BAT-29

BAT-29. BATMAN "BATPHONE" (Marx 1966)
8"long red plastic battery-operated phone programmed with
ten different phrases. Voice is activated when receiver is
picked up and button pressed. Box is 10x10x5" deep and
has flip-open display lid. **$125-175**

BAT-30

BAT-30. BATMAN "BATCRAFT" (Marx 1966)
Battery operated 6.5" yellow, hard plastic one-man
helicopter with figure of Batman at controls. Craft moves
forward and siren flashes. Box is 7x5x4" and illustrated on
all sides. Although made by Marx, this toy was distributed
almost exclusively in Great Britain. **$200-250**

BAT-31

BAT-31. BATMAN UTILITY BELT (Ideal 1966)
Adjustable yellow soft vinyl plastic belt comes equipped with

rope and grappling hook, two Bat-grenades (each a different
size), Batarang, handcuffs, flashlight, Bat-pistol and two-
way radio belt buckle with secret compartment. **$1000 and
up.**

BAT-32

BAT-32. BATMAN "BATCAVE" CARRY CASE (Ideal
1966) Colorful 11x18x6" deep vinyl case was made as an
accessory for the 3" Batman figures Ideal also made. Case
has secret side door entrance for 6" Batmobile. Inside of
case is designed like the Batcave with three-dimensional
computer equipment, stairs and Bat-ramp. **$75-100**

BAT-33

BAT-33. BATMAN "BEND-A-BITTY" FIGURE (Marx
1966) 5" soft rubber bendable figure comes on 5x8" display
card. **$25-40**

BAT-34

BAT-34. BATMAN PILLOWS (mfg unknown, 1966)
Each pillow is approx. 10x12" with old style Forties Batman
logo and action scene. Two different pillows known to exist.
$50

BAT-39

BAT-40

BAT-35 **BAT-36**

BAT-39. BATMAN COLORING BOOK PREMIUM STORE POSTER (Holoway Candy, 1966) 18x24 yellow store display poster announces three new Batman coloring books which are free inside six-packs of MilkDuds, Slow Poke and Black Cow candies. **$35-40**

BAT-35. BATMAN FORK & SPOON SET (Imperial Knife 1966) Stainless steel fork and spoon have embossed 1.5" figures of Batman and Robin on handles and the word "Batman" engraved further down the handles. Set comes on 10x4" display card. **$25-40**

BAT-36. BATMAN CHOCOLATE FLAVOR MILK CARTON (Sealtest 1966) Side panels have cut-out Batman mask and villain. Sealtest also made Batman Pink Lemonade in a carton with cut-out Batmobile and villain. **EACH $25-30**

BAT-40. BATMAN "CRUSADER-SUNDAE" FUDGE SICLE (Pop-sicle 1966) 7" white and brown wrapper. **$8-10**

BAT-41

BAT-41. BATMAN DINNER PLATE (1966) Plastic 8" diameter plate with color illustration. **$20-25**

BAT-37 **BAT-38**

BAT-37. BATMAN "SLAM BANG" BANANA MASHMELLOW ICE CREAM CARTON (1966) Colorful 8x5x4" carton with illustrations on all four sides. **$35**

BAT-38. BATMAN "PUNCH-O" DRINK MIX (1966) Small 4x3" Koolaid-sized packet with Batman on front. Short-lived due to its sacharin content. **$35-50**

BAT-42

BAT-42. BATMAN CERAMIC DINNER SET (mfg unknown, 1966) Three-piece set consists of plate, bowl and cup, all with illustrations of Batman and Robin which are from the animated opening of the television series. Our photo shows the 10" diameter dinner plate. **SET $75-100**
INDIVIDUAL PIECES $20-25

BAT-43   BAT-44

BAT-48

BAT-43. BATMAN CUP (1966)
Small 4" white plastic cup with color decal of Batman. **$8-10**

BAT-44. BATMAN COFFEE MUG (1966)
White glass mug with black/white illustrations of Batman on each side. **$15**

BAT-48. BATMAN NOTEBOOK BINDER (1966)
Yellow vinyl three-ring note book binder with wing-tipped bottom. **$25**

BAT-49

BAT-45

BAT-49. BATMAN HELMET AND CAPE (Ideal 1966)
Hard shell-like blue plastic helmet designed to fit over child's head. Comes with full-length blue wing-tipped cape. Box is 12x12x14". **$50-85**

BAT-45.   BATMAN CARTOON KIT (Colorforms 1966)
8x12" box contains vinyl plastic pieces of Batman, Robin, villains, etc, that affix to Gotham City background. **$40-50**

BAT-46. BATMAN HALLOWEEN COSTUME (Ben Cooper 1966) Comes in 8x10" box. **$25-35**

BAT-50

BAT-46

BATMAN RECORD ALBUMS: A variety of Batman record albums were produced between 1966-68. We've listed the 8 most collectible 33 1/3 LP albums.

BAT-47.   BATMAN HALLOWEEN COSTUME STORE POSTER (Ben Cooper 1966) 12x24" yellow store display poster. **$35-50**

BAT-50. BATMAN SOUNDTRACK ALBUM (20th Century Fox 1966) Official exclusive soundtrack with color photo of West and Ward in Batmobile on cover. **$35-50**

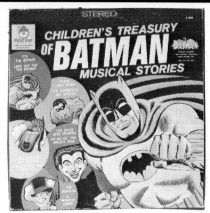

BAT-51

BAT-51. BATMAN THEME BY NEIL HEFTI ALBUM (20th Century Fox 1966) Bat-logo cover. **$25-30**

BAT-52. A CHILDREN'S TREASURY OF BATMAN MUSICAL STORIES (Peter Pan 1966) **$15-20**

BAT-53. OFFICIAL ADVENTURES OF BATMAN & ROBIN ALBUM (Leo 1966) Illustration of Batman and Robin swinging in front of Batmobile. **$20-25**

BAT-54. MORE OFFICIAL ADVENTURES OF BATMAN & ROBIN ALBUM (Leo 1966) Illustration of Batman and Robin on rooftop. **$20-25**

BAT-55. BATMAN & ROBIN ALBUM (Tiny Tim 1966) Illustration of Batman & Robin swinging on ropes with full moon background. **$20-25**

BAT-56. BATMAN TV THEME ALBUM (Panda 1966) Illustrated Bat-like man among other animals set inside a gold framed cover. **$25-35**

BAT-57. BATMAN ALBUM (Golden Record 1966) Red cover with Batman & Robin swinging on ropes. Record includes feature story book, Crime Fighter button, flasher ring and membership card. **$35-50**

BAT-58

BATMAN GUM CARD SETS (Topps 1966-68) Topps made five different Batman gum card sets, all different from each other.

BAT-58. BATMAN GUM CARDS (55 card set) Illustrations on front with **black** bat title logo. Back of card contains story explaining illustration.
SET $60-75
WRAPPER (red with illustration of Batman & Robin) $25
DISPLAY BOX $75-125

BAT-59. BATMAN "SERIES A" GUM CARDS (44 card set) Illustrations on front with **red** bat title logo. Story and puzzle on back.
SET $50-65
WRAPPER (Bat logo) $20-30
DISPLAY BOX $75-125

BAT-60. BATMAN "SERIES B" GUM CARDS (44 card set) Illustration on front with **blue** Bat-logo. Back of card comes with story and puzzle **or** with story over blue bat logo.
SET $65-85
WRAPPER $20-25
DISPLAY BOX $75-125

BAT-61

BAT-61. BATMAN "REAL PHOTOS" GUM CARDS (55 card set) Color photo cards from the TV series with "Bat-Laffs" jokes and photo puzzle on back.
SET $85-100
WRAPPER (blue with photo of Batman) $25-40
DISPLAY BOX $100-150

BAT-62

BAT-62. BATMAN PHOTO CARDS (38 card set) Color photo cards with "Riddler's Riddle" on back with scrambled answer to be decoded by a decoder which was included in every pack. **SET $75-100**
WRAPPER (Batman punching) $35-50
DISPLAY BOX (color photo scene of Batman and Robin in Batcave) $200-250

CAPTAIN ACTION

CAPTAIN ACTION DOLL (Ideal 1966)

Jointed 12" hard plastic doll comes dressed in black/blue one-piece outfit with blue captain's cap, black boots, blue belt, ray gun and a lightning bolt-shaped sword. There is a triangular foil decal on the chest of the uniform with the initials "C/A". The back of the doll's neck is marked "Copyright Ideal Toy Company 1966". Box is 6x13x4" deep. Three different box styles were made, the last two being in production for very short periods.

CAP-1

CAP-1. 1st ISSUE BOX: Illustrated box showing the nine characters the doll can change into. **$200-300**

CAP-2. 2nd ISSUE "FREE PARACHUTE" BOX: Same illustrated design as first issue box with added illustration on top of box of Captain Action descending from parachute. **$300-350**

CAP-3. 3rd ISSUE "PHOTO" BOX: Color photo box of the Captain Action doll standing over a defeated Dr. Evil doll. **$300-350**

ACTION BOY DOLL (Ideal 1967)

With the success of Captain Action firmly secured the first year, Ideal did the next logical thing and introduced a side kick for him. Action Boy stood 8" tall and, like his mentor, is jointed and fully posable. The doll comes packaged two different ways in two different boxes. Box is 9x4x4" deep.

CAP-4. 1st ISSUE BOX: Illustrated box also shows the three characters the doll can change into. Doll is dressed in blue/red one-piece costume with a triangular foil emblem on chest with the initials "A/C". Doll is also comes with blue beret, black boots, belt, boomarang and black panther cat on leash. **$300-350**

CAP-5

CAP-5. 2nd ISSUE "PHOTO" BOX: Color photo box shows Action Boy dressed in a silver space suit. Doll comes dressed in silver space suit with familiar triangular emblem on chest, helmet, silver gloves, utility-style belt and ray gun. Box is titled; "Action Boy-the Bold Adventurer". **$350-400**

CAP-6. DR. EVIL DOLL (Ideal 1967)

Every hero needs a good villain, and Ideal provided just that when it introduced Dr. Evil. This 12" jointed doll with light blue skin has bulging eyes and an exposed brain! Doll comes dressed in a blue metallic two-piece outfit with gold medallion, ray gun and human pull-over face mask. Box is 13x6" and features a color photo of a Dr. Evil doll standing triumphantly over a fallen Captain Action as he's pulling off his human mask. Alter-ego costumes were planned for this doll as well and included the Joker (Batman) and the Red Skull (Captain America), but the doll was discontinued after the Batman television series was cancelled and the popularity of superheroes quickly faded. **$250-300**

CAP-7

CAP-7. DR. EVIL DOLL & LAB SET (Ideal 1968)

13x16" window display box contains one Dr. Evil doll, one mannequin dressed in lab coat with bearded face mask, a

Thought Control Helmet, extra face mask of an Oriental, Hypnotic Eyeball, Laser Gun Ray, an Ionized Hypo Needle and Reducing Ray. This set was produced just before the series was discontinued and had limited distribution. **$500-700**

CAPTAIN ACTION COSTUMES (Ideal 1966-68)

All costumes come in a 10x14" window display box with the costume and accessories laid out neatly on a color display card. Of the first nine costumes, Sgt. Fury was dropped from the production line in 1967. The remaining eight are offered with a premium flasher ring which shows Captain Action one way and a superhero when the ring is tilted. Four new costumes were added (Spiderman, Green Hornet, Buck Rogers and Tonto) and also come with flasher rings. There was also a slight change in the Lone Ranger's costume, the shirt being changed from light blue to red/black, and the pants being changed from light blue to black.

CAP-8. AQUAMAN (includes costume, mask, fins, swordfish sword, conch horns, trident spear, knife with sheath) **$150-250, Box w/ring: $300**

CAP-9

CAP-9. BATMAN (includes costume, cape, mask, boots, utility belt, flashlight, grappling hook, laser beam and Batarang) **$200-250, Box w/ring: $300**

CAP-10

CAP-10. BUCK ROGERS (includes silver space suit, mask, boots, space belt, twin jet pack, space helmet, space gun, space light and canteen) **$300-400**

CAP-11. CAPTAIN AMERICA (includes costume, mask, boots, shield, laser gun w/hoster, laser rifle) **$250-300, Box w/ring: $350**

CAP-12. FLASH GORDON (includes white space suit, mask, helmet, boots, space gun w/holster, oxygen guidance ('Zot" gun) **$200-250, Box w/ring: $300**

CAP-13

CAP-13. GREEN HORNET (includes green overcoat with gold linen lining, mask, hat, white shirt, black pants, shoes, stinger cane, gas pistol, shoulder holster, wrist watch message receiver, TV radar scanner w/phone adapter and gas mask) **$1000 and up.**

CAP-14

CAP-14. LONE RANGER (includes shirt and pants, hat, boots w/spurs, two-gun holster w/pistols, rifle and mask) Blue costume: **$200-250,** Red/Black costume w/ring: **$350-400**

CAP-15. PHANTOM (includes costume, mask, boots, rifle w/scope, two-gun holster w/pistols or revolvers, knife, and skull-shaped brass knuckles) **$200-250, Box w/ring: $300**

CAP-16

CAP-16. SGT. FURY (includes camouflage outfit, mask, boots, machine gun, holster and .45 revolver, ammo belt, walkie talkie, helmet and three grenades) **$300-450**

CAP-17

CAP-17. SPIDER-MAN (includes costume, mask, boots, belt, web-tank w/hose, spider webbing, flashlight and yellow spider) **$1000 and up.**

CAP-18. STEVE CANYON (includes green flight jumpsuit, mask, pilot's helmet, boots, holster and .45 automatic, parachute pack, garrison belt, oxygen mask and knife) **$150-200, Box w/ring: $250**

CAP-19

CAP-19. SUPERMAN (includes costume, cape, mask, boots, Kryptonite, Phantom Zone projector, chains and shackles and Krypto the Super Dog w/cape) **$250-300, Box w/ring: $350**

CAP-20. TONTO (includes two-piece buckskin outfit, mask, moccasins, headband w/feather, gun belt w/pistol, bow, quiver, four arrows and eagle) **$350-450**

ACTION BOY COSTUMES (Ideal 1967-68)
Only three costumes were produced for Action Boy, although, had the series continued another year, Kato (Green Hornet) and Bucky (Captain America) costumes were planned for 1969. Each costume comes in a 10x14" window display box which features the costume and accessories on a color display card.

CAP-21

CAP-21. AQUA LAD (includes costume, mask, belt w/sheath and sea horse knife, sea shell axe and octopus) **$400-450**

CAP-22

CAP-22. ROBIN (includes costume, cape, mask, gloves, boots, belt, Bat-shaped Launcher, Bat-A-Rang, two Bat Grenades and two hand-held, suction-cup wall-climbers) **$400-450**

CAP-23

CAP-23. SUPERBOY (includes costume, cape, mask, boots, belt, telepathic space scrambler, interspace language translator and space chem lab unit) **$400-500**

CAPTAIN ACTION ACCESSORY SETS (Ideal 1966-68) Six different accessory sets were produced, each packaged in a red/blue 8x9" window display box. Each set comes with a variety of painted plastic weapons, helmets, jet packs and space gadetry. (Loose pieces have little value).
CAP-24. ANTI-GRAVITATIONAL POWER PACK: $100
CAP-25. FOUR FOOT WORKING PARACHUTE: $75

CAP-26

CAP-26. INTER-GALACTIC JET MORTAR: $100-125
CAP-27. INTER-SPACIAL DIRECTIONAL
      COMMUNICATOR: $100-150
CAP-28. SURVIVAL KIT: $100
CAP-29. WEAPONS ARSENAL: $100

CAP-30

CAP-30. CAPTAIN ACTION'S "SILVER STREAK" AMPHIBIAN CAR (Ideal 1967) 21" long silver plastic futuristic jet car with tri-wheel design. Two large missiles are mounted to each side of car and can be fired. Both Captain Action and Action Boy can be seated in the car. Car is advertised as an amphibious jet car and can float in water. Box is 18x24x14" deep. **$500-600**

CAPTAIN ACTION DEPARTMENT STORE EXCLUSIVES (1966-68) During the popularity of Captain Action, some of the larger national department stores offered special exclusive accessories as a way of boosting sales. Five different exclusives were offered.

CAP-31

CAP-31. CAPTAIN ACTION "SILVER STREAK" GARAGE (Sears 1967) Offered by Sears stores exclusively, this 24x18x12" tall color cardboard garage features open dual doors, beacon light and radar dish. The words "Captain Action" are above entrance. **$200-300**

CAP-32

CAP-32. CAPTAIN ACTION'S HEADQUARTERS CARRY CASE (Sears 1967) By far the most mass produced exclusive was Sears vinyl "Headquarters". The square-like 12x14x5" case opens to reveal a two-room secret headquarters. One room has a door which conceals a vacu-form seat and computer control panel. **$100-150**

CAP-33

CAP-33. CAPTAIN ACTION'S QUICK CHANGE CHAMBER (Sears 1967) Cardboard 18x13x5" vault-designed chamber with plastic swivel seat which sits behind a large computer control board with a global map. There is a vault door that opens up to a small closet room. Chamber is two tone blue with red computer room. **$300-400**

CAP-34. CAPTAIN ACTION'S "ACTION CAVE" CARRY CASE (Montgomery Wards 1967) Colorful 11x18x6" vinyl case with twin peaks opens to reveal a hidden cave hideaway with computer equipment. This is the same case Ideal used a year earlier for its Batman playset series and the inside of the cave is almost identical. **$200-250**

CAP-35. DR. EVIL'S SANCTUARY (Speigel's 1967) 10x15" pentagonal vinyl carrying case with computerized interior and colorful superheroe graphics on the outside. Because Speigel's was a smaller department store, distribution was limited, making this store exclusive the most difficult to locate. **$400-600**

CAP-36

CAP-36. CAPTAIN ACTION MODEL KIT (Aurora 1966) The Aurora model kit company, known for its wide range of figure kit subjects, capitalized on the popularity of Captain Action and issued an 11" plastic assembly kit of the hero. The same artwork from the doll box was used, making the two products indistinguishable at first glance. Box is 13x4". **$150-200**

CAP-37. CAPTAIN ACTION HALLOWEEN COSTUME (Ben Cooper 1966) 10x12" box with window display lid contains one-piece synthetic fabric suit and plastic mask. **$150-200**

CAP-38. CAPTAIN ACTION "WATER FUN" INNER-TUBE (1967) Child's vinyl plastic lifesaver/inner-tube with illustrations of Captain Action and superheroes. **$50-100**

CAP-39. CAPTAIN ACTION PLAYING CARDS (Cool Pops 1967) Deck of playing cards with illustrations of Captain Action, Action Boy, Silver Streak Car, and the superheroes he can change into. Comes in 3x4" protective box. These cards were offered as a mail order premium from Cool Pops, obtainable by sending Cool Pop wrappers in to the company. **$35-50**

© 1963 BY NATIONAL PERIODICAL PUBLICATIONS INC

DC COMIC CHARACTERS

DC-3

DC-3. AQUAMAN JIGSAW PUZZLE (Whitman 1967) 100-piece puzzle shows Aquaman and Mera fighting giant squid. Box is 8x11". **$25-30**

DC-4

DC-4. AQUAMAN & THE JUSTICE LEAGUE OF AMERICA GAME (Hasbro 1967) 9x17" box contains playing board, spinner and four playing pieces. The object is to be the first player to reach home. **$75-125**

DC-1. AQUAMAN/CAPTAIN ACTION COSTUME: See "Captain Action", #CAP-8 of this chapter.

DC-2

DC-2. AQUAMAN HALLOWEEN COSTUME (Ben Cooper 1967) 10x12" box contains one-piece yellow/green synthetic bodysuit with illustration of Aquaman. The plastic mask of Aquaman has blonde hair with a red shell-mask which covers the eyes. **$50-100**

DC-5

DC-5. AQUAMAN'S WIFE "MERA" DOLL (Ideal 1967) 12" posable doll comes in costume with belt, trident and crown. Window display box is 5x15x4" deep. **$400-650**

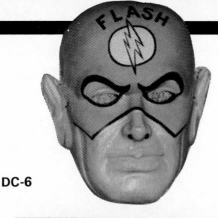

DC-6

DC-8

contains five pre-numbered canvas sketches, ten vials of paint and brush. **$75-150**

DC-6. THE FLASH HALLOWEEN COSTUME (Ben Cooper 1967) 8x12" window display box contains red one-piece synthetic fabric body suit with illustration of the Flash on chest and red plastic mask. **$50-100**

DC-7. THE FLASH FIGURE (Ideal 1967) 3" painted figure of the Flash in a running pose. This figure came with The Justice League of America playset and was also sold on a 5x8" display card which also contained Aquaman or Wonder Woman and two unpainted villains. The price we quote is for a loose, unpackaged figure. **$50**

DC-8. THE FLASH & THE JUSTICE LEAUGE OF AMERICA GAME (Hasbro 1967) 9x17" box contains playing board, spinner and four playing pieces. The object is to be the first player to reach home. **$100-150**

DC-9. GREEN LANTERN HALLOWEEN COSTUME (Ben Cooper 1967) 8x12" window display box contains green/yellow one-piece synthetic fabric costume with illustration of Green Lantern on chest. Plastic mask has brown hair and green or blue mask. **$50-80**

DC-10. JUSTICE LEAUGE OF AMERICA PAINT BY NUMBER SET (Hasbro 1967) 10x11" window display box

DC-11

DC-11. JUSTICE LEAUGE OF AMERICA PLAYSET (Ideal 1967) The title on the box reads "Batman & the Justice League of America", but this set is universally referred to as simply the "Justice League of America" playset. This 20-piece playset comes in a 22x12x11" deep window display box. The inside display is a two-level illustrated cardboard landscape diorama consisting of a battle between the JLA and villains. Set includes six painted 3" plastic figures of (Batman, Robin, Superman, Aquaman, Flash and Wonder Woman), seven villains molded in purple, orange and green plastic, Batplane w/launcher, Batmobile, Batcave (marked "Sanctuary" across entrance), laser ray weapon and computer console. **$1000 and up.**

DC-12. SUPERBOY/ACTION BOY COSTUME (See "CAPTAINACTION" section in this chapter)

DC-13

DC-16

DC-13. SUPERBOY MODEL KIT (Aurora 1965)
13x4" box contains all plastic assembly kit of Superboy and Krypto fighting a dragon. **$100-125**
(**Note:** This kit was re-issued in 1974 as part of Aurora's "Comic Book Scenes" series and came in a large white box with a comic book. Value is about 25% of the original issue kit.)

DC-16. SUPERMAN CARTOON KIT (Colorforms 1964)
8x12" box contains thin plastic vinyl character pieces which affix to illustrated backboard of Metropolis. **$25-50**

DC-14   DC-15

DC-17   DC-18

DC-14. SUPERGIRL DOLL (Ideal 1967)
12" posable doll comes with costume, cape, boots, Krypto (same Krypto figure as in the Captain Action-Superman costume set), and a dress for her alter-ego Linda Lee Danvers' identity. Window display box is 15x5x4" deep. **$400-750**

DC-15. SUPERMAN FORK & SPOON EATING SET
(Imperial Knife Co. 1966) Stainless steel fork and spoon set have embossed 1.5" figures of Superman on handles and the word "Superman" engraved further down the handle. Comes on colorful 10x5" display card. **$20-35**

DC-17. SUPERMAN FIGURE (Ideal 1966)
3" painted figure with removable cape came in the Batman playset, Justice League of America playset and also on a 6x9" display card which also contained a painted Aquaman or Wonder Woman and two unpainted villains. The price we quote is for a loose (mint) Superman figure. **$20-25**

DC-18. SUPERMAN "FLYING" BINGO GAME (Whitman 1966) The Superman Flying Bingo game is a perfect example of the wave of character licensing that began in the Sixties and found its way onto the packaging of what would otherwise be a completely generic toy. The game consists of a plastic tray containing 25 small spaces and an assortment of plastic chips. The object is to toss the chips into the spaces. The only reference or tie-in to Superman is on the box lid. Box is 12x12". $15-25

DC-19

DC-22   DC-23

DC-19. SUPERMAN IN THE JUNGLE GUM CARD SET
(Topps 1966) Set of 66 illustrated color cards with story on back. This set was test marketed on a small area of the nation for a very short time and is consequently very hard to find. It has been reported that no display for this set exists, although one turned up in 1990. The display box and wrapper is considered very rare. **Gum Card Set: $2000 ($25-35 per card), Gum Card Wrapper: $350-500, Gum Card Display Box: Estimated at $3000 and up.**

DC-22. SUPERMAN PUPPET (Ideal 1966)
12" vinyl head/cloth body hand puppet comes in poly bag with color header card showing illustration of Superman and Batman. This header card was also used to package the Batman hand puppet Ideal also made that year. Puppet has also been found having a vinyl plastic body. **$25-40**

DC-23. SUPERMAN PUSH BUTTON MARIONETTE
(Kohner 1966) 3" plastic jointed mechanical figure with cape moves when bottom of base is pressed in. **$35-50**

DC-20

DC-20. SUPERMAN JIGSAW PUZZLE (Whitman 1964)
10x12" box contains 150 piece 14x18" jigsaw puzzle of Superman fighting several Brainiacs on jet sleds. **$20-25**

DC-21

DC-21. SUPERMAN PARTY PLACE SET (1966)
Bright blue three piece paper set consists of plate, cup and napkin and shows an illustration of Superman breaking chains with his chest. **$10-20**

DC-24. SUPERMAN MODEL KIT (Aurora 1963, 1966)
13x4" box contains all plastic 1/8 scale assembly kit of Superman punching through brick wall. There are two different box lid designs to this kit. The first issue is an oil painting style lid (1963), and the second issue (1966) is line art illustration like that found in a comic book, complete with the sound effect "crash" on the box. The reason for the art change was to make the Superman kit look like the rest of Aurora's superhero series (1964-68) which, with exception to the Batmobile and other superhero vehicles, were all line art. **1st Issue Box: $150-200, 2nd Issue Box: $200-250** (**Note:** This kit was re-issued in 1974 as part of Aurora's "Comic Scenes" series and came in a large white box with a free comic book. Value is about 20% of a 1st issue original. It should also be noted that Monogram re-issued this kit in 1980 and the value of that kit is $10)

GREEN HORNET

The Green Hornet was originally broadcast in the 1930's and 40's as a radio program and then as a movie serial. The television show was introduced to a superhero-infatuated audience at the peak of **Batman**'s success. The new show offered dramatic intrigue for adult viewers and exciting gadgetry and action for the kids. Despite these concepts, the show did not attract the viewing audience it had hoped for and, to make matters worse, its massive merchandising campaign was not successful. The series lasted only one season. Today, Green Hornet items are highly sought after by an ever-increasing number of Green Hornet and Kato (Bruce Lee) fans.

GH-2

GH-2. GREEN HORNET "BLACK BEAUTY" CAR MODEL KIT (Aurora 1966) 13x4" box contains all-plastic assembly kit molded in black of Chrysler Imperial sedan used in the ABC television series. Kit contains no figures. **$300-400**

GH-3

GH-3. GREEN HORNET "BLACK BEAUTY" SLOT CAR (Aurora 1966) 2.5" black Chrysler Imperial with circular Green Hornet logo on roof. Sold separately but adaptable to any of the Aurora race car sets. Comes in 3x2x2" clear plastic case. **$50-125**

GH-1

GH-1. GREEN HORNET "BLACK BEAUTY" CAR (Corgi 1966) Black 5" metal die-cast car features shooting projectiles from hidden missile launcher in front grille of car and a Flying Radar Scanner which sails several feet into the air when trunk is opened by way of hidden lever. There is also a small figure of the Green Hornet leaning out the back window of the back seat aiming a pistol which can be moved slightly by way of lever underneath car. There is a figure of Kato behind the wheel. Car comes with pull-out display stand in a 6x3x3" deep box. **$300-400**

GH-4

GH-4. GREEN HORNET CARTOON KIT (Colorforms 1966) 8x12" box contains plastic vinyl character pieces of the Green Hornet, Kato and villains and accessories, which affix to an illustrated cardboard background. **$75-125**

GH-5

GH-5. GREEN HORNET FRAME TRAY PUZZLE SET (Whitman 1966) Boxed set contains four 9x12" frame tray puzzles. Box is 9x12x2" deep. **$50-75**

GH-6

GH-6. GREEN HORNET ELECTRIC DRAWING SET (Lakeside 1966) 12x16" plastic light table comes with large envelope which contains several illustrated sheets that can be placed over the light board to trace from. Box is 12x20x4" deep. **$175-225**

GH-7

GH-7. GREEN HORNET GUM CARDS (Donross 1966) Set of 44 color photo cards based on the ABC television series starring Van Williams and Bruce Lee. Backs of cards feature a photo puzzle and story text. **Gum Card Set: $75-125, Wrapper: $35-50, Display box: $175-225**

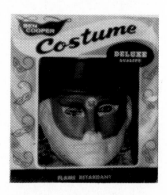

GH-8

GH-8. GREEN HORNET HALLOWEEN COSTUME (Ben Cooper 1966) 12x14" window display box contains synthetic fabric one-piece costume and plastic mask. **$150-200**

GH-9

GH-9. GREEN HORNET HAT & MASK (Arlington Hat Co. 1966) Child's dark green or black felt hat with pull down felt mask which covers eyes and nose. There is an illustrated fabric label on the front crown of hat which reads "Green Hornet" and features the hornet logo. **$50-75**

GH-10

GH-10. GREEN HORNET KITE (Roalex 1967)
Large plastic kite with full illustration of the Green Hornet walking with his stinger cane. Kite comes in long 34x6" package. **$75-125**

GH-11

GH-11. GREEN HORNET MAGIC RUB-OFF SET (Whitman 1966) 9x12" box contains eight glossy cardboard slates with illustrations to color which can be rubbed off and re-colored. Set also includes eight crayons and cloth. **$75-125**

GH-12

GH-12. GREEN HORNET PLAYING CARDS (Ed-U-Cards 1966) Standard deck of 52 playing cards, each with a black/white photo of Van Williams or Bruce Lee from the ABC television series. The two jokers are illustrations of the Green Hornet. Deck comes in 2.5x3.5" box. **$10-20**

GH-13

GH-13. GREEN HORNET PRINT PUTTY (Colorforms 1966) Colorful 7x8" display card holds secret print putty which comes in green canister with the Hornet logo on lid. The secret print putty is actually Colorform's own brand of Silly Putty and its main feature is that it will lift and transfer prints from and to paper. There is also a print transfer booklet included with illustrations of the Green Hornet. **$35-50**

GH-14

GH-14. GREEN HORNET OIL PAINT-BY-NUMBER SET (Hasbro 1966) Large 26x18" window display box contains one 14x20" pre-sketched, pre-numbered canvas, ten vials of oil paints, brush and large green plastic frame. **$350-500**

GH-15

GH-15.   GREEN HORNET "QUICK SWITCH" GAME
(Milton Bradley 1966) 10x20" box.   **$200-250**

GH-16

GH-16. GREEN HORNET SOCKS (1966)
6x5" display card contains three different pairs of children's
socks, each in a different color and with a different
illustration.   **$75-100**

GH-17

**GH-17.   GREEN HORNET STARDUST "TOUCH OF
VELVET" PAINT SET** (Hasbro 1966) 11x14" box contains
large pre-sketched, pre-numbered black velvet canvas, six
vials of paint and brush.   **$150-200**

GH-18

GH-18. GREEN HORNET "THING MAKER" MOLD (Mattel
1966) 6x9" display card holds metal mold which is to be
used with the Mattel line of Thing Maker Mold and Oven
sets. Mold is of three hornet insects of varying sizes. Also
included is a bottle of plastic "goop", mold handle, plastic
knife, and pins and materials to make rings and badges.
$75-125

GH-19

GH-19. GREEN HORNET WALKIE-TALKIES (Remco 1966)
10x10x4" deep color photo box contains two 9" long, green,
hard plastic two-way "electromagnetic" walkie-talkies. Each
walkie-talkie has a pull-out antenna, connecting wire and
soft earpiece.   **$150-225**

GH-20.   GREEN HORNET WALLET (1966) Plastic vinyl
green wallet comes with membership card. **$25-30**

MARVEL SUPERHEROES

When Marvel Comics first published Fantastic Four #1 in November of 1961, little did they realize the revolutionary change it would initiate in the comic book industry--on the same level as the influence the Beatles exercised in the music world of the 60's.

With the success of the Fantastic Four firmly established, Spiderman, Thor and the Hulk were created in 1962. Classic Marvel heroes from the 1940's, including Captain America and the Sub-Mariner, were re-vamped and found renewed interest in a new generation of comic book readers. What Marvel comics offered over the more conservative DC Comics superheroes was in-depth character studies of the alter-egos of its stars, and a soap-opera-like continuation of the problems of those characters. This off-beat but realistic formula was popular with pre-teens, teens, college students and even adults--an audience DC had lost over the years. Peak merchandising on Marvel characters in the Sixties was made between 1965-68.

MAR-1

MAR-1. CAPTAIN AMERICA COLORING BOOK (Whitman 1966) 8x11", 80+ pages. **$25-35**

MAR-2. CAPTAIN AMERICA/ CAPTAIN ACTION COSTUME (See "CAPTAINACTION"in this chapter.)

MAR-3

MAR-3. CAPTAIN AMERICA "FLYING" FIGURE (Trans0gram 1966) 11x15" display card holds 12" vacuform plastic figure with glider wings. **$35-50**

MAR-4

MAR-4. CAPTAIN AMERICA GAME (Milton Bradley 1966) Object of the game is to be the first player to complete successfully a mission by overcoming obstacles and reaching the Radar Tower. Game includes stand-up cardboard figures of Captain America and Bucky, playing board and dice. Also included in every game was a free Marvel comic book. Box is 10x20". **$50-65**

MAR-5. CAPTAIN AMERICA HALLOWEEN COSTUME (Ben Cooper 1966) 12x14" window display box contains fabric one-piece red, white and blue body suit and plastic mask. **$50-75**

MAR-8

MAR-8. DAREDEVIL T-SHIRT (Marvel Comics 1966-68) At the peak of Marvel's popularity, 11 different t-shirts were offered through the Marvel comic books as a mail order premium. T-shirt is white and comes in three sizes and sports a bright color graphic of Daredevil on the front. **$35-50**

MAR-6

MAR-6. CAPTAIN AMERICA MODEL KIT (Aurora 1966) 13x4" box contains all-plastic assembly kit molded in flat blue plastic of Captain America running across a battlefield. **$200-250**

(**Note:** This kit was re-issued by Aurora in 1974 as part of its "Comic Scenes" series and was molded in bright blue plastic and came in a large white box with a free comic book. The value of this kit is about 20% of the original.)

MAR-9

MAR-9. DOCTOR DOOM HALLOWEEN COSTUME (Ben Cooper 1967) 10x12" window display box contains green/yellow one-piece synthetic fabric bodysuit and plastic mask. **$100-150**

MAR-10. FANTASTIC FOUR "THING" HALLOWEEN COSTUME (Ben Cooper 1966) 10x12" window display box contains orange one-piece synthetic fabric bodysuit and orange plastic mask. **$75-100**

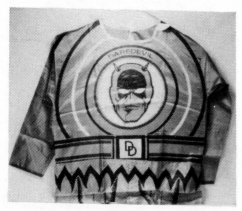

MAR-7

MAR-7. DAREDEVIL HALLOWEEN COSTUME (Ben Cooper 1967) 10x12" window display box contains red one-piece synthetic fabric bodysuit and red plastic mask. **$75-125**

MAR-11. FANTASTIC FOUR "BIG LITTLE BOOK" JIGSAW PUZZLE (Whitman 1969) 5x6x1" box designed like a "Big Little" book contains 99-piece jigsaw puzzle. The scene is from a previously published "Big Little" book by Whitman. **$10-15**

MAR-12

MAR-12. HULK MODEL KIT (Aurora 1966)
13x4" box contains all-plastic assembly kit molded in metallic green featuring the Hulk bending a steel girder. **$200-250**
(**Note:** This kit was re-issued in 1974 as part of Aurora's "Comic Scenes" series, was molded in drab green plastic and came in a large white box with a free comic book. The value of this kit is about 20% of the original.)

MAR-13

MAR-13. HULK SWEAT SHIRT (Marvel Comics 1966)
Available exclusively through Marvel comic books as a mail order premium. The front of the shirt shows a frontal view of the Hulk and reads "Here Comes the Incredible Hulk". The back of the sweat shirt shows the back of the Hulk and reads "There Goes the Incredible Hulk". The sweat shirt is long sleeved and white. **$50-100**

MAR-14

MAR-14. IRON MAN HALLOWEEN COSTUME (Ben Cooper 1967) 10x12" window display box contains red/yellow one-piece flannel body suit and yellow plastic mask. **$50-75**

MAR-15

MAR-15. IRON MAN FIGURE (Marx 1966)
Plastic 6" figure molded in red, blue or grey plastic of Iron Man breaking chain. The grey plastic figures were available only through Marvel Comics as a mail order premium. Our photo shows the figure painted. **RED/BLUE: $5-10, GREY: $15**

MAR-16. MARVEL SUPERHERO BIKE PLATES (Marx 1967) Colorful 2x4" tin license plates made for bicycles. Four different plates were made: **Captain America, Hulk, Spider-man, Thor. EACH: $5-15**

MAR-17

MAR-20

MAR-20. MARVEL SUPERHERO GUM CARDS (Donross 1966) Set of 66 color illustrated cards with humorous captions. Cards feature six different characters (**Captain America, Daredevil, Hulk, Iron Man, Spider-man, Thor**) and the illustrations are from previously published comic books. Back of card is a color illustrated puzzle. **Gum Card Set: $50-100, Wrapper: $20-30, Display Box: $100-150**

MAR-17. MARVEL SUPERHERO BUTTONS (Button World 1965) A set of 12 different 3.5" diameter color buttons were produced featuring Marvel Superhero characters. Each button reads "OfficialMember Superhero Club" and came in a poly bag with colorful 4x3" header card. Characters include: **Fantastic Four, Doctor Strange, Captain America, Daredevil, The Hulk, Spider-man, Iron Man, Sub-Mariner, Thor, Avengers, Sgt. Fury, X-Men.** **EACH: $10-20**

MAR-21

MAR-21. MARVEL SUPERHERO JIGSAW PUZZLE (Milton Bradley 1966) 8x12" box contains 100 piece jigsaw puzzle. Scene shows illustration of **Thor, Iron Man, Hulk** and **Sub-Mariner** (Hulk not shown on box) fighting alien sea creatures. Iron Man is in his old second series gold suit. **$40-65**

MAR-18

MAR-18. MARVEL SUPERHERO FIGURES (Marx 1966) Well detailed solid plastic 6" figures molded in red, blue and grey plastic. The grey figures were available through Marvel Comics only as a mail order premium. Characters include: **Captain America, Daredevil, Hulk, Iron Man, Spier-man, Thor.** **EACH: Red/Blue $5-10, EACH: Grey $15** (**Note:** These figures are currently being re-manufactured by a small company in New York and are molded in various colors other than the three original colors listed above. The plastic is more brittle and the value of these figures is about $1 each.)

MAR-19. MARVEL SUPERHERO "FLICKER" RINGS (Vari-Vue 1966) Also known as "flasher" rings or "flicker-flasher" rings. The ring would produce two different images when turned right to left or up and down. A series of 12 different rings was produced and was available only from gum ball machines. **EACH: $3-10**

MAR-22

MAR-22. MARVEL SUPERHERO PENNANTS (RMS Sales Co. 1966) Set of five 9" felt pennants with one color illustration of hero and title logo of hero. Heroes include: **Captain America, Hulk, Iron Man, Sub-Mariner, Thor.** Pennants come in polybag with illustrated header card.

MAR-23

MAR-23. MARVEL SUPERHERO POSTERS (Marvel Comics 1966) Set of eight 12x16" color posters of **Captain America, Doctor Strange, Hulk, Human Torch, Iron Man, Spider-man, Sub-Mariner, Thor.** Posters come in 12x20" polybag with illustrated header card. **$35-50**

MAR-25

MAR-25. MARVEL SUPER-HERO "SPARKLE" PAINTS (Kenner 1966) Kenner's sparkle paints series became the best-selling paint sets in America in the early Sixties. Two sets were produced featuring the Marvel Superheroes. The first set comes in a 8x12" box and contains five pre-numbered sketches, (**Captain America, Daredevil, Hulk, Spider-man, Thor**) five vials of paint which contain glitter, and three brushes. A second, larger set comes in a 10x13" box and contains eight pre-numbered sketches which feature all the super heroes in the smaller set and include new heroes such as the **Silver Surfer** and the **Sub-Mariner,** ten vials of sparkle paint and six brushes. **Small Set** (Captain America on box) **$30-45, Large Set** (Silver Surfer on box) **$50-65**

MAR-24

MAR-24. MARVEL SUPER-HEROES "SEE-A-SHOW" STEREO VIEWER SET (Kenner 1966) Kenner's see-a-show was similar to Sawyer's viewmaster reels except that the viewing reels were rectangular and not circular, and that the reels were moved manually instead of by lever. The see-a-show viewer came with five different view cards on a 8x5" display package. **$25-35**

MAR-26

MAR-26. MARVEL SUPER-HERO STATIONARY SET (Marvel Comics 1964-68) Offered exclusively by Marvel Comics through its line of comic books as a mail order premium. Stationery comes in large portfolio-size illustrated envelope showing all the Marvel characters. The stationery is illustrated with 12 characters and there is an illustration of the "Thing" on the envelope. Also included is a bonus 8x11" page with illustrations of all the Marvel characters and their autographs. **$40-65**

MAR-27. MARVEL SUPER-HERO TRICYCLES (Marx 1968) Series of four tricycles made by Marx in the last days of the superhero craze of the mid-Sixties. Colorful 4x4" window display box contains a 3" plastic figure of a hero (**Captain America, Hulk, Spider-man, Thor**) on a metal wind-up tricycle with ringing bell. **$35-50**

MAR-28

MAR-28. MECHANICAL MARVEL SUPER-HEROES (Marx 1968) Series of three plastic 4" wind-up mechanical figures of **Captain America, Spider-man, Thor.** Each come in a colorful 5.5x3x3" deep window display box. **$50-75**

MAR-29

MAR-29. MERRY MARVEL MARCHING SOCIETY MEMBERSHIP KIT (Marvel Comics 1964-68) Offered exclusively by Marvel comics through its comic books as a mail order premium. Membership kit comes in large, illustrated 9x12" envelope and includes one large 3" diameter button reading "I Belong to the Merry Marvel Marching Society", five smaller 1" diameter buttons that have sayings such as "Face Front" and "Hang Loose", a membership card, an 8x10" membership certificate, several 3x4" orange paper stickers of the Thing saying "The M.M.M.S. wants you!", a Marvel bullpen newsletter, and a 33-1/3 rpm record with illustrated sleeve featuring the Marvel staff welcoming the member into the club. There are also color page ads for the Marvel line of t-shirts and posters.
$50-100

MAR-30

MAR-30. SPIDER-MAN GAME (Milton Bradley 1966) 10x20" box contains stand-up cardboard figures of Spider-man, playing board and dice. The box lid also shows the Hulk, Iron Man, Sub-Mariner and Thor running to the aid of Spider-man, who is battling two villains. **$50-100**

MAR-31

MAR-31. SPIDER-MAN MODEL KIT (Aurora 1966) 13x4" box contains all-plastic assembly kit, molded in tan, of Spider-man shooting his webbing over a defeated Kraven the Hunter. **$225-275**
(**Note:** This kit was re-issued in 1974 by Aurora as part of their "Comic Scenes" series and came molded in red plastic in a large box with a free comic book. The value of this kit is about 20-25% of the original.)

MAR-32. THOR CANDY CONTAINER (Pez 1960s) Plastic 4" Pez candy container with detailed head of Thor. Helmet is silver and has protruding wings on each side. **$25-50**

TV/ADVENTURE

Television shows from the Sixties offered some of the most imaginative and enduring characters ever created by networks. Some, such as *Star Trek*, have been immortalized on the Big Screen, while many still play in syndication, continually growing in popularity and forming cult followings. *Lost in Space, Gilligan's Island, Bewitched, The Monkees,* and the *Twilight Zone* are just a few of the Sixties' "Hall of Famers."

With the popularity of television and its infinite range of entertaining shows and characters came a licensing frenzy in the toy industry that still dictates sales today. When a toy was made in the image of a television character, the television program became, in essence, a 30-60 minute promotion for the toy itself. The age of mass marketing had arrived.

TV/ADV-2. BEN CASEY M.D. PLAY HOSPITAL SET (Transogram 1962) 16x18x4" window display box contains black plastic medical bag with medical certificate and hospital charts, a medicine chest filled with medical supplies and instruments, and a doctors cap. **$35-50**

TV/ADV-3.

TV/ADV-3. DARK SHADOWS "HORROR HEADS" PILLOWS (Centsable Products 1969) Series of three stuffed character head pillows of a **Witch, Vampire, Werewolf** come in bright fluorescent day-glo colors, each in a 10x10x14" window display box. **EACH: $50-100**

TV/ADV-4. DARK SHADOWS BARNABAS COLLINS GAME (Milton Bradley 1969) 10x20x3" deep box contains plastic/cardboard coffin which contains bone parts to four skeletons. Object is to be the first player to build a skeleton. Also included in the game is a pair of fangs for each player to wear. **$25-50**

TV/ADV-5. DARK SHADOWS BARNABAS MODEL KIT (MPC 1968) 13x5" box contains all-plastic 1/8 scale assembly kit molded in black plastic of Barnabas Collins. **$150-200**

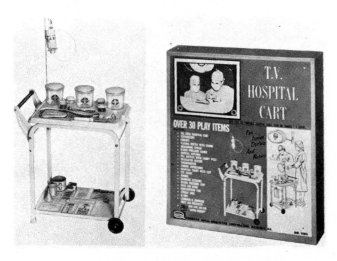

TV/ADV-1.

TV/ADV-1. BEN CASEY "TV" HOSPITAL CART (Transogram 1962) Large 18x22" box contains an all steel constructed hospital cart and 30 related items including stethoscope, forceps, plasma bottle and blood stand, blood pressure gauge, thermometer, various Johnson & Johnson products, charts and books. **$100-150**

TV/ADV-5   TV/ADV-6

TV/ADV-6. DARK SHADOWS GAME (Whitman 1968) 10x18" box contains fold-out paper playing board, four stand-up monster playing pieces and deck of playing cards including a color photo card of Barnabas. **$35-50**

TV/ADV-2.

TV/ADV-7

TV/ADV-10

TV/ADV-7. DARK SHADOWS GUM CARDS (Philly 1968) Two gum card sets were made on Dark Shadows. The first set of 66 cards features black/white photos on a PINK border with a photo puzzle on back. The second series of 66 cards features black/white photos on a GREEN border with a photo puzzle on back. Both sets are numbered #1-66. The sets are the same in value. **Gum Card Set: $100-150, Gum Card Wrapper: $20-35, Gum Card Display Box: $100-200**

TV/ADV-10. DARK SHADOWS "WEREWOLF" MODEL KIT (MPC 1969) 13x5" box contains all-plastic 1/8 scale assembly kit molded in dark brown of the Werewolf. Kit comes with extra glow-in-the-dark pieces. **$150-200**

TV/ADV-8

TV/ADV-11

TV/ADV-8. DARK SHADOWS JOSETTE'S MUSIC BOX (1969-1970) Plastic 4" tall cylinder-shaped music box with a 2.5" diameter is copper in color with a repeating Victorian pattern. The lid detaches from the box and is also copper color. Bottom of the box has a built-in key feature and when wound up plays "Quentin's Theme". Inside of the music box is marked "Dark Shadows/Josette's Music Box/ Copyright 1970, Dan Curtis Productions". Comes in 5x3x3" brown cardboard box with a dark purple photo of Barnabas on front side. This was a mail order premium not available in stores. **$250-400**

TV/ADV-11. DR. KILDARE GAME (Ideal 1962) Object of the game is to be the first player to complete his rounds, decode his diagnosis card and analyze his patient's illness correctly. Game includes hospital playing board, spinner/analyzer, diagnosis and doctor cards and four playing pieces. Box is 10x20". **$20-25**

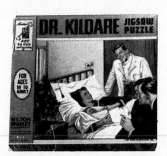

TV/ADV-12.

TV/ADV-9. DARK SHADOWS VIEWMASTER REEL SET (GAF 1968) Three reel set comes in photo envelope with 16-page booklet. **$25-40**

TV/ADV-12. DR. KILDARE JIGSAW PUZZLE (Milton Bradley 1962) 10x12" box contains over 100 piece jigsaw puzzle. **$15-20**

TV/ADV-14.

TV/ADV-13

TV/ADV-17

TV/ADV-17. FLIPPER MODEL KIT (Revell 1965) 6x10" box contains all-plastic assembly kit of Flipper diving out of water and Sandy riding along his side. **$40-60**

TV/ADV-13. DR. KILDARE JUNIOR DOCTOR PUNCH-OUT KIT (Golden Funtime 1962) 13x7" book contains colorful punch-outs of medical instruments and such. **$10-20**

TV/ADV-14. DR. KILDARE MAGIC SLATE (Lowe 1962) 8x13" cardboard slate with lift-up plastic drawing sheet. **$15**

TV/ADV-15. FLIPPER ERASABLE MAGIC SLATE (Lowe 1963) 8x13" color cardboard slate back with lift-up drawing sheet and wooden stylus pencil. This is presumably the very first Flipper item to be made. **$15-25**

TV/ADV-18

TV/ADV-15.

TV/ADV-18. HONEY WEST DOLL (Gilbert 1965) 12" plastic posable doll with synthetic blonde hair dressed in black jumpsuit. The right arm is spring-activated and raises to shoot pistol she is holding. Box is 12x4x2" deep. **$100-150**

TV/ADV-16

TV/ADV-19

TV/ADV-16. FLIPPER "FLIPS" GAME (Mattel 1965) 10x20" box contains four miniature dolphins, treasure chest and playing board. The object of the game is to be the first diver to return safely to boat with the treasure. **$20-25**

TV/ADV-19. HONEY WEST "THE GIRL PRIVATE EYE" GAME (Ideal 1965) Object of the game is to be the first player to catch the criminal at large by successfully solving clues. Box is 10x20". **$35-50**

TV/ADV-20

TV/ADV-20. LAND OF THE GIANTS CARTOON KIT
(Colorforms 1968) 8x12" box contains plastic vinyl character
parts and accessories which stick to illustrated background
board. **$40-75**

TV/ADV-21

**TV/ADV-21. LAND OF THE GIANTS NUMBERED PENCIL
COLORING SET** (Hasbro 1968) 16x13" box contains ten
pre-numbered sketches, 12 color pencils, and pencil
sharpener. **$100-125**

TV/ADV-22

TV/ADV-22. LAND OF THE GIANTS GAME (Transogram
1968) Players move through the Land of the Giants,
competing to be the first to collect material essential to the
repair of their damaged space ship. Game includes playing
board, two giants, four little people, 16 material tokens and
dice. Box is 20x10". **$75-125**

TV/ADV-23

TV/ADV-23. LAND OF THE GIANTS GUM CARD SET
(Topps 1968) Color photo set of 55 cards with narratives or
puzzle on back. This card set was a test market product
and distribution was very limited.
Gum Card Set: $500 and up
Gum Card Wrapper $100-200
Gum Card Display Box: $700 and up.

TV/ADV-24

**TV/ADV-24. LAND OF THE GIANTS HALLOWEEN
COSTUME** (Ben Cooper 1968) 10x12" window display
contains a male scientist outfit. The fabric body suit shows
three little people climbing up the shirt pockets and the tie
clip reads "Land of the Giants". The plastic mask is of a
bearded angry looking giant. **$75-125**

TV/ADV-25

TV/ADV-25. LAND OF THE GIANTS HAND MOVIE VIEWER (Acme 1968) Plastic 3" hand-held viewer with turning knob and two boxes of film come on 5x8" color photo display card. **$25-50**

TV/ADV-26

TV/ADV-28

TV/ADV-26. LAND OF THE GIANTS JIGSAW PUZZLE (Whitman 1968) Square 11x11" box contains 125 piece circular jigsaw puzzle of the little people fighting a cat. **$20-35**

TV/ADV-28. LAND OF THE GIANTS MODEL KIT (Aurora 1968) 13x7" box contains all-plastic assembly kit molded in metallic green of the little people fighting off an attacking rattle snake. **$250-375**

TV/ADV-27.

TV/ADV-29

TV/ADV-27. LAND OF THE GIANTS OIL PAINT BY NUMBERS SET (Hasbro 1968) 10x11" box contains five pre-numbered sketches, ten vials of paint and brush. **$100-150**

TV/ADV-29. LAND OF THE GIANTS MOTORIZED FLYING ROCKET (Remco 1968) Plastic glider plane with thin plastic wings and working motor and propeller which flies and performs stunts by way of a hand-held cable attached to its base. Comes in large 18x20" box. **$100-175**

TV/ADV-30. LAND OF THE GIANTS SHOOT N STICK TARGET RIFLE SET (Remco 1968) Brown plastic 28" long spring-loaded rifle with paper decal logo on stock comes with six firing darts and a 9x9" target with the Giant logo. Box is 12x32x4" deep. **$175-275**

TV/ADV-31

TV/ADV-31. LAND OF THE GIANTS SIGNAL-RAY SPACE GUN (Remco 1968) Plastic ray gun with three color turrets at the end of the barrel which produce a colored beam of light when the small lightbulb inside the gun is switched on. A loud buzzing noise is also made when switch is activated. This particular gun was originally made back in the 50's as a generic space gun, but Remco has used it many times since as a character pistol by simply changing the decals and box in which it was packaged. **$45-75**

TV/ADV-32

TV/ADV-32. LAND OF THE GIANTS SPACE SHIP CONTROL PANEL (Remco 1968) Plastic 9x11x7" control panel with stand-up die-cut top control panel featuring the Giant logo. Wheel turns, horn honks, levers and switches move up and down and some light up. If this toy looks familiar it's because it's the popular FIREBIRD 99 car dashboard Remco had been making for the past eight years. With a few changes and new set of decals applied, Remco saved tens of thousands of dollars on new molds. Box is 12x18x8" deep. **$350-500**

TV/ADV-33

TV/ADV-33. LAND OF THE GIANTS SPACE SLED (Remco 1968) Remco was as clever at re-packaging old toys as the Louis Marx Company. A perfect example is the LOG Space Sled, which was originally the successful battery-operated SUPERCAR just six years earlier. The car is still molded in original orange plastic and has Mike Mercury still behind the driver's seat! The Space Sled comes with four directional discs, each containing two directional programs which, depending on the disc used, would drive forward in a figure-8 pattern, loop-the-loop pattern and so on. Sled is 11" long with a 10" wingspan and comes in a 14x12x3" deep box. **$350-500**

TV/ADV-34

TV/ADV-34. LAND OF THE GIANTS SPINDRIFT MODEL KIT (Aurora 1968) 14x7" box contains all-plastic assembly kit of the little people's space ship. **$200-300**
(**Note:** This kit was re-issued by Aurora in 1975 and its value is about 1/2 of the original)

TV/ADV-35. LAND OF THE GIANTS SPINDRIFT TOOTHPICK CRAFT KIT (Remco 1968).
10x10" box contains die-cut sheets that form a Spindrift spaceship shell and toothpicks to fill in the void. **$35-60**

TV/ADV-36. LAND OF THE GIANTS VIEWMASTER REEL SET (GAF 1968) Three reel set comes in photo envelope with 16-page booklet. **$25-35**

TV/ADV-37. LAND OF THE GIANTS TARGET GAME (Hasbro 1968) Set consists of 14x10" tin litho target, target gun and plastic darts with suction cup tips. **$200-225**

TV/ADV-41

TV/ADV-41. LOST IN SPACE GAME (Milton Bradley 1965) Object of the game is to be the first player to reach his designated color space. Box is 9x17". **$35-60**

TV/ADV-37   TV/ADV-38

TV/ADV-38. LAND OF THE GIANTS WALKIE TALKIES (Remco 1968) Pair of 3x5" red plastic walkie-talkies with 20 feet of hollow plastic tubes to connect them for "sound transmission". Each walkie-talkie has a paper decal of the Giant logo. Box is 9x16". **$150-250**

TV/ADV-39. LOST IN SPACE 3-D ACTION GAME (Remco 1966) Three-level playing board with four small detailed plastic playing figures. Comes in large 20x24" box with color photo of children playing the game and photo of cast members in upper right corner. **$200-250**

TV/ADV-42

TV/ADV-42. LOST IN SPACE GAME (1966) Made in Greece, this game had no U.S. distribution. Playing board features photos of cast members and some of the enemies encountered in the series. Box shows Dr. Smith and Will Robinson in the foreground, an alien monster behind them, the Robot in the background and head shots of the other cast members in the distance. Box is 10x17". **$350-500**

TV/ADV-40

TV/ADV-40. LOST IN SPACE BATTERY-OPERATED ROBOT (Remco 1966) All plastic 12" robot moves forward and chest panel lights up and blinks. The arms can be moved by way of two levers in the back of robot. Each side of the bottom track of robot has a colored-paper decal reading "Lost in Space". This robot was produced in several color combinations (red/black, blue/black, green/black, blue/red) the most desirable color being a metallic blue body. The box is 8x10x14". **$300-400**

TV/ADV-43

TV/ADV-43. LOST IN SPACE GUM CARD SET (Topps 1966) Set of 55 black/white photo cards with narration on back.
Gum card Set: $200-300
Gum Card wrapper: $35-65
Gum Card Display Box: $350-500

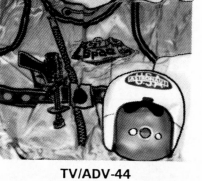

TV/ADV-44

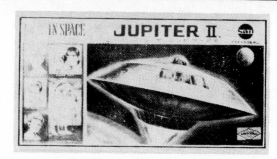

TV/ADV-46

TV/ADV-44. LOST IN SPACE HALLOWEEN COSTUME
(Ben Cooper 1965) 10x12" window display box contains
silver one-piece synthetic fabric body suit and plastic
astronaut mask. This costume was originally a 1960 U.S.
Astronaut's costume, but with a few alterations to the name
on the body suit, it sold very well in 1965 as a Lost in Space
costume. **$100-200**

TV/ADV-46. LOST IN SPACE JUPITER II MODEL KIT
(Marusan 1966) 18x12" box contains all-plastic assembly kit
molded in orange of the Robinson Family's Jupiter II space
ship. The kit also comes with a motor which, when
completely assembled, will drive forward. The interior is
detailed and figures are included. This kit was made in
Japan and was not distributed in the U.S. **$1000 and up.**

TV/ADV-45

TV/ADV-47

TV/ADV-45. LOST IN SPACE HELMET & GUN SET
(Remco 1966) Blue plastic helmet with clear plastic dome
"beacon" top piece and colorful decals on front and sides of
helmet. The 10" plastic Signal Ray Gun has a three-color
turret at the end of barrel which, when switch on gun is
activated, will turn light on inside and produce a colored
beam of light. This gun was originally made back in the
Fifties by Remco, but was continually re-issued to be sold
as a licensed character ray gun when the right television
show came along. This gun was also used as a Star Trek,
Land of the Giants and Voyage to the Bottom of the Sea ray
gun. Box is 9x9x11". **$250-350**

TV/ADV-47. LOST IN SPACE LUNCHBOX (Aladdin 1966)
Metal dome-top lunchbox with generic steel thermos which
shows various flying spaceships.
Box: $200-300, Thermos: $20-25

TV/ADV-48

TV/ADV-48. LOST IN SPACE MAGIC EYES STORY SET
(Sawyer 1965) 10x12" display card holds three 4x6" film cards. Made for a GAF Magic Eyes film viewer which, unlike Sawyer's view master reel sets, was less popular and soon discontinued. **$25-40**

The larger deluxe kit comes in a 13x10" box and contains all the same pieces as the smaller kit plus a two-piece rock cliff formation to give the cyclops added height, and an additional large base section which allows room for the Space Chariot which is also included. This kit is sometimes referred to as the "Cyclops with Chariot" kit.
Small Kit: $500-800
Large Kit w/Chariot: $1000 and up.

TV/ADV-50

TV/ADV-49

TV/ADV-49. LOST IN SPACE MODEL KITS (Aurora 1966-67)
This model kit was made in a small and deluxe edition. The smaller kit comes in a 14x13" box and contains five Robinson figures running and fighting a giant cyclops monster which is about to hurl a large boulder down upon them. The cyclops is standing on a rock formation which reads "Lost in Space".

TV/ADV-50. LOST IN SPACE ROBOT MODEL KIT
(Aurora 1968) 13x4" box contains all-plastic assembly kit molded in silver and clear plastic of the Robot. **$650-900**

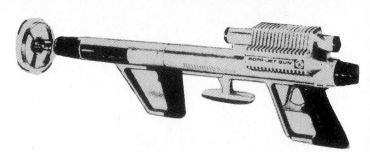

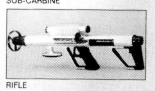

LAUNCH ROTO-MISSILES FIVE
DIFFFRENT WAYS

SUB-CARBINE

RIFLE

ROTO-LAUNCHER

PISTOL
HAND LAUNCHER (not shown)

TV/ADV-51

TV/ADV-51. LOST IN SPACE ROTO-JET GUN (Mattel 1966) Authentic looking silver laser rifle like the one used on the television series. Features five different weapons in one: Sub-Carbine, Roto Launcher, Pistol and Hand Launcher. Rifle shoots spinning Roto-missiles. Window display box is 24x18". The flip side of the box features a painting on heavy foil paper of Will Robinson fighting off cyclops monsters with the Roto-Jet gun. The side panels are illustrated with various members of the family (including Dr. Smith) demonstrating the different variations of the gun. **$1500 and up.**

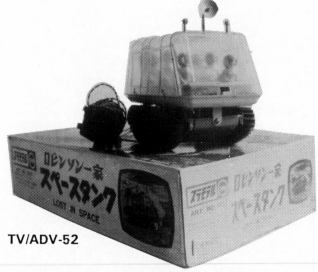

TV/ADV-52

TV/ADV-52. LOST IN SPACE SPACE CHARIOT MODEL KIT (Marusan 1966) 18x12" box contains all-plastic assembly kit of the Robinson's space chariot. There is a small motor included which, when installed, allows the chariot to move forward. Five Robinson figures are included. This kit was made in Japan and had no U.S. distribution. **$1000-1500**

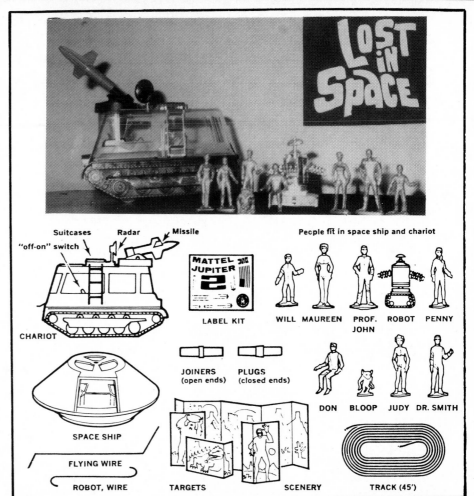

TV/ADV-53

TV/ADV-54

TV/ADV-55.

TV/ADV-53. LOST IN SPACE SWITCH & GO PLAYSET
(Mattel 1966) Playset contains large two-piece 17x7"
styrofoam Jupiter spaceship with clear plastic windows,
plastic battery-operated Space Chariot with missile launcher,
40 feet of air hose for the space chariot to run on, several
plugs and joiners to assemble air hose track, four color
cardboard stand-up targets of space creatures, nine silver
plastic 3" figures of the entire television cast including Dr.
Smith, Bloop and the Robot. The Robot has a chrome finish
and is two pieces. There is also a hooked wire which can be
connected to the Robot so that he can be pulled along
behind the chariot. A chrome finished jet pack attaches to
John and a wire can attach to him from the Jupiter II to
simulate flying. The Jupiter II comes with a sheet of decals
and interior rooms including a parking space for the Space
Chariot. The Space Chariot has a clear plastic body and
detachable chrome finish ladder, luggage and radar dish.
The battery-powered chariot moves on the air hose track
and fires missiles at cardboard targets. Box is 14x20x4"
deep and has colorful foil paper graphics. **$1000 and up.**

TV/ADV-54. LOST IN SPACE TRAY PUZZLES (Milton
Bradley 1965) Series of three 10x14" frame tray puzzles, all
depicting battles with the cyclops monster. One puzzle is
the same illustration as that used on the Milton Bradley
board game. **EACH: $40-75**

TV/ADV-55. LOST IN SPACE VIEWMASTER REEL SET
(Sawyer 1965) Three reel set comes in color photo envelope
and 16-page booklet. **$35-65**

TV/ADV-56

TV/ADV-60

TV/ADV-56. MOD SQUAD GAME (Remco 1968)
Object of the game is to be the first player to solve the crime and catch the criminal. Box is 10x20". **$50-75**

TV/ADV-57. MOD SQUAD STATION WAGON MODEL KIT (Aurora 1970) 10x10" color photo box contains 1/25 scale all-plastic assembly kit and includes figures of Linc, Pete and Julie. **$75-100**

TV/ADV-60. OUTER LIMITS GAME (Milton Bradley 1964)
Object of the game is to locate and liquidate monsters to prevent a series of catastrophies. Game includes playing board which is divided into four "Tracking Laboratories", each with an electronic viewing screen on which an image of a monster can be seen. Each monster's image is divided into four parts (playing cards). Monster must be assembled to be destroyed. There are 42 monster cards included. Box is 10x20". **$50-100**

TV/ADV-57   TV/ADV-58.

TV/ADV-61

TV/ADV-58. NURSES PAPER DOLL SET (Whitman 1963)
6x10" hard cardboard color photo envelope contains cardboard dolls of cast plus several sheets of clothes which can be cut-out and applied to dolls. **$15-25**

TV/ADV-59.

TV/ADV-59. NURSES GAME (Ideal 1963) Object of the game is to be the first player to graduate from nursing school. Box is 20x10". **$30-40**

TV/ADV-61. OUTER LIMITS GUM CARD SET (Bubbles, Inc. 1964) Color illustrated set of 50 cards, each featuring a monster from the series and a narrative on back. Cards have a black border.

Gum Card Set: **$150-225**
Gum Card Wrapper: **$50-100**
Gum Card Display Box: **$400-500**

TV/ADV-66

TV/ADV-62

TV/ADV-66. ROUTE 66 TRAVEL GAME (Transogram 1962) Object of the game is to travel across country while stopping to work and be the first player back that has saved the most money. Game includes road map-style playing board, four yellow plastic cars, play money and markers. Box is 9x17". **$40-75**

TV/ADV-62. OUTER LIMITS JIGSAW PUZZLES (Milton Bradley 1964) A series of six puzzles were produced, each comes in a 8x13" box and contains 100 jigsaw pieces which make a 19x21" puzzle when assembled. **$100-150**

TV/ADV-63. OUTER LIMITS HALLOWEEN COSTUME (Collegeville 1964) 10x12" window display box contains green one-piece synthetic fabric costume with monster illustration on front and plastic monster mask. **$150-200**

TV/ADV-64. RIP CORD GAME (Lowe 1962) Object of the game is to win $10,000 by completing rescue mission. Game includes playing board, four plastic airplanes, play money and working parachute with ejector. **$50-100**

TV/ADV-67

TV/ADV-67. SEA HUNT UNDERWATER ADVENTURE GAME (Lowell 1960) Object of the game is to be the player to recover the sunken treasure. Box is 9x17". **$50-60**

TV/ADV-65

TV/ADV-68

TV/ADV-65. RIP CORD SKY-DIVING PARACHUTIST (Ray-Line 1962) 6x9" display card contains hollow 5" plastic figure with red/white thin plastic parachute attached. When figure is tossed in air, it will "parachute" gently downward. **$20-35**

TV/ADV-68. STAR TREK ASTRO-WALKIE-TALKIES (Remco 1968) 9x14" display card holds two yellow/red plastic hand-held intercom-shaped walkie talkies that operate by 20 feet of hollow plastic "transmission line". **$35-50**

TV/ADV-69

TV/ADV-69. STAR TREK ASTRO BUZZ-RAY GUN
(Remco 1968) Plastic 10" ray gun with three color turrets at
the end of barrel which projects beams of colored light
when switch is activated. Gun also produces a loud buzzing
sound. This gun dates back to the early Fifties, but Remco
kept it in almost continual production with the aid of
licensed characters and television shows. Box is 9x14x3"
deep. **$100-150**

TV/ADV-72

TV/ADV-70

TV/ADV-72. STAR TREK LUNCHBOX (Aladdin 1968)
Metal dome-top lunchbox with matching steel thermos. The
front shows the USS Enterprise and the back shows Kirk
and Spock with phasers. **$400-600**

TV/ADV-70. STAR TREK COLORING BOOK
(Artcraft/Saalfield 1968) 8x11", 75+ pages. **$25-30**

TV/ADV-71

TV/ADV-73

TV/ADV-71. STAR TREK GAME (Ideal 1967)
Object of the game is to be the first player to complete his
mission by visiting three designated planets and returning to
Earth. Game includes Spaceship Tokens, Fuel Unit cards,
Mission Destination Cards, Fuel Ship Discs and solar system
playing board. Box is 10x20". **$50-75**

**TV/ADV-73. STAR TREK "MR. SPOCK" HALLOWEEN
COSTUME** (Collegeville 1967) 10x12" box contains one-
piece blue/black synthetic fabric body suit with USS
Enterprise graphic on front and a plastic mask of Spock.
$75-125

TV/ADV-74

TV/ADV-74. STAR TREK OIL PAINT SET (Hasbro 1967) 28x20" window display box contains a pre-numbered sketched canvas, eight vials of oil paints and a red plastic frame. **$200-250**

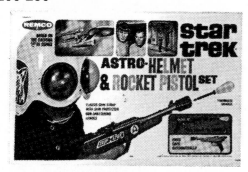

TV/ADV-75

TV/ADV-75. STAR TREK ROCKET PISTOL & ASTRO-HELMET COMBO (Remco 1968) 18x13x8" deep box contains yellow plastic helmet with large, bubbled, clear plastic eye slots and color decals on each side. The Pistol is 10" long and shoots a missile or roll of caps and has a "Star Trek" decal on each side. Both the helmet and pistol were originally made for the short-lived Hamilton Invaders playsets four years earlier. **$175-250**

TV/ADV-76

TV/ADV-76. STAR TREK ROCKET PISTOL (Remco 1968) Remco also packaged the pistol to the above pistol & helmet set separately. Box is 14x10" and shows a color photo of Mr. Spock firing pistol. **$100-150**

TV/ADV-77

TV/ADV-77. STAR TREK TRACER GUN (Grand 1966) 8x11" display card contains 6" plastic spring-loaded gun which fires small plastic "jet" discs (included). **$35**

TV/ADV-78

TV/ADV-78. T.H.E. CAT CARD GAME (Ideal 1966) 6x9" plastic case with clear plastic lid contains playing cards and chips. **$35-50**

TV/ADV-79

TV/ADV-79. T.H.E. CAT GAME (Ideal 1966) Object of the game is to be the successful "Cat" who safely brings three jewels back to his "Cat Lair". Game includes color plastic imitation jewels, Cat Tokens, Inspector Tokens, Deck of Equipment Cards, playing board and spinner. **$75**

TV/ADV-80. T.H.E. CAT HALLOWEEN COSTUME (Collegeville 1966) 10x12" window display box contains one-piece yellow/black synthetic fabric costume and black hooded mask covering top of head, eyes and nose with the words "T.H.E.Cat" on the forehead. **$50-75**

TV/ADV-81

TV/ADV-84

TV/ADV-81. T.H.E. CAT HIDE-A-WAY GUN SET (Ideal 1966) 11x7x2" deep window display box contains 4" black plastic cap-firing pistol with silver inscription "T.H.E.Cat" on the barrel. There is also a 7" plastic black/silver stiletto with working pop-up blade and a plastic wrist scabbard. Also included is an official T.H.E. Cat ID card and a chrome plated ring of a cat's head with green plastic "emerald" eyes. **$500-650**

TV/ADV-84. TIME TUNNEL GAME (Ideal 1966) Object of the game is to be the first successful "Time Traveller" to travel through four different "Time Areas". Game includes "Time Tunnel" cards, "Time Tunnel" Zone Spinner, colored tokens, four playing pieces and playing board. Box is 10x20". **$75-150**

TV/ADV-82

TV/ADV-85

TV/ADV-82. TIME TUNNEL CARD GAME (Ideal 1966) 6x9" plastic case with clear plastic lid contains cards and chips. Players travel through four time zones (Prehistoric, middle Ages, the Present and Future) to collect the most "Time Travelling" chips. **$40-50**

TV/ADV-83. TIME TUNNEL COLORING BOOK (Saalfield 1967) 8x11", 80+ pages. **$30-40**

TV/ADV-85. TIME TUNNEL MODEL KIT (Fujimi 1966) 10x6" box contains all-plastic assembly kit of the Time Tunnel. Kit also includes small film slides which can be placed at the end of the Tunnel to create a "view from the past". This kit was made in Japan and had no U.S. distribution. **$250-350**

TV/ADV-86. TIME TUNNEL VIEWMASTER REEL SET (Sawyer 1966) Three reel film set comes in color photo envelope with 16-page booklet. **$25-40**

TV/ADV-87

TV/ADV-87. TIME TUNNEL "SPIN TO WIN" GAME (Pressman 1967) 10x16" box contains two spin tops and playing board of the Time Tunnel which has various scoring holes. Object of the game is to take a trip into the past to desired year and return safely. **$100-150**

TV/ADV-88

TV/ADV-88. TWILIGHT ZONE GAME (Ideal 1964) Object of the game is to be the first player to move his marker along the Road of Reality thru the Twilight Zone and reach his destination. Game includes playing board, spinner, playing markers and 12 Closed Door cards. Box is 10x20". **$100-200**

TV/ADV-89

TV/ADV-89. UNTOUCHABLES ELLIOT NESS .38 SPECIAL WATER PISTOL (Knickerbacher 1961) 7x10" display card holds 5" plastic water gun. **$20-30**

TV/ADV-90

TV/ADV-90. UNTOUCHABLES GAME (Transogram 1961) Object of the game is for players to raid illegal breweries and round up and arrest as many mobsters as possible. Player with the most points wins. Game includes 120 playing tiles, 24 mobster gun markers, 24 gun cards, playing board. Box is 10x20". **$35-50**

TV/ADV-91. UNTOUCHABLES PLAYSET (Marx 1961) 14x26x3" box contains two tin litho warehouse buildings, two metal friction drive sedans, warehouse accessories including ramps, barrels, policemen, agents, gangsters, character figures of Elliot Ness and Al Capone, plastic layout sheet and several more small accessories. **$1500 and up.**

TV/ADV-93

TV/ADV-92. VOYAGE TO THE BOTTOM OF THE SEA COLORING BOOK (Saalfield 1964) 8x11", 75 pages. **$25**

TV/ADV-93. VOYAGE TO THE BOTTOM OF THE SEA JUNIOR JIGSAW PUZZLES (Milton Bradley 1965) 19x10" boxed puzzles, featuring the same artwork as the Milton Bradley board game and card game. Each: **$20-35**

TV/ADV-94

TV/ADV-94. VOYAGE TO THE BOTTOM OF THE SEA GUM CARD SET (Donross 1964) Set of 66 black/white photo cards with narrative on back.
Gum Card Set: $50-75
Gum Card Wrapper: $25-30
Gum Card Display Box: $200-250

TV/ADV-95

TV/ADV-95. VOYAGE TO THE BOTTOM OF THE SEA "SEAVIEW" MODEL KIT (Aurora 1966) 13x4" box contains all-plastic assembly kit of the Seaview submarine. **$150-225** (**Note:** This kit was re-issued in 1975 by Aurora and value is about 50% of the original)

TV/ADV-96

TV/ADV-96. VOYAGE TO THE BOTTOM OF THE SEA "SEAVIEW" PLAYSET (Remco 1964)
24x12x10" deep window display box contains yellow 18" plastic Seaview Submarine with metallic blue trim. The sub is rubber-band powered to move across water or floor. Set also includes two underwater figures, octopus and two torpedoes. **$350-450**

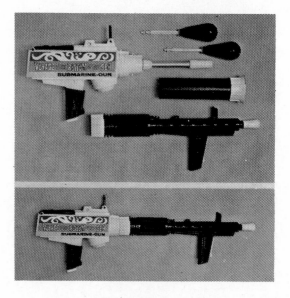

TV/ADV-97

TV/ADV-97. VOYAGE TO THE BOTTOM OF THE SEA "4-WAY" SUB GUN SET (Remco 1966)
10x16x3" window display box contains 12" plastic pistol with interchangeable features which allow it to become a tommy gun, bazooka gun, submarine gun and torpedo gun. Comes with two torpedoes and gun attachments. **$300-350**

TV/COMEDY

Gimmicks and slapstick were the comedy formuli of the Sixties and seemed to be aimed at a younger generation of viewers than that of the previous decade. The more outlandish the premise of a show, the better chance it seemed to have of getting on the air. "My Mother the Car" (1965) was about a mother reincarnated into a 1928 Porter owned by her son. "My Living Doll" (1964) revolves around a sexy female robot being trained to act human by a bumbling man hiding her secret. Martians, witches and genies all became part of the "idiot sitcom" era of the sixties, as well as ghoulish families ("Munsters", "Addams Family",) spies, ("Get Smart"), military ("Gomer Pyle", "Hogan's Heroes", "F-Troop", "McHale's Navy",) stranded castaways ("Gilligan's Island") and Superheroes ("Batman", "Mr. Terrific", "Captain Nice"). Hillbillies moved to High Society ("Beverly Hillbillies"), High Society moved to hillbillies ("Green Acres"). There was hardly a comedy show that went by that didn't inspire some form of toy.

TV/COM-2   **TV/COM-3**

TV/COM-2. ADDAMS FAMILY BOP-BAG (1965) 42" tall vinyl plastic bop bag with blinking eyes and beeping nose. Bottom is weighed down with sand and bevelled to rock back and forth. **Lurch** and **Fester** were produced. **$75-100**

TV/COM-3. ADDAMS FAMILY CARTOON KIT (Colorforms 1965) 10x12" box contains thin vinyl plastic character parts and accessories which stick to illustrated background of the Addams' Family living room. **$50-100**

TV/COM-4

TV/COM-1

TV/COM-1. ADDAMS FAMILY BOARD GAME (Ideal 1965) 10x20" box. **$40-50**

TV/COM-4. ADDAMS FAMILY ELEMENTARY PUZZLES (Milton Bradley 1965) 12x9" box contains two color photo frame tray puzzles. One features Uncle Fester, the other Lurch. **$40-60**

TV/COM-5. ADDAMS FAMILY FLICKER-FLASHER RINGS (Vari-View 1965) Series of six silver band two-way flicker rings, each showing a member of the Addams Family. **EACH: $5-8**

TV/COM-6

TV/COM-6. ADDAMS FAMILY GUM CARD SET (Donross 1965) Set of 66 black/white cards with humorous sayings and photo puzzle on back.
Gum Card Set $100-150
Gum Card Wrapper $20-25
Gum Card Display Box $250-350

TV/COM-8

TV/COM-8.   ADDAMS FAMILY HAUNTED HOUSE MODEL KIT (Aurora 1965) 10x11" box contains all-plastic assembly kit molded in light grey plastic of the Addams Family house. The house features bobbing ghosts inside which can be seen from the windows and are controlled by an outside lever. Another ghost opens the two front doors. There are also cardboard sheet illustrations of the Addams Family which can be cut out and placed behind remaining windows. House stands 8" tall. **$450-550**

TV/COM-7

TV/COM-7.   ADDAMS FAMILY HANDPUPPETS (Ideal 1965) 11" puppets with soft vinyl heads and cloth bodies come both boxed and in poly bags with illustrated header card. The boxes are designed like a haunted house with a frontal window display and measure 6x8x3" deep. Three characters were produced: **Gomez, Morticia, Uncle Fester.** There were plans to release three more puppets of Pugsly, Lurch and Grand Mamma, but the television show was cancelled before actual production began.
BOX: $200-250
POLY BAG: $100-150, LOOSE: $50-60

TV/COM-9

TV/COM-9. ADDAMS FAMILY "LURCH" HALLOWEEN COSTUME (Ben Cooper 1965) 10x12" window display box contains black one-piece synthetic fabric body suit with silver glitter illustrations of Lurch and Thing. A plastic mask of Lurch is also included.   **$100-200**

TV/COM-10

TV/COM-12

TV/COM-10 ADDAMS FAMILY "MONSTER EYES" FLASHLIGHT (Bantam-lite 1965) 6x4" display card holds 4" plastic pen-style flashlight with illustration of eyes and Addams Family logo. **$100-200**

TV/COM-12. ADDAMS FAMILY MYSTERY JIGSAW PUZZLE (Milton Bradley 1965) 8x10" box contains a jigsaw puzzle which, upon completion, solves a mystery. Two different puzzles were made; "Cleopatra's Plight" and "Ghost at Large". **$25-50**

TV/COM-11

TV/COM-13

TV/COM-11. ADDAMS FAMILY "MORTICIA" HALLOWEEN COSTUME (Ben Cooper 1965)
10x12" window display box contains purple one-piece synthetic fabric body suit with illustration of a dress adorned with small creatures. Plastic mask of Morticia comes with painted face or clear plastic face. **$100-150**

TV/COM-13. ADDAMS FAMILY T-SHIRT (Nazareth 1965) Shirt depicts all seven characters (including "Thing") in a "family tree". Four color shirt of purple, red, flesh, and black. **$50-60**

TV/COM-14

TV/COM-14. ADDAMS FAMILY RECORD ALBUM (RCA 1965) Original 33-1/3 RPM soundtrack album with cover photo of cast. **$25-40**

TV/COM-15

TV/COM-15. ADDAMS FAMILY TARGET SET (Ideal 1965) 12x16" window display box contains four die-cut cardboard figures of Gomez, Morticia, Lurch, and Fester which are attached to a plastic base. The targets flip backwards to reveal a score when hit. Plastic spring powered pistol and three rubber-tipped darts included. **$200-300**

TV/COM-16

TV/COM-16. ADDAMS FAMILY "THING" BANK (Poynter Products, 1964) 3.5x4.5" black plastic square box features a creeping hand that slowly reaches out for coin and, once grabbing it, quickly disappears. Comes in 3.5x4.5" box showing front and back illustration of the Addams Family house and side photos of the family. **$35-60**

TV/COM-17. ADDAMS FAMILY "UNCLE FESTER" HALLOWEEN COSTUME (Ben Cooper 1965) 10x12" window display box contains black one-piece synthetic fabric body suit and mask and plastic mask. **$100-200**

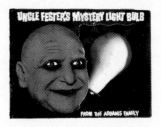

TV/COM-18

TV/COM-18. ADDAMS FAMILY UNCLE FESTER'S "MYSTERY" LIGHT BULB (1964) 7x5.5" window display box contains battery-powered lightbulb which lights up when held to mouth. Comes with a monster flicker-flasher ring. **$100-150**

TV/COM-19

TV/COM-19. ADDAMS FAMILY VIEWMASTER REEL SET (Sawyer 1965) Three reel film set comes in color photo envelope with 16-page booklet. **$75-125**

TV/COM-20

TV/COM-20. BEVERLY HILLBILLIES COLORING SET (Standard Toykraft 1963) 12x18" window display box contains ten pre-numbered sketches, crayons and plastic paint pallete with eight paints and brush. **$35-50**

TV/COM-21   TV/COM-22

TV/COM-21. BEWITCHED MAGIC COFFEE SET (Amsco 1965) Amsco, which made a line of girls household items, capitalized on the success of Bewitched and produced a line of household "Bewitched" items. The Magic Coffe Set features a coffee set with a Bewitched logo, toaster, and kichen accessories in a 14x18" display box that does little to promote the set was in fact a Bewitched toy. **$100-125**

TV/COM-22. BEWITCHED HI-CHAIR & FEEDING SET (Amsco 1965) 29x14" display box contains pink steel baby doll hi-chair, baby plate and utentsils, and Amsco's famous patented Magic Feeding Bottle which now sported a Bewitched logo. **$150-200**

TV/COM-24

TV/COM-24. BEWITCHED DOLL (Ideal 1965) 12" posable doll comes in red dress with matching hat and a broom in a 10x14" window display box. **$300-400**

TV/COM-25. BEWITCHED HALLOWEEN COSTUME (Ben Cooper 1965) 10x12" window display box contains black/yellow synthetic fabric dress with illustration of Samantha flying on broom. Plastic mask included. **$50-75**

TV/COM-23

TV/COM-26

TV/COM-23. BEWITCHED BROOM (Amsco 1965) 36" long broom with 5" hollow detailed head of Samantha in a witch's hat. **$35-50**

TV/COM-26. BEWITCHED "SAMANTHA & ENDORA" GAME (Gems 1965) Object of the game is to be the first player to overcome bizarre obstacles and make it to Vacationland. Box is 10x20" and comes with color discs and markers of Darrin, Samantha and Endora. **$50-75**

TV/COM-27

TV/COM-27. BEWITCHED DOLL FEEDING SET (Amsco 1965) 8x14" box contains vinyl travel bag with Bewitched logo, Magic Feeding Bottle with Bewitched logo and several doll feeding accessories. The Magic Feeding Bottle was also sold seperately as an accessory to most Amsco bewitched sets and came in a 5x8" display box. **SET: $100-150. BOTTLE ACCESSORY: $35-65**

TV/COM-28

TV/COM-28. CAR 54 WHERE ARE YOU GAME? (Allison 1961) Object is to reach or overtake Car 54. Game includes 13 plastic cars, cardboard radio control unit, thirty Car 54 Location Cards, Dispatch Cards, Location Cards and a playing board which features a four-precinct city with 29 locations and a Police Headquarters. Box is 10x23". **$100**

TV/COM-29

TV/COM-29. DICK VAN DYKE GAME (Standard Toykraft 1965) Box is 10x20". **$40-75**

TV/COM-30

TV/COM-30. F-TROOP COLORING BOOK (Saalfield 1965) 8x11", 70+ pages. **$15-20**

TV/COM-31

TV/COM-31. F-TROOP GAME (Ideal 1965) Box is 10x20". **$50-75**

TV/COM-32

TV/COM-32. GET SMART EXPLODING TIME BOMB GAME (Ideal 1965) Object is to collect clue cards to make a picture of a KAOS agent while avoiding time bomb. Game includes 16 clue cards, playing board, four playing pieces and a spring-loaded time bomb. **$35-50**

TV/COM-33

TV/COM-33. **GET SMART GUM CARDS** (Topps 1966)
Set of 66 black/white photo cards with quiz riddles on back.
Gum Card Set: $50-75
Gum Card Wrapper: $20-25
Gum Card Display Box: $100-150

TV/COM-36

TV/COM-36. **GET SMART CAR MODEL KIT** (AMT 1967)
5x9" box contains all-plastic 1/25 scale assembly kit of
Maxwell Smart's '65 Sunbeam sports car. **$50-75**

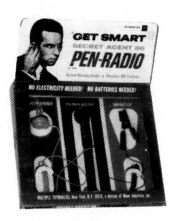

TV/COM-34

TV/CCOM-34. **GET SMART & AGENT 99
PEN RADIO** (MPC 1966) 7x7" window display box contains
AM radio shaped like a pen and comes with earpiece and
small clip. **$35-65**

TV/COM-37

TV/COM-37. **GIDGET FORTUNE TELLING CARD GAME**
(Milton Bradley 1965) 6x10" box contains playing cards and
fold out playing mat. **$10-15**

TV/COM-35

TV/COM-35. **GET SMART & AGENT 99 LIPSTICK-
RADIO** (MPC 1966) 8x12" window display box contains AM
radio shaped like a lipstick container and comes with an
earpiece and small clip. **$40-75**

TV/COM-38

TV/COM-38. **GILLIGAN'S ISLAND GAME** (Gems 1965)
10x20" box. Object is to get off the island. **$100-125**

169

TV/COM-39

TV/COM-39. GILLIGAN'S ISLAND GUM CARDS (Topps 1965) Set of 55 black/white photo cards. The backs have a film clip photo puzzle which, when assembled, features a short action sequence.
Gum Card Set: $125-225
Gum Card Wrapper: $20-30
Gum Card Display Box: $175-275

TV/COM-40

TV/COM-40. GOMER PYLE GAME (Transogram 1965) Object of the game is to be the first player to get all 25 of his men out on the grounds and in formation. Box is 9x17".
$20-25

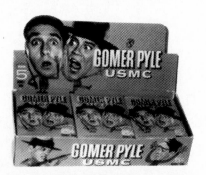

TV/COM-41

TV/COM-41. GOMER PYLE GUM CARD SET (Fleer 65) Set of 66 black/white cards with jokes on back.
Gum Card Set: $20-35
Gum Card Wrapper: $20-30
Gum Card Display box: $75-100

TV/COM-42. GOMER PYLE LUNCHBOX (Aladdin 1965) Steel box with matching steel thermos.
Box $35-45, Thermos $15-20

TV/COM-43

TV/COM-43. GREEN ACRES GAME (Standard Toykraft 1965) 10x20" box. $50-75

TV/COM-44

TV/COM-44. HOGAN'S HEROES "BLUFF OUT" GAME (Transogram 1966) Object of the game is to be the first player to escape successfully from Stalag 13. Game includes four Hogan figures, 48 Color Code Cards, 18 Equipment Cards, plastic Duffle Bag and playing board of Stalag 13. $50-75

TV/COM-45

TV/COM-45. HOGAN'S HEROES WWII JEEP MODEL KIT (MPC 1968) 6x9" box contains all-plastic assembly kit of a 1944 Willey's Jeep. $35-45

TV/COM-46

TV/COM-46. HOGAN'S HEROES LUNCHBOX (Aladdin 1966) Steel dome-top lunchbox with matching thermos. **Box $150-225, Thermos $35-50**

TV/COM-47

TV/COM-47. I DREAM OF JEANNIE DOLL (Ideal 1966) 18" posable doll fully dressed in genie outfit including veil. Box is 20x8x7". **$250-325**

TV/COM-48

TV/COM-48. I DREAM OF JEANNIE GAME (Milton Bradley 1965) Object of the game is to be the first player to spell the word JEANNIE. Box is 10x20". **$20-30**

TV/COM-49

TV/COM-49. IT'S ABOUT TIME GAME (Ideal 1967) Object of the game is to capture four different monsters. Game includes Monster Cards, Monster Discs, Direction Cards, Rock Money, four playing pieces and playing board. Box is 10x20" **$100-150**

TV/COM-50

TV/COM-50. IT'S ABOUT TIME GUM CARDS (Topps 1967) Test market card set with very low distribution. Exact number of cards in the set are unknown, but assumed at either 55 or 66, a standard Topps set. Each card is black/white photo with a humorous saying and joke on back.
Cards: $20 per Card   Wrapper: $150-250
Gum Card Display Box: $500 and up.

TV/COM-51. IT'S ABOUT TIME LUNCHBOX (Aladdin 1967) Steel dome-top lunchbox with matching thermos. **Box $150-200, Thermos $50-75**

TV/COM-52

TV/COM-52. LAUGH-IN ELECTRIC DRAWING SET (Lakeside 1968) 10x15x4" deep box contains plastic light table and large envelope of illustrated sheets, tracing paper and color pencils. **$35-50**

TV/COM-53

TV/COM-56

TV/COM-53. LAUGH-IN FUN KIT (Hasbro 1968)
12x15" box contains ten different gags and and party tricks such as phony plastic donut, dripping glass, facial disguises and more. **$35-45**

TV/COM-56. McKEEVER & THE COLONEL "SHAVE & SHINE" MESS KIT (Transogram 1962) 12x18" window display box contains Army mess kit which includes vinyl carry case, shaving mug, brush, razor, shoe polish, comb and soap. **$100-150**

TV/COM-54

TV/COM-57

TV/COM-54. LAUGH-IN NOTEBOOK BINDER (1968)
Illustrated vinyl plastic three-ring notebook binder. **$15**

TV/COM-57. McKEEVER AND THE COLONEL HOLSTER & CANTEEN SET (Transogram 1962) 15x15" window display box contains plastic automatic pistol, grenade, whistle, canteen and leather holster and belt. **$100-150**

TV/COM-55

TV/COM-58

TV/COM-55. LAUGH-IN WASTE PAPER BASKET (1968)
Colorful metal lithograph waste basket with one side featuring photos of the cast with silly quotes and the other side a large illustration of the tricycle rider in raincoat. **$25-30**

TV/COM-58. MISTER ED TALKING HAND PUPPET (Mattel 1962) 7x12" window display box contains 12" handpuppet with plastic head and cloth body and a pull-string which activates concealed voice box to produce a variety of programmed phrases. **$40-75**

MONKEES: See "Music, Movie & Personality" Chapter

TV/COM-59

TV/COM-59. MUNSTERS "AT HOME WITH THE MUNSTERS" RECORD ALBUM (AA Records 1964) Original cast recording, stories and songs. **$25-35**

TV/COM-60

TV/COM-60. MUNSTERS BOWLING SET (Ideal 1965) 12x16" window display box contains four 6" hollow plastic figures of **Herman, Lilly, Grandpa, Eddie** and two plastic bowling balls. **$300-400**

TV/COM-61

TV/COM-61. MUNSTERS CARTOON KIT (Colorforms 1964) Colorforms made two different sets on the Munsters. The small set shows the family riding on the Koach car and consists of a Koach car illustrated background board and plastic vinyl character parts. Box is 10x12.
The larger deluxe set shows the family sitting together on a sofa and consists of a living room scene background board with plastic vinyl character parts. Box is 13x17".
Small Edition (Munster Koach box): $150-200
Large Edition (Family on Sofa box): $250-350

TV/COM-62. MUNSTERS CARD GAME (Milton Bradley 1964) 6x10" box contains playing cards and roll out playing mat. Two box lids exist for this game. One shows the family playing cards with a frightened boy, the second lid shows the boy replaced by a cheerful Eddie Munster. Neither box is especially difficult to locate and there is no difference in price. **$18-30**

TV/COM-63

TV/COM-63. MUNSTERS CASTEX 5 MOLDING SET (Emenee 1964) Large 21x12x4" box contains four two-piece figure molds of **Herman, Lilly, Grandpa** and **Eddie**, plus a bag of plaster and paints. **$500-700**

TV/COM-64. MUNSTERS COLORING BOOK (Whitman 1964) 8x11", 75+ pages. **$25-35**

TV/COM-65. MUNSTERS DELUXE RUB-ON SET (Hasbro 1964) 12x14" box contains several sheets of rub-on characters and accessories which, when rubbed with pencil, transfer to large color illustrated background. **$200-300**

TV/COM-66

TV/COM-66. MUNSTERS DOLLS (Remco 1964) Remco made a series of three dolls, **Herman, Lilly** and **Grandpa**. Each doll is 5-6" tall and has a large soft plastic head with life-like synthetic hair and a small hard plastic body. Each doll came in a 4x6" window display box designed like a stone castle dungeon. **Herman; $450-500, Grandpa & Lilly: 400-450**

TV/COM-67

TV/COM-67. MUNSTERS DRAG RACE GAME (Hasbro 1964) 10x18" box. **$200-250**

TV/COM-68

TV/COM-72.

TV/COM-68. MUNSTERS DRAGULA MODEL KIT (AMT 1964) 5x9" box contains all-plastic assembly kit of Grandpa's wild coffin dragster. **$100-150**

TV/COM-69

TV/COM-70

TV/COM-69. MUNSTERS FLASHLIGHT PEN (Bantam lite 1965) 4x6" display card holds 4" plastic flashlight with decal of Herman and Munster logo. **$75-125**

TV/COM-70. MUNSTERS "HERMAN" KITE (Pressman 1964) 32x6" illustrated package contains giant 3' plastic kite. **$100**

TV/COM-71

TV/COM-71. MUNSTERS GUM CARD SET (Leaf 1964)
Set of 72 black/white photo cards with humorous sayings and jokes on back.
Gum Card Set: $175-250
Gum Card Wrapper: $20-25
Gum Card Display Box $100-150

TV/COM-72. MUNSTERS HAND PUPPETS (Ideal 1964) 10" puppets with plastic vinyl head and cloth body of **Herman, Lily, Grandpa**. Puppets come packaged in poly bags with illustrated header card _or_ 4x7" window display boxes designed like a haunted house.
Poly Bag: $100-150
Box: $200-250
Loose: $50

TV/COM-73

TV/COM-73. MUNSTERS "HERMAN" HALLOWEEN COSTUME (Ben Cooper 1964) 12x14" window display box contains black/yellow one-piece synthetic fabric body suit and plastic mask. **$200-225**

TV/COM-74.

TV/COM-75

TV/COM-85

TV/COM-85. MUNSTERS KOACH MODEL KIT (AMT 1964) 5x9" box contains all-plastic assembly kit of the famous car. Two box variations exist. The first features Beverly Owens in the cast photo and the second features Pat Priest. **$150-225**

TV/COM-74. MUNSTERS "HERMAN" TALKING DOLL (Mattel 1964) 20" stuffed cloth doll with plastic head and hands and a string in back which produces a variety of sayings when pulled. Comes in 10x6x6" deep box. **$375-550**

TV/COM-75. MUNSTERS "HERMAN" TALKING HAND PUPPET (Mattel 1964) 12" puppet with same plastic head and hands as the Herman talking doll. String in back produces a variety of sayings when pulled. This puppet comes packaged in a closed box and a window display box. **$300-400**

TV/COM-86

TV/COM-86. MUNSTERS KOACH TOY (AMT 1964) 12" plastic black/red car with chrome trim features a real motor sound from the back wheels when car is in motion. Car comes in 7x15x5" deep box with pop up display lid. **$400-600**

TV/COM-76. MUNSTERS HYPODERMIC SQUIRT GUN (Hasbro 1964) Plastic 8" hypodermic needle squirts water from tip. Comes on 9x10" display card. **$125-200**

MUNSTERS JEWELRY (Harry Klitzner Co. 1964) A series of seven different pieces of jewelry was produced featuring the Munsters. All came on a display card about 3x4 or 5x6"

TV/COM-77. TIE CLIP (Photo of Herman) **$50-75**
TV/COM-78. BOLO TIE (Photo of Herman) **$50-75**
TV/COM-79. CUFF LINKS (Photo of Grandpa) **$50-75**
TV/COM-80. KEY RING (Photo of cast) **$40-60**
TV/COM-81. BRACELET (Photo of cast) **$75-100**
TV/COM-82. EARRINGS (Photo of Lilly or cast) **$50-75**
TV/COM-83. NECKLACE (Photo of cast) **$75-100**

TV/COM-87

TV/COM-87. MUNSTERS LUNCHBOX (King Seeley Thermos 1965) Steel Box with matching thermos.
Box: $100-200, Thermos $35-65

TV/COM-84. MUNSTERS JIGSAW PUZZLES (Whitman 1964) A series of four puzzles known to be made, each comes in a 8x12" box and contains 100 pieces. **$25-35**

TV/COM-88

TV/COM-93

TV/COM-88. MUNSTERS "MAD DOCTORS" DOLLS
(Ideal 1965) These 8" movable plastic vinyl dolls of **Herman, Lilly** and **Eddie** were originally designed as Munsters dolls, but when the show was cancelled, Ideal quickly redressed them in medical uniforms and re-marketed them as "Mad Doctors" and "Mini-Monsters". **EACH: $50-100**

TV/COM-89. MUNSTERS MASQUERADE PARTY GAME
(Hasbro 1964) 10x17" box. **$200-275**

MUNSTERS MASKS (Don Post Studios 1965)
Thin pull-over rubber latex masks were produced of **Herman, Grandpa** and **Lilly**. Each mask was made two different ways, either with painted hair or life-like hair. We list the masks with hair. The painted hair masks are 50% the value of a mask with hair.
TV/COM-90. HERMAN w/HAIR: $200-250

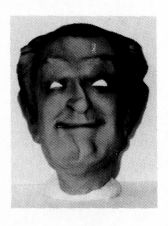

TV/COM-91   TV/COM-95

TV/COM-91. GRANDPA w/HAIR: $200-250
TV/COM-92. LILLY w/HAIR: $175-200

TV/COM-93. MUNSTERS MODEL KIT (Aurora 1964)
11x14" box contains all-plastic assembly kit of **Herman, Lilly, Grandpa** and **Eddie** all sitting (or hanging) in front of a living room with fireplace and television set. **$750-1000**

TV/COM-94. MUNSTERS NOTEBOOK BINDER (1964)
Plastic vinyl three-ring notebook binder. **$35-60**

TV/COM-95. MUNSTERS OIL PAINT-BY-NUMBER SETS
(Hasbro 1964) Series of three different sets were produced (**Herman, Grandpa** and **Lilly**). Each comes in a 10x11" box and contains an 8x10" pre-numbered, sketched canvas, five vials of paint and brush. **EACH: $200-300**

TV/COM-96. MUNSTERS PAPER DOLLS (Whitman 1965)
9x12" cardboard folder contains cardboard stand-up figures of **Herman. Lilly, Grandpa, Eddie** and **Marilyn** plus six sheets of cut-out costumes. **$40-75**

TV/COM-97. MUNSTERS PENCIL BY NUMBER SET
(Hasbro 1964) 9x12" box contains 12 pre-numbered sketches and 12 colored pencils. **$200-300**

TV/COM-103. MUNSTERS "TOUCH OF VELVET" ART SET

(Hasbro 1964) 12x14" box contains a 10x12" pre-numbered black velvet sketched canvas, eight vials of paint and brush. **$200-275**

TV/COM-98   TV/COM-99

TV/COM-98. MUNSTERS PICNIC GAME (Hasbro 1964) 10x20" box. **$200-275**

TV/COM-99. MUNSTERS SLIDE PUZZLE (Roalex 1964) 5x6" display card hold 3x3" plastic tile puzzle with illustration of the Munster Family. The object is to slide the tiles about to complete a picture. **$75-100**

TV/COM-101.   TV/COM-104

TV/COM-104. MUNSTERS TRAY PUZZLE (Whitman 1964) Two different frame tray puzzles were produced and are 10x14". **$25-35**

TV/COM-100.

TV/COM-100. MUNSTERS SOUVENIR HAT (Arlington Hat Co. 1964) Child's felt hat with cloth picture label of **Herman** on front. Hat comes in blue, black and green. **$50-75**

TV/COM-101. MUNSTERS STICKER FUN BOOK (Whitman 1964) 8x12" book with pages of cut-out and stick-on illustrations which are used in the book. **$50-60**

TV/COM-102

TV/COM-102. MUNSTERS TARGET GAME (Ideal 1965) 12x16" window display box contains four die-cut cardboard stand-up figures of **Herman, Lilly, Grandpa** and **Eddie** which are attached to a plastic base. The targets flip over backwards and reveal a score when hit. Plastic spring-loaded pistol and three rubber-tipped darts are included. **$200-300**

TV/COM-105

TV/COM-105. MUNSTERS WALL PAINT-A-PLAQUES (Standard Toykraft 1964) Series of three different boxed wall plaques were produced and sold separately of **Herman, Grandpa** and **Lilly**. Each comes in an 11x14" window display box and contains a 10x12" plastic 3-D embossed portrait. **EACH: $200-250**

TV/COM-106

TV/COM-106. MUNSTERS VIEWMASTER REEL SET
(Sawyer 1964) Three reel film set comes in color photo
envelope with 16 page booklet. **$75-125**

TV/COM-107

**TV/COM-107. MY FAVORITE MARTIAN COLORING
BOOK** (Whitman 1964) 8x11", 65+ pages. **$20-25**

TV/COM-108

TV/COM-108. MY FAVORITE MARTIAN COLORING SET
(Standard Toykraft 1963) 13x18" window display box
contains plastic paint pallette with 19 colors, brush, eight
crayons and eight pre-numbered sketches. **$100-150**

TV/COM-109

**TV/COM-109. MY FAVORITE MARTIAN CRAYON BY
NUMBER & STENCIL SET** (Standard Toykraft 1963)
15x10" window display box contains four pre-numbered
sketches, four stencil sheets containing illustrations and 12
crayons. **$100-125**

TV/COM-110

**TV/COM-110. MY FAVORITE MARTIAN "MARTIAN
MAGIC TRICKS" SET** (Gilbert 1963) 14x20" box contains
16 different magic tricks which include a plastic replica of
Uncle Martin's spaceship, a 4" Martian figure, assorted alien
figures and other space related items. **$200-250**

TV/COM-111

TV/COM-111. MY THREE SONS COLORING BOOK
(Whitman 1967) 8x11", 70+ pages. **$20**

TV/COM-112

TV/COM-115.

TV/COM-112. MY THREE SONS TRIPLETS DOLLS (Remco 1968) 13x18" box contains three 10" posable babies of Little Steve, Charlie and Robbie and includes three bottles and a blanket. **$150-200**

TV/COM-115. PATTY DUKE GLAMOUR SET (Standard Toykraft 1963) 15x12" window display box contains plastic comb, brush, mirror, talc, perfume and soap. **$35-65**

TV/COM-113

TV/COM-113. PATTY DUKE CHARM JEWELRY SET (Standard Toykraft 1963) 18x13" window display box contains a variety of small charms in metallic shades and includes chain material for looping charms together. Also included is a jewelry box. **$35-65**

TV/COM-116

TV/COM-116. THREE STOOGES GUM CARD SET (Fleer 1966) Set of 66 black/white photo cards with photo puzzle on back.
Gum Card Set: $50-85
Gum Card Wrapper: $15-20
Gum Card Display Box: $75-125

TV/COM-114.

TV/COM-114. PATTY DUKE DOLL (Horseman 1963) 12" plastic doll comes dressed in slacks and sweater and comes with telephone in a 10x14" window display box which includes a 5x7" autographed photo of Patty Duke. **$100**

TV/COM-117

TV/COM-117. THREE STOOGES HAND PUPPETS (Ideal 1961) 11" puppets with soft vinyl heads and cloth bodies of Larry, Curly and Moe. **EACH: $75-100**

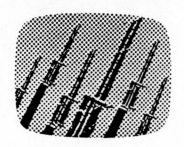

TV/WAR

With successful box-office hits such as *"The Longest Day"* (1961) and *"The Guns of Navarone"* (1962), the entertainment industry saw that there was money to be made in 're-fighting' World War II. Between 1962 and 1967, over a dozen WWII drama and comedy shows premiered on prime time television. Of these, *"Combat"* (1963-1968) was by far the most popular and longest running show, placing in the top ten highest rated television shows in 1965, and opening the door for other WWII shows. Four lasted to 1968, the peak of the Viet Nam War controversy. Only *"Hogan's Heroes"* survived into the Seventies. As television brought the Viet Nam War right into our living rooms everyday, it became more and more a focal point of Americans' daily life, and the glamour of reliving the second World War had begun to lose its appeal.

TV/WAR-2

TV/WAR-2. COMBAT BATTLE GEAR PLAYSET (Diamond 1963) Large 24x36" display card holds plastic Thompson machine gun, pistol with holster belt, knife, grenade and helmet, all molded in army geen color plastic. **$100-200**

TV/WAR-3. COMBAT CARD GAME (Milton Bradley 1963) 6x10" box contains oversize playing cards. **$15-25**

TV/WAR-4. COMBAT COLORING BOOK (Saalfield 1963) 8x11", 70+ pages. **$15-20**

TV/WAR-5

TV/WAR-5. COMBAT GAME (Ideal 1963) Object of the game is to capture the other side's headquarters. Box is 10x20". **$25-30**

TV/WAR-1.

TV/WAR-1. COMBAT "AT ANZIO BEACH" GAME (Ideal 1963) 14x26" glossy hard cardboard envelope contains playing board, cards and playing pieces. **$50-75**

TV/WAR-6

TV/WAR-6. COMBAT GUM CARD SET (Donross 1963) Series of two gum card sets totalling 132 black/white photo cards with narratives on back.
Gum Card Set 1 (1-66): $50-75
Gum Card Set II (67-132): $50-75
Gum card Wrapper: $20-25
Gum Card Display Box: $100-150

TV/WAR-7. COMBAT JIGSAW PUZZLE (Milton Bradley 1964) 10x12" box contains 125 piece puzzle. Two different puzzles are known to have been produced. **$20-25**

TV/WAR-10

TV/WAR-10. COMBAT PLAYSET (T. Cohn 1963) 15x30" box contains a 72 piece playset with tanks, trucks, jeeps, trailers, howitzers, soldiers and accessories. **$175**

TV/WAR-8

TV/WAR-8. COMBAT OFFICIAL COMBAT SET (Diamond 1963) Boxed set includes plastic 25" long roll-cap repeating Thompson machine gun, .45 cap pistol with white stag handles and flap leather holster, OD belt with garrison buckle, Patrol binoculars with real lenses, screw-top canteen and two hand grenades. Box is 32x16". **$200-275**

TV/WAR-11

TV/WAR-11. COMBAT "SONGS OF THE COMBAT YEARS" RECORD ALBUM (Columbia Records/AC Sparkplug 1963) Premium record offered through AC Sparkplug features original soundtrack theme and a variety of WWII songs. **$50-75**

TV/WAR-9

TV/WAR-9. COMBAT OIL PAINT BY NUMBER SET (Hasbro 1963) Two different paint sets were made by Hasbro. One features a 15x17" carry case box and comes with three 12x16" pre-numbered sketched canvases, 28 vials of paint and three brushes. **Carry Case Set: $100-125** The second paint set comes in a large 14x20" box and contains a 12x14" pre-numbered sketched canvas, 14 vials of paint and brush. **Boxed Set: $75-100**

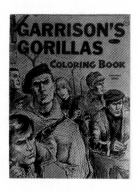

TV/WAR-12

TV/WAR-12. GARRISON'S GORILLAS COLORING BOOK (Whitman 1968) 8x11", 65+ pages. **$10-15**

TV/WAR-13

TV/WAR-17

TV/WAR-13. GARRISON'S GORILLAS GAME (Ideal 1967) 20x10" box. **$40-75**

TV/WAR-17. RAT PATROL "DESERT COMBAT" GAME (Transogram 1967) Object of the game is to beat the German tanks. Game includes several jeep and tank markers, playing board. Box is 10x17". **$35-45**

TV/WAR-14

TV/WAR-14. GARRISON'S GORILLAS GUM CARD SET (Leaf 1967) Set of 72 black/white photo cards with photo puzzle back.
Gum Card Set: $35-50
Gum Card Wrapper: $15-20
Gum Card Display box: $45-75

TV/WAR-18. RAT PATROL GUM CARD SET (Topps 1966) Set of 66 color photo cards with puzzle back.
Gum Card Set: $35-50
Gum Card Wrapper: $20-25
Gum Card Wrapper: $100-150

TV/WAR-15. GARRISON'S GORILLAS HALLOWEEN COSTUME (Ben Cooper 1967) 10x12" window display contains red/yellow/tan one-piece synthetic fabric body suit designed like a military tunic. Comes with plastic mask. **$45**

TV/WAR-19. RAT PATROL HALLOWEEN COSTUME (Ben Cooper 1967) 10x12" window display box contains tan one-piece synthetic fabric body suit designed like a desert patrol outfit and comes with plastic mask wearing bush hat. **$40-50**

TV/WAR-16

TV/WAR-16. THE LIEUTENANT "COMBAT TOWN" GAME (Transogram 1963) From the short-lived television show starring Gary Lockwood and Robert Vaughn. Object of the game is to be the first player to complete successfully three dangerous missions. Box is 10x17". **$50-65**

TV/WAR-20

TV/WAR-20. RAT PATROL JEEP W/DOLLS (Marx 1967) 14" long tan plastic jeep features a detachable .50 caliber machine gun which mounts in the back. Two 8" dolls in molded tan uniforms are included and come with a variety of accessories including helmet, cap, beret, bush hat, walkie-talkies, pistols w/holsters and two M-16s! (a historical oversight on the part of the Louis Marx Company). There are also two M-16 holsters that hang from the jeep. Box is 14x8x7" deep. **$250-350**

TV/WAR-21. RAT PATROL LUNCHBOX (Aladdin 1967) Steel box with matching thermos.
Box: $25-50, Thermos: $15-20

TV/WAR-22. RAT PATROL MIDGET MOTOR JEEP (Remco 1967) 4x6" box contains plastic 6" motorized jeep with tires which are designed to grab and climb steep grades. Jeep also features a swivel .50 caliber machine gun in the back and real engine sound when the jeep is in motion. Rat Patrol decals on sides. **$50-100**

TV/WAR-23

TV/WAR-23. RAT PATROL MODEL KIT (Aurora 1967) 10x15" box contains all-plastic H/O assembly kit playset diorama with jeeps, tanks, soldiers, sand dunes, palm trees and accessories. **$50-100**

TV/WAR-24

TV/WAR-24. RAT PATROL "SGT. JACK MOFFITT" DOLL (Marx 1967) For a very brief time Marx test marketed their 8" Rat Patrol doll separately and not with the jeep (See TV/WAR-20 above). This figure comes on a 10x12" display card with helmet, rifle, pistol w/holster and walkie-talkie. **$150-250**

TV/WAR-25

TV/WAR-25. TWELVE O'CLOCK HIGH CARD GAME (Milton Bradley 1965) 6x10" box contains oversized playing cards. **$15-20**

TV/WAR-26

TV/WAR-26. TWELVE O'CLOCK HIGH GAME (Ideal 1965) Object of the game is to score the highest number of points by commanding the most "Accurate Stategic Bombing Squadron". Game includes Playing board with aerial view of German landscape and cities, Squadron Markers, Bomb Cards, Direct Hit Cards and dice. There are two box lid variations to this game. The first issue features **Robert Lansing** on the lid, the second issue features **Paul Burke**. There is little difference in value but the first issue Robert Lansing box is more difficult to locate. Box is 20x10". **$35-50**

TV/WAR-27

TV/WAR-27. TWELVE O'CLOCK HIGH JIGSAW PUZZLE (Milton Bradley 1965) 9x11" box contains 100-piece puzzle. Two different puzzles are known to have been produced. **$15-20**

TV WESTERNS

The television western peak years were 1957-1962, with more than 30 different westerns showing on prime time in the 1959-1960 season. Gunsets and western playsuits were very popular sellers in the early Sixties, but as the shows themselves began dropping off the air so did the sales of the toys drop. By 1964, only "Bonanza" and "Gunsmoke" appeared unscathed in TV ratings and merchandise sales.

TV/WES-2

TV/WES-2. BONANZA JIGSAW PUZZLE (Milton Bradley 1964) 10x12" box contains 125 piece puzzle and a 12x14" color poster of the cast. **$25-35**

BONANZA DOLLS (American Character 1966) A series of four 6" posable dolls were made of the cast. A moustache was given the Adam Cartwright doll at the last minute when Pernell Roberts left the show, and was re-packaged as the Villain. All dolls come with hats, gun and holsters and accessories. Box is 4x8".

TV/WES-3

TV/WES-3. BEN CARTWRIGHT: $75-100

TV/WES-1

TV/WES-4   TV/WES-5

TV/WES-1.   BONANZA COLORING BOOKS (Artcraft/Saalfield 1965) Two different coloring books on Bonanza were produced by Artcraft in 1965. Each are 8x11" and have 60+ pages. **EACH: $15-20**

TV/WES-4. HOSS CARTWRIGHT: $100-125
TV/WES-5. LITTLE JOE CARTWRIGHT $125-140
TV/WES-6. VILLAIN: $50-75

TV/WES-7

TV/WES-7. BONANZA FOUR-IN-ONE WAGON (American Character 1965) 25" plastic wagon made for the 8" dolls American Character also produced (see above). Wagon can be designed into an Ore Wagon, Chuck Wagon, Ranch Wagon or Covered Wagon and comes with over 70 pieces of equipment. **$50-75**

TV/WES-8

TV/WES-8. BONANZA MODEL KIT (Revell 1965) 10x10" box contains all-plastic assembly kit of **Hoss, Little Joe** and **Ben.** Figures stand 7" tall and stand on base. **$50-100**

TV/WES-9

TV/WES-9. CIMARRON STRIP GAME (Ideal 1967) Object of the game is to be the first player to claim four matching pieces of land. Game includes Claim Markers, Hit-and-Miss Bullet Cards, Cowboy Tokens, playing pieces and playing board. Box is 18x10". **$35-50**

TV/WES-10

TV/WES-10. FESS PARKER AS DANIEL BOONE COLORING BOOK (Saalfield 1964) 8x11", 70+ pages. **$20**

TV/WES-11

TV/WES-11. FESS PARKER AS DANIEL BOONE "FRONTIER ATTACK" PLAYSET (MPC 1964) 32x28x3" deep box contains plastic snap together fort, frontiersmen, Indians, cannons, wagons, tee-pees and accessories. This set was offered exclusively through Grant department stores. **$100-125**

TV/WES-12

TV/WES-12. FESS PARKER AS DANIEL BOONE LUNCHBOX (King Seeley Thermos 1964) Steel lunchbox with matching thermos. **Box: $40-65, Thermos: $20-25**

TV/WES-13

TV/WES-13. FESS PARKER "TRAIL BLAZERS" GAME
(Milton Bradley 1964) Object of the game is to protect fort.
Box is 20x10". **$20-30**

TV/WES-14

**TV/WES-14. FESS PARKER-DANIEL BOONE OIL PAINT-
BY-NUMBER AND PENCIL-BY-NUMBER SET** (Standard
Toykraft 1964) 18x12" window display box contains eight
craycil color pencils, eight vials of paint, eight pre-numbered
sketches and two pre-numbered canvas sketches of Daniel
Boone. **$50-75**

TV/WES-16

TV/WES-15

TV/WES-16. REBEL FIGURE ON HORSE (Hartland 1960)
Hard plastic 5" painted figure with detailed likeness to Nick
Adams. Figure is wearing a yellow mustard-colored shirt,
grey-blue pants and a silver belt buckle with the initials
"CSA",and a black gun holster which holds a replica brown
or red scattergun. Figure also wears a Confederate cap.
Horse is two-tone grey and cream with a black mane and
tail and black spots on rear flanks. Saddle included. Box is
10x12x7". **$500-750**

TV/WES-15. THE LEGEND OF JESSE JAMES (Milton
Bradley 1966) Object is to make it home safely. Box is
20x10". **$35-50**

TV/WES-17

TV/WES-17. REBEL SCATTERGUN (Kilgore 1960) 15x4x3" red box contains plastic/metal 16" double barrel shotgun with dual working triggers. **$350-500**

TV/WES-18

TV/WES-18. RIFLEMAN "TV STAGE" PAINT BY NUMBER SET (Standard Toykraft 1960) 10x15" box contains two die-cut canvas town buildings, two die-cut canvas figures of Lucas and Mark McCain which can be painted and stood up to create one large western diorama scene. Set also includes seven oil paints and brush. **$100**

TV/WES-19

TV/WES-19. SHOTGUN SLADE GAME (Milton Bradley 1960) 20x10" box. **$25-45**

TV/WES-20. STAGECOACH WEST ADVENTURE GAME (Transogram 1961) Early short-lived western with **Wayne Rogers** of future M.A.S.H. fame. Object is to be the first player to get his stagecoach safely home. Box is 9x17". **$25-45**

TV/WES-21

TV/WES-21. TALES OF WELLS FARGO PLAYSET (Marx 1960) 25x16x4" deep box contains stagecoach, horses, cowboys and Indians, stagecoach depot, town and accessories. **$400-600**

TV/WES-25

TV/WES-22

TV/WES-22. WAGON TRAIN PLAYSET (Marx 1960)
24x13x4" deep box contains covered wagons, cowboys and
Indians, character figures of Flint McCullough and Major
Seth Adams and accessories. **$400-600**

TV/WES-26.

TV/WES-25. WILD WILD WEST LUNCH BOX (Aladdin
1969) Steel lunchbox with matching plastic thermos. **Box:
$50-80, Thermos: $20-30**

TV/WES-26. ZORRO GAME (Whitman 1965)
Object of the game is to be the first player to complete the
trail and collect cards which spell out ZORRO. Box is 14x8"
and features photo of children playing game. **$10-20**

TV/WES-23

TV/WES-27

TV/WES-23. WAGON TRAIN TRAY PUZZLE (Whitman
1960) 11x14" frame tray puzzle of Major Seth Adams and
Flint McCullough on a covered wagon. **$10-15**

TV/WES-24. WILD WILD WEST GAME (1967)
20x10" box. **$50-100**

TV/WES-27. ZORRO GAME (Parker Bros. 1966)
Object of the game is to be the first player to reach the
finish space. White 10x18" illustrated box of Zorro riding
horse. **$25-35**

TV/WES-28. ZORRO MODEL KIT (Aurora 1965)
13x7" box contains all-plastic assembly kit molded in black
of Zorro riding a rearing horse. **$175-250**

TOP TEN TOY COMPANIES

Listed below are the ten most popular toy companies of the Sixties. The first four companies were known as the "Big Four" and were the largest. Of the ten companies listed, only Mattel and Hasbro still exist today.

Louis Marx & Company (1919-1972): DisneyKins, Rock-em Sock-em Robots, Big Loo Robot, Johnny West Doll, plastic soldier playsets (particularly Fort Apache and Civil War sets).

The undisputed leader of toy manufacturers, grossing more than three to four times as much as its closest competitor, Marx developed the playset, invented the yo-yo, and produced some of the most ingenius tin wind-ups, guns, dolls, trains, trucks, and cars, and just about any other type of toy imaginable. Marx sold in high volume and only to larger chain stores such as Sears, Montgomery Wards, and Kresge's, shutting the door on smaller "mom-and-pop" stores and even most distributors and wholesalers! In the 1960's Marx offered over 6000 items in its toy line and often forced buyers to take slower-moving toys in order to get first crack at the "hot sellers". Louis Marx sold his company to Quaker Oats in 1972 for $51 million. At that time he had manufacturing plants in Japan, Hong Kong, Mexico, Wales, France, and South Africa. After four years of losing money each year, Quaker sold the company for $15 million.
Slogan: "One of the many Marx toys--do you have all of them?"

Ideal Toy Corporation (1907-early 1980's): Mr. Machine, Robot Commando, King Zor, Baby Thumbelina, Motorific, Mousetrap, U.N.C.L.E. gunsets, Pebbles/Bamm Bamm dolls, Zeroids.

Ideal excelled at producing extremely imaginative toys, some of which revolutionized the toy world and became pop-icons of the Sixties. This is largely due to Marvin Glass and Associates, the leading toy designer of the Sixties. Morris Michtem, owner of a small Brooklyn, New York stationery store, founded Ideal in 1907 after reading a political cartoon featuring President Teddy Roosevelt and a small bear cub. When Mitchem wrote asking permission from the President to use his name on some small bears his wife had sewn, the President actually wrote back with the response, "I doubt my name will mean much in the toy business, but you may use it if you wish." Thus was born the "Teddy Bear", an enormous success upon which the Ideal Toy and Novelty Company was formed. Until the Sixties, Ideal was primarily known for production of sophisticated girls' dolls. CBS bought Ideal in the early 1980's in order to benefit from Ideal's international distribution network. CBS had also just purchased the licensing rights from Coleco to mass market a new computer called Adam. When Adam failed, CBS auctioned off pieces of the company and various molds which went to several companies including Hasbro, Milton Bradley and Toy Biz. Viewmaster bought the name "Ideal" and the rights to many of its classic toys, including Mr. Machine, which has been re-released twice since the 1970's.
Slogan: "It's a wonderful toy--it's Ideal!"

Mattel, Inc. (1945-present) Barbie doll, talking pull-string puppets and dolls, Major Matt Mason, Thingmaker set, Liddle Kiddles, Zero-M Secret Agent Guns, Switch 'N Go race sets.

Founded in 1945 by Elliot and Ruth Handler, Mattel produced simple, conventional toys until its enormously successful Barbie doll, which Ruth designed, in 1959. Shortly after, Mattel developed a large Research and Development staff headed by master electronic engineer Jack Ryan. It was Ryan who brought the talking, pull-string, voice boxes for Mattel's dolls to the company, which then led the industry as the first toy company to take full advantage of modern technology in the Sixties. Mattel's quest for greater technology in toys and its willingness to take risks is what has kept it the only remaining survivor of the "Big Four" toy giants (Marx, Ideal, Mattel, and Remco) that ruled the industry in the Sixties. Today, Mattel makes over 75% of its income from the Barbie line of dolls and accessories.

Slogan: "You can tell it's Mattel...it'sswell!"

Remco Industries, Inc. (1949-1970's): Barracuda Sub, Big Caeser War Ship, Beatles dolls, Fascination game, Mighty Matilda Battleship, Bulldog Tank, Monkey Division Guns, Duffy's Daredevils, Snugglebun Doll, Electric Radio Station, Firebird 99 Dashboard.

Founded in 1949, Remco mainly produced conventional toys in the Fifties, such as dolls, play phones, and science related toys. Its most creative years were 1958-66 when wide diversification of its product line produced a succession of hits with big, battery-operated, plastic toys. The Seventies were bleak years for the toy industry as a whole and Remco, like other giants of the industry, suffered a string of losses and sold out to Azrak/Hamway in the Seventies.

Hasbro (Hassenfeld Brothers) (1923-present) GI Joe, Mr. & Mrs. Potato Head, games, paint sets, TV- and cartoon-licensed items.

Hassenfeld Brothers got its start in the early Twenties as a textiles and school supplies manufacturer. The company entered the toy business in 1943, with it's first big hit being Mr. Potato Head in 1952. In 1963, free-lance toy designer Stan Weston sold his GI Joe doll concept to Hasbro. When introduced in 1964, G.I. Joe transcended the word "doll" to become "action soldier", and millions of boys were playing with dolls, to the surprise of their fathers. Hasbro has increasingly gained in strength with its acquisitions of Knickerbocker, Milton Bradley, Kenner, Tonka and Parker Brothers, and is today the very largest toy company. Hasbro also holds the licensing rights to Charles M. Schultz' Peanuts comic strip characters.

Wham-O: (1948-1982) Frisbee, Hula-Hoop, Superball

This company's first product was the "Wham-O Slingshot", from which the company took its name, and Wham-O has since produced some thirty different products, many of which, like the Frisbee, are not only still selling briskly today, but have become American icons. Kransco bought out Wham-O in the late 1980's, but still manufactures the Frisbee.

Kenner Products Company (Early 50's-1989): Girder & Panel sets, Give-A-Show Projectors, Spirograph, Doozies, Sparkle Paints, Easy-Bake Oven.)

Kenner grew in strength when it introduced its famous Girder & Panel sets in the late Fifties. The Sixties was the best decade for the company with hits including Give-A-Show Projector, Sparkle Dust Paint Sets, Spirograph, and the famous Easy-Bake oven. Kenner was recently purchased by Hasbro.

Slogan: "It's Kenner--It's Fun!"

Gilbert (1915-1960's) Erector sets, science sets, spy dolls)

Gilbert has been a long time producer of erector, science, chemistry, and magic sets. During the TV-movie licensing rage that was dominating sales in the mid-Sixties, Gilbert gambled on producing James Bond 007 dolls and figures with moderate success. The company's 007 Super Road Race set, which was to be mass-produced and sold exclusively at Sears for a whopping $35.00, met with disaster from the start. Production delays and deadlines forced the company to have the slot cars and electronic parts produced in Hong Kong so they would be finished in time for the Christmas season of 1965. Millions of dollars had already been spent on advertising. The sets arrived on time, barely, but over 70% of the slot cars were mechanically unsound and did not operate correctly. Sears was inundated with returns after Christmas and Gilbert was obligated to make good on its defective merchandise. The company's staple line of erector sets and science sets had been poor sellers for years, continually losing ground to flashier toys, and couldn't save the company from its financial bind. Gilbert was soon bought out by a larger interest.

Transogram: (1915-1970) Trik-Trak, games, doctor/nurse sets, plastic toys of all kinds.

Transogram grew larger in 1962 when it offered its stock to the public and sold directly to the quickly rising discount and chain stores. The company grew to four factories producing over 300 different items. Transogram diversified into other businesses and by 1970, sold its toy stock interests.

Deluxe Reading Corporation/Topper Toys: (1960-1970's) Johnny 7 OMA Gun, Secret Sam spy toys, Johnny Eagle Guns, Penny Brite doll

In the early 1960's, Deluxe Reading produced large plastic toys and sold exclusively to grocery stores. The company officially entered the conventional toy market in 1964 with its new line of toys named "Topper", and introduced the Johnny Seven One-Man-Army Gun, which was the runaway hit of 1964. D-R continued to produce sophisticated gun sets and high quality toys throughout the Sixties and ran the world's largest toy plant out of Elizabeth, New Jersey.

A CHRONOLOGY of EVENTS
of the
1960's TOY INDUSTRY

1960:   Toys based on characters from TV Western shows were the top sellers. Firmly established in popularity since 1959 were products licensed from the landmark Hanna-Barbera animated cartoons, such as *Yogi Bear* and *The Flintstones*.

Mr. Machine is introduced and becomes the biggest selling mechanical toy up to that time. It also opened the door for other large plastic toys which could be sold for high prices.

The game market begins to expand and several toy companies diversify their lines to compete with giants such as Milton Bradley and Parker Brothers.

The Aurora Plastics Corporation introduces table top slot car racing and an industry is born.

The Etch A Sketch is introduced on the U.S. toy market and becomes an instant success.

Mattel, still riding high from the previous year's blockbuster Barbie doll, introduces the first pull-string talking dolls and puppets, which remain strong sellers throughout the Sixties.

Kenner's Give-a-Show Projector is introduced, and enjoys strong popularity for the next decade.

Marx introduces nearly twenty new playsets to its already prolific line.

Milton Bradley introduces its highly successful Game of Life.

Elvis Presley is honorably discharged from the U.S. Army--no toys are planned.

1961:   TV Westerns begin to lose ground to trendy TV detectives and private eyes including *77 Sunset Strip*, *Peter Gunn*, and *Hawaiian Eye*.

Aurora Plastics Corporation issues Frankenstein, the first in a series of wildly successful model kits based on monsters from the classic Universal horror films of the 1930's and '40's. Demand for this kit is so great that a second mold had to be produced and run non-stop.

Disney's *101 Dalmations* movie is greeted with great marketing success.

Marx introduces two of its best-ever sellers, Disneykins, and the Rock 'Em Sock 'Em Robots. The Robots were created by Marvin Glass and Associates of Mr. Machine fame.

Ideal releases Robot Commando, also created by free-lance designer Marvin Glass.

Remco introduces its line of Monkey Division military weapons with great success.

Marvel Comics publishes Fantastic Four #1, giving Superman a run for his money and forever changing the format of comics.

The National Association of Broadcasters and the Federal Trade Commission lower the axe on toy companies with exaggerated commercials which falsely represent the performance of the toy. Robot Commando is singled out as an example for giving the erroneous impression that the toy responds to voice commands.

1962: Another wave of cartoon favorites, including *Alvin* and *Top Cat*, offer fresh characters for toys. The rage in live-action TV is doctor shows, such as *Ben Casey* and *Dr. Kildare*, each with a viewing audience of 23 million. Both generate an epidemic of merchandise. TV comedy sitcoms grow in audience and licensing.

Shari Lewis dominates the child host market, followed by *Captain Kangaroo*; *Kukla, Fran, and Ollie*, and *Jon Gnagy's "Learn to Draw"*.

The toy industry, encouraged by the past two years of winning sales of large plastic toys, begins mass production of ships, tanks, car dashboards, cannons, animals, and dinosaurs.

Marvel Comics publishes Spiderman #1 and The Hulk #1.

Lego building sets are introduced.

Aurora Plastics releases its Wolfman and Dracula kits to an increasingly ravenous market.

Disney's re-release of *Pinocchio* does moderately well in the toy market.

1963: The monster craze is a howling success with The Aurora Plastics Corporation's release of the Mummy and The Phantom, with monsters appearing on every imaginable product.

The Rat Fink and Weird-Ohs are introduced and develop an immediate cult following.

The plastic revolution continues to dominate manufacturing, causing slow sales of steel/metal cars and trucks.

Ideal introduces the now legendary Mouse Trap game, revolutionizing the way board games were played.

Ideal collaborates with Hanna-Barbera on *The Magilla Gorilla Show*. H-B produces the 30-minute cartoon while Ideal manufactures a slew of toys to go with it.

Combat TV series premieres and taps into a nostalgia for World War II. It is heavily duplicated in similar TV shows and a wave of military toys begins.

1964:   The original format GI Joe doll is created by toy designer Stan Weston and introduced by Hasbro.

Rock 'n Roll performs a succesful crossover to the toy industry as Beatles memorabilia becomes the hottest merchandising trend of the year.

Deluxe Reading, a grocery store-only toy distributor, formally enters the conventional toy industry as "Topper Toys" with its introduction of the highly successful Johnny 7 O.M.A. gun. Over 1.6 million units are sold the first year with an average <u>wholesale</u> price of $5.00. Topper's TV advertising budget of $800,000 nets a return of ten times the investment.

Milton-Bradley sponsors the *Shenanigans* children's game show, capturing eight million viewers/potential consumers of its games.

Kenner introduces the Easy-Bake Oven, starting a wave of food-preparation and -serving toys.

Ideal introduces Motorific Torture Track Race Set.

Toy designer Stan Weston gambles on a potential spy trend and purchases licensing rights for the new *Man From U.N.C.L.E.* series.

Thingmaker sets (and burned fingers!) debut from Mattel.

Cap'n Crunch cereal debuts from the Quaker Oats Company and becomes the second-largest pre-sweetened cereal in only two years.

Remco's Hamilton's Invaders "ugly sci-fi bug" playsets are introduced and promptly fail despite heavy ad campaigns.

1965:   James Bond and Man From U.N.C.L.E. lead the new spy craze.

Wham-O introduces the Superball and millions of units are sold the first six months.

Disney re-releases the 1950's TV show **Zorro** and capture a viewing audience of 30 million, or 68% of all homes.

Benay-Albee's Zorro hat and mask are a complete sell-out their first week.

Re-introduction of *Gumby* "claymation" show features that flexible green fellow and his sidekick Pokey.

194

The Gabriel Toy Company purchases the Hubley and Lido toy companies. Hubley, primarily a producer of western gunsets, lost most of its market share with the decline of the "western" craze in 1961.

King-Seeley-Thermos buys out Structo, the leading manufacturer of steel trucks since 1908. Declining sales cause the phasing out of the steel trucks.

Lost in Space TV series premieres and is heavily licensed.

1966:   Mid-season replacement TV show *Batman* opens the floodgates for a superhero craze and comic books gain an exalted status.

Stan Weston designs and markets Ideal's Captain Action 12" moveable doll, which can change into other superheroes.

Premiere of *Star Trek*.

Mattel introduces its See 'N Say pull-string talking teaching toys for pre-schoolers.

Cartoons in general experience a decline in quality as they begin to be mass-produced assembly-line style.

Astro Boy, a cartoon of Japanese origin, reigns in quality and popularity as one of the highest rated prime-time animated series created.

1967:   The made-for-TV Rock group "The Monkees" become the newest merchandising rage with their own 30 minute weekly commercial, thinly disguised as a TV sitcom.

Made-for-TV originals Space Ghost, Birdman, and the Galaxy Trio battle for toy store shelf space with established superheroes Superman, Spiderman and Aquaman.

The Viet Nam conflict and urban rioting sour the public's infatuation with war toys.

Mattel introduces Astronaut Major Matt Mason, a 6" bendable rubber doll.

Increased labor costs force manufacturers to cut corners in production and packaging, and the elaborate toys of 1960-66 are no longer economically feasible.

American Characters, maker of the Bonanza doll series, is liquidated.

T. Cohn, manufacturer of tin litho toys and playsets, is liquidated.

1968:   The Beatles ride another wave of merchandising with the release of the animated film *Yellow Submarine.*

Major Matt Mason figures and playsets lead the latest fad of space-oriented toys.

Ideal introduces Zeroids battery-operated robots and Boatarific.

Successful manufacturers are producing space toys and educational/computer-type toys.

Plush toys make a come-back.

Land of the Giants premieres, with highly sought after licensed items.

1969:   American astronauts land on the moon, and space toys close out the decade skyrocketing in popularity.

Topper's Johnny Lightning and Mattel's Hot Wheels small, metal die-cast cars enjoy popularity, along with technologically-advanced, battery-operated toys.

The pace of life in America accelerates, and leisure toys, crafts, and models experience a decline in popularity.

Winky Dink, originally aired in 1954, makes a come-back with a new five-minute cartoon series.

Standard Toykraft's Winky Dink TV Activity Kit sells a half million its first ten days on the market.

Cox Toy Company, manufacturer of engine-powered planes, folds.

Milton-Bradley purchases The Amsco Company, producers of Toon-a-Vision and The Magic Baby-Feeding Bottle.

Hasbro sponsors *H.R. Pufnstuff* and becomes the first toy manufacturer in NBC's history to sponsor fully a Saturday morning program.

The Pennsylvania Department of Labor and Industry bans distribution of stuffed toys deemed "dangerously flammable" and starts an era of safer stuffed toys.

Milton Bradley spends $4 million on TV commercials to boost slumping sales, the biggest advertising effort of a game business in history.

BIBLIOGRAPHY

PLAYTHINGS, The National Magazine of the Toy Trade, Nov. 1959-Dec. 1969.

MODEL AND TOY COLLECTOR MAGAZINE, 1986-1991,Issues 1-18.

Brooks, Tim & Marsh, Earle. *The Complete Directory to Prime Time Network TV Shows, 1946-Present.* (Revised Edition) New York: Ballantine Books, 1988.

Bruegman, Bill. *Toy Scouts, Inc. Mail Order Catalog*, 1983-1991.

Sears Roebuck & Co. Mail Order Catalog, 1959-1970.

JC Penny Company Mail Order Catalog, 1959-1970.

Montgomery Ward Mail Order Catalog, 1959-1970.

Spiegel Mail Order Catalog, 1959-1970.

Aldens Mail Order Catalog, 1959-1970.

Louis Marx and Company Product Catalog, 1960-1969.

Ideal Toy Company Product Catalog, 1960-1969.

Mattel, Inc. Product Catalog, 1960-1969.

Remco Industries Product Catalog, 1960-1969.

Hasbro Product Catalog, 1960-1969.

Transogram Toy Company Product Catalog, 1960-1969.

Eldon Industries Product Catalog, 1960-1969.

Deluxe Reading Corporation/Topper Toys Product Catalog, 1960-1969.

A.C. Gilbert Company Product Catalog, 1960-1969.

Standard ToyKraft Company Product Catalog, 1960-1969.

INDEX

202

ABOUT THE AUTHOR

In just ten years, Bill Bruegman has become an internationally recognized leader in the profitable hobby of collecting memorabilia. Starting as a dealer in vintage records, Bill soon noticed many of his customers wanted music and collectibles from the TV cartoons of their childhoods.

Spotting a trend toward 1950's and 1960's memorabilia, Bill turned to selling and trading model kits, board games and other toys which led to the formation of his mail-order firm, **Toy Scouts, Inc.**, in 1983. Since that time, Toy Scouts has grown to supply customers around the world.

To better serve his clientele, Bill created in 1986 **Model and Toy Collector Magazine**, a quarterly publication devoted to Fifties and Sixties collectibles, and watched it skyrocket in popularity among hobbyists and investors.

Because of his expertise, Bill has been recognized in leading news sources including Rolling Stone, USA Today, The Wall Street Journal, Entrepreneur, and Pronto, the prestigious Japanese trend monitor. He has also been sought out by motion picture studios such as Warner Brothers and Columbia Pictures as a source for the purchase and rental of period props.

Items from the Toy Scouts inventory and Bill's personal collection were recently on display at the Smithsonian Institute in Washington, DC as part of "It's Your Childhood, Charlie Brown," an exhibit of post-World War II children's life. Other museums, including the Henry Ford Museum and the "Please Touch" Museum for children in New York, have also featured pieces of the Toy Scouts inventory in their displays.